M. François Guizot

Great Christians of France, Saint Louis and Calvin

M. François Guizot

Great Christians of France, Saint Louis and Calvin

ISBN/EAN: 9783337028176

Printed in Europe, USA, Canada, Australia, Japan

Cover: Foto ©Lupo / pixelio.de

More available books at **www.hansebooks.com**

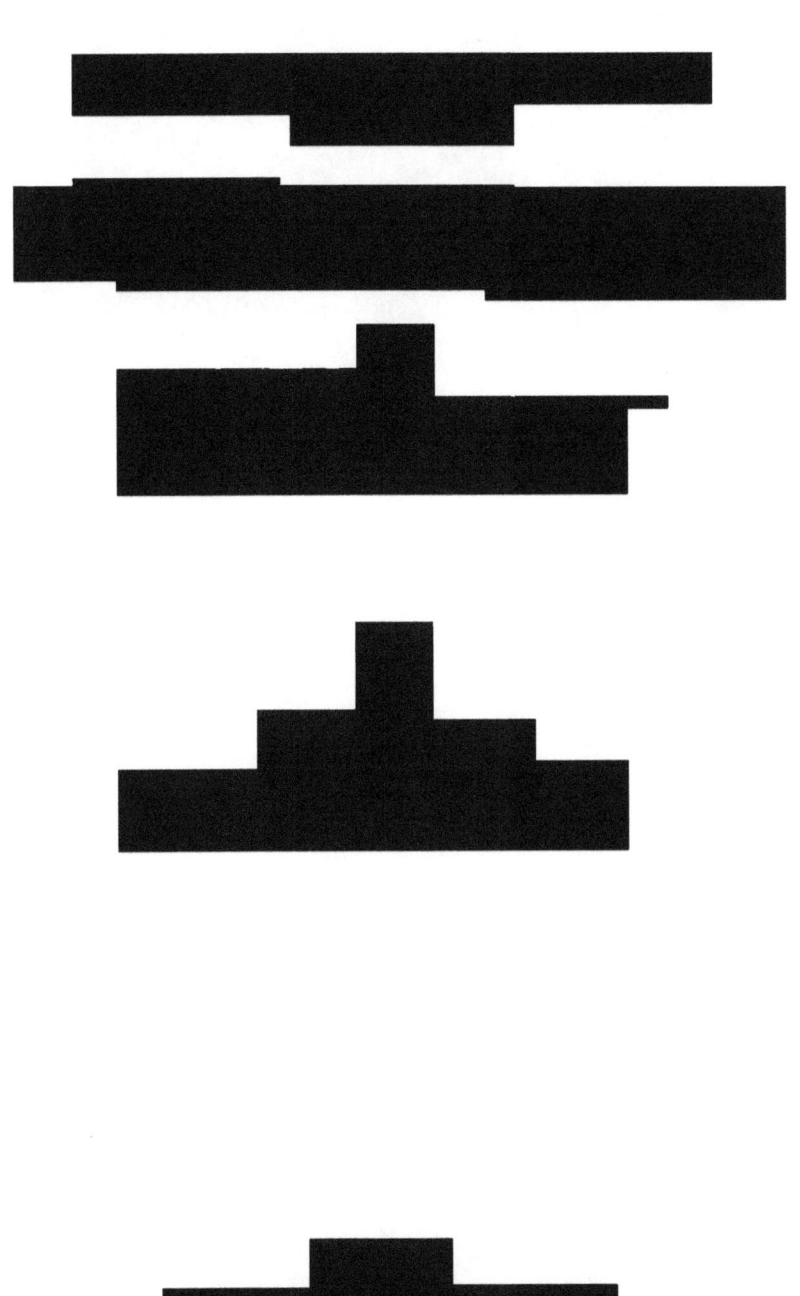

CHAPTER I.

...OST CHRISTIAN
... CANONIZATIO...

CHAPTER II.

...S. INFLUENCE OF ...
THE FORMATION O...

CHAPTER III.

...OUIS—HIS MARRIAGE, AND T...
MENT OF HIS GOVERNMENT . . . . .

CHAPTER IV.

RELATIONS OF ST. LOUIS WITH HIS VASSALS. HIS FEUDAL
CONFLICTS. WAR WITH HENRY III. OF ENGLAND . . . 26

CHAPTER V.

ATTITUDE OF ST. LOUIS IN THE STRUGGLE BETWEEN THE
GERMAN EMPIRE AND THE PAPACY 37

CHAPTER VI.

CHRISTIAN EUROPE AND MAHOMETAN ASIA IN THE THIRTEENTH
CENTURY 43

CHAPTER VII.

ORIGIN OF THE PASSION FELT BY ST. LOUIS FOR THE CRUSADES.
HIS SICKNESS IN 1244. HIS VOW. HIS DEPARTURE ON HIS
FIRST CRUSADE IN 1248 51

CHAPTER VIII.

CHAPTER III.

CALVIN THE LAW STUDENT, AT ORLEANS AND BOURGES. CALVIN THE REFORMER, IN PARIS 157

CHAPTER IV.

CALVIN A FUGITIVE. PERSECUTION OF THE PROTESTANTS IN PARIS 165

CHAPTER V.

CALVIN THE THEOLOGIAN 173

CHAPTER VI.

CALVIN'S BELIEF IN THE PLENARY INSPIRATION OF THE BIBLE . 181

CHAPTER VII.

CALVIN'S THEORY OF FREE-WILL AND PREDESTINATION . . 189

CHAPTER VIII.

CALVIN PREACHES RELIGIOUS REFORM IN ITALY. THE DUCHESS OF FERRARA. CALVIN'S FLIGHT FROM AOSTA 202

CHAPTER IX.

WILLIAM FAREL. CALVIN IN GENEVA 212

CHAPTER X.

CALVIN'S POLEMICS 232

CHAPTER XI.

CALVIN, LUTHER, AND MELANCTHON. CALVIN IN SEARCH OF A WIFE 241

CHAPTER XII.

CALVIN RETURNS TO GENEVA 250

CHAPTER XIII.

CALVIN'S ECCLESIASTICAL POLITY 258

CHAPTER XIV.

CALVIN'S CIVIL LEGISLATION 266

DIVISION OF THE RELIGIOUS AND CIVIL AUTHORITIES ON THE
QUESTION OF THE LORD'S SUPPER 278

CHAPTER XVI.
DEFEAT OF THE LIBERTINES 283

CHAPTER XVII.
CALVIN'S THEOLOGICAL CONTROVERSIES. SERVETUS . . . 290

CHAPTER XVIII.
SERVETUS IN GENEVA. HIS TRIAL AND EXECUTION . . . 312

CHAPTER XIX.
THE TWO OPPONENTS. CALVIN'S LETTER TO SOCINUS . . . 326

CHAPTER XX.
CALVIN'S INFLUENCE OVER THE REFORMED CHURCHES. HIS
PRESBYTERIANISM 333

CHAPTER XXI.
CALVIN THE AUTHOR. HIS CHURCH CATECHISM. HIS RE-
SPECT FOR THE INTELLECT 345

CHAPTER XXII.

PREFACE.

'Go ye and preach to all nations, baptizing them in the name of the Father, and of the Son, and of the Holy Ghost.'

This was the last injunction of Jesus Christ to His Apostles.

Universality is therefore the first principle and ultimate aim of Christianity. It has been designed for and is intended to become, in fundamental belief, the religion of the universe.

The *Universality* of Christianity in fundamental belief is accompanied by *Diversity* in institutions and forms of worship, which are secondary and external developments; for this *Diversity* is the inevitable result of difference of place, of time, of degrees of civilization, and of all those events which mould the destiny and constitute the history of nations.

When the Apostles were commanded to instruct all nations 'in the name of the Father, and of the Son, and of the Holy Ghost,' they also received the gift of tongues. This gift, which was a consequence of the *Diversity* of their means and methods of instruction, also bore witness to it, and at the same time manifested the *Unity* and *Universality* of their mission.

The whole history and progress of Christianity verifies these two facts. There has been great *Diversity* in the numerous developments of the Christian religion which we find over the face of the whole earth, and it has often entailed deplorable strife. But Christian *Unity* has never ceased to be the fundamental principle of these different manifestations, and *Universality* has remained the ultimate aim of Christianity, in spite of the different methods which it has adopted and forms in which it has been clothed, as it has spread from land to land.

In Europe, and in the states which have grown out of European colonies, Catholicism and Protestantism are the two great branches which have sprung from the Christian stem. For a long time a grievous and sanguinary war was waged between these two Churches. They triumphed or succumbed on different battle-fields. But where Catholicism has conquered, as in France, Protestantism has not perished; where Protestantism has been the victor, as in England, Catholicism still survives. After having subjected each other to so many trials and so much suffering, these two Churches have at last learnt that they can and ought to live together in peace, and that liberty must be their watchword and their safeguard.

From the brightest epochs of Catholicism and Protestantism, I have endeavoured to select some of their most earnest and noble representatives,— men whom no intelligent and well-informed man of the present day can refuse to recognise as Christians

PREFACE.

I was born a Protestant, and the experience of life, as well as the study of history, have more and more confirmed me in the faith of my forefathers; but, at the same time, they have taught me to recognise and to revere those true Christians who are members of Churches not my own.

The thirteenth and the seventeenth centuries are the two noblest and fairest epochs of French Catholicism. The sixteenth century and the beginning of the seventeenth are the two noblest and fairest periods of French Protestantism.

Among French Catholics I have chosen St. Louis in the thirteenth century and St. Vincent de Paul in the seventeenth, as two great and noble Christians, two earnest and illustrious representatives of the Christian faith and life, as well as of the loftiest thought and purest morality of their country and their generation. Among the Protestants of the sixteenth century, Calvin and Du Plessis Mornay present the same characteristics and deserve an equal glory.

These four men were emphatically and first of all Christians, in thought and life. Christian faith and piety shone out in all of them, notwithstanding their profound divergence and their fierce controversies. That is why I have selected them; and I have tried to depict them as glorious and profitable examples of Christianity, and of its persistent *Unity* in the midst of its most striking *Variety*.

GUIZOT.

VAL RICHER, 1868.

ST. LOUIS, KING OF FRANCE.

BORN AT POISSY, NEAR PARIS, *April* 25, 1215.
DIED BEFORE TUNIS, *August* 25, 1270.

CHAPTER I.

ORIGIN OF THE TITLE 'MOST CHRISTIAN KING,' AS GIVEN TO THE KINGS OF FRANCE. CANONIZATION OF CHARLEMAGNE AND ST. LOUIS.

IT was one of the chief glories of the kings of France to be called 'Most Christian King.' This was a title of traditionary honour rather than a testimony to their personal and religious merits, for, to tell the truth, the majority of these monarchs were very indifferent Christians. It is not mere external profession which makes the Christian, but the condition of a man's soul and the manner of his life.

By a startling coincidence, it was under the reign of one of the most villanous, knavish, and yet able sovereigns France ever had—Louis XI.—that the title 'Most Christian King' became the permanent and official attribute of French royalty. Before the middle of the fourteenth century we sometimes find it in letters from the popes to the kings of France, but rarely and casually, or else in documents of questionable authenticity. In 1286, Pope Honorius IV. writing to Philip the Fair, styled him 'the Catholic King,' a name, he said, 'belonging specially to the kings of France.' And even in 1456, Pope Calixtus III. addressed a brief to Charles VII. under no other title than that of 'Illustrious King of the Franks.' Twelve years after, in 1468, Pope Paul II., in replying to the complimentary address which had been conveyed to him by Guillaume de Montreuil, envoy of Louis XI., recalled all that the kings of France had done for the Holy See since the days of Pepin le Bref and Charlemagne, and declared that, if his predecessors had not always given the title of 'Most Christian' to these sovereigns, he himself had begun, and intended to continue so to designate them. Since that time, both at home and abroad, the French monarchs have claimed and received this august title.

Another title, more august still—that of 'Saint' —has been received by only two, Charlemagne and Louis IX., out of this long line of sovereigns. We must not exact a very strict proof of the right of Charlemagne to this title in the Catholic Church. He was only canonized in 1165 or 1166 by the Antipope Pascal III. and through the influence of the Emperor Frederick Barbarossa. Since then, not one of the legitimate popes has ever officially recognised or proclaimed his canonization, but still they have tolerated and tacitly admitted it, no doubt on account of his services to the Papacy. Nevertheless, besides emperors and popes, Charlemagne had warm and powerful admirers; he was the great man, the popular hero, of nearly the whole German race, who acknowledged his sanctity with enthusiasm, and have always religiously honoured it. From the earliest days of the University of Paris, Charlemagne has been the patron-saint of all the German students there. In France, however, his position in the calendar remained obscure and uncertain until the end of the fifteenth century, when, from some motive which we cannot now discover, (perhaps to snatch from his great enemy, Charles the Bold, Duke of Burgundy, possessor of the finest German provinces in Charlemagne's empire, the exclusive privilege of showing reverence to the memory of so great a man,) Louis XI. ordained saintly honours to be paid to the illustrious emperor, and fixed as his fête-day the 28th of January, threatening with death all who refused to acknowledge this new object of worship. In vain: the sanctity of Charlemagne has never been generally recognised by the Church of France; but the University of Paris has remained faithful to her tradition, and in 1661, two centuries after the death of Louis XI.—without expressly bestowing the title of *Saint* —she publicly proclaimed Charlemagne her patron, and ordered his fête-day to be solemnly kept every year. In spite of the hesitations of the 'Parlement'[1]

[1] The French 'Parlement' was not a representative assembly like the English Parliament. It consisted originally of the great vassals of the King, who were called together to deliberate on the general affairs of the kingdom on the 1st of March or the 1st of May every year, or if any urgent necessity arose, were summoned whenever the King had need of their advice. By degrees this assembly was transformed into a great judicial court; at first it also preserved its political character, and this was strongly manifested even as late as the sixteenth century, in the so-called religious wars. But starting from the reigns of Louis XIII. and Louis XIV., the 'Parlement' became merely a court of justice, which was joined on solemn occasions by the royal princes, and the dukes and peers of the realm.

of Paris, and the revolutions of our century, it is still celebrated as the chief fête-day of the great classical schools in France. Thus the University of France has repaid her emperor for his benefits towards her: he protected her students and her learning, she has protected his saintship.

That of Louis IX. did not require such pertinacious and erudite defence, nor suffer such uncertainties of fate. Proclaimed immediately after his death, not only by his son, Philip the Bold, and the barons and prelates of the kingdom, but by the public voice of France and of Europe, it became immediately the object of papal inquiry and deliberation. For twenty-four years, nine popes—Gregory X. Innocent V. John XXI. Nicholas III. Martin IV. Honorius IV. Nicholas IV. St. Celestine, and Boniface VIII.—swift successors in the papal chair, pursued the customary inquiry into the faith and life, virtues and miracles of the defunct king; and it was at last Boniface VIII. (afterwards destined to maintain a fierce conflict with the grandson of St. Louis, Philip the Fair) who, on August 11, 1297, decreed the canonization of the most Christian of all the monarchs of France, nay, of one of the truest Christians, monarch or peasant, that either France or Europe ever knew.

CHAPTER II.

EDUCATION OF ST. LOUIS. INFLUENCE OF HIS CENTURY, AND OF HIS MOTHER, ON THE FORMATION OF HIS CHARACTER.

BORN to a throne, a powerful monarch, a valiant soldier, and a noble knight, the object of devoted attachment to those about his person and of admiring respect to those further removed from him, whether friends or enemies,—these honours and pleasures failed either to dazzle or intoxicate King Louis. They held the first place neither in his thoughts nor his actions. Before all things and above all things, he desired to be—and was—a Christian, a true Christian, guided and governed by the determination to keep the faith and fulfil the law of Christianity. If he had been born in the lowest worldly estate, or if he had occupied a position in which the claims of religion would have been most imperative; if he had been poor, obscure, a priest, a monk, or a hermit, he could not have been more constantly and passionately pre-occupied with the desire to live as Christ's faithful servant, and to insure by pious obedience upon earth his eternal salvation hereafter. It is this peculiar and original feature in the character of St. Louis,—the rare, perhaps the sole instance of the kind in the annals of monarchs,—which I wish now to bring forward into the light.

The causes which could influence and produce such a character have been sometimes sought in the general or special influences of the age in which St. Louis lived. The thirteenth century was one of faith and religious observances. The creeds and ordinances of Christianity exercised a very strong influence over all classes. The mother of Louis IX., Queen Blanche of Castile, was a remarkable woman in mind and character, and as pious as she was clever. She gave her son a sound Christian education in his youth, and wise counsel and valuable support during the whole course of her life. Some writers have considered that these facts are sufficient to account for the spiritual development and life of the King. But this is a very superficial view, for neither the religious spirit of the thirteenth century nor the influence of Queen Blanche could have produced such a lofty moral nature as that of St. Louis; nor will they suffice to account for its existence.

Though the thirteenth century was fruitful in faith and Christian observances, still the Christians of that age were neither so numerous nor so influential as, in order to shame our present day, is often averred. The Crusades, that great outbreak of Christian zeal, had introduced tastes, passions, and habits of great licence into all classes. I find, in a learned and judicious 'History of St. Louis,' to which the French Academy has lately awarded a prize, the following faithful and authentic summary of the moral disorders of the time: '"People start on these sacred expeditions in order to become holy," says Rutebeuf, the contemporary poet, "and they come back—those who do come back—reprobate vagabonds." Their faith was tainted by association with the Mussulmen, and their lives by the manners and customs of the East. The clergy even did not escape corruption. . . . . The priests were so despised by the laity that they looked down upon them as if they had been Jews, saying, "I'd rather be a priest than do so-and-so." The young priests, when they appeared in public, hid the tonsure, which they wore close to the forehead, by drawing the hair from the back of the head over it. The nobles no longer allowed their sons to take holy Orders; they found it more convenient to appoint to the churches the children of their vassals, from whom they could exact some share of the pecuniary dues. The bishops had no chance of choosing their own priests, but were reduced to accept any who would condescend to enter such a discreditable profession.'

At the same time, the luxury of the higher orders of the clergy was a subject of great scandal. 'The councils of the Church had often attempted to check it, and in 1179 the third Council of Lateran suggested the following regulation as a reform:— " The archbishops on their journeys shall have at the utmost from forty to fifty horses, the cardinals twenty-five, the bishops twenty or thirty, the archdeacons seven, and the deans and their inferiors two." The progress of the legates of the Holy See was justly dreaded as causing absolute ruin. "Wherever they went," says Abbé Fleury, "they exacted magnificent entertainment from the bishops and abbots; and in order to defray these expenses the monasteries were sometimes even compelled to sell the sacred vessels from their churches."[1] Such a clergy,' adds the historian, 'was unable to check the evil tendencies of the age, either by setting the example of a life of self-denial or by teaching a pure and enlightened religion.' Nor could such a period produce religious kings. The history of the thirteenth century gives a striking proof of this fact, for the grandfather and grandson of Louis IX., though able and energetic princes, who served both the throne and the nation well, showed much more tendency towards worldly policy and keen self-interest than towards Christian faith. Philip Augustus was no type of St. Louis, and Philip le Bel no imitation of him.

Nor will the education he received from his mother, and her influence over him, both during a regency of ten years and even after he had attained his majority and assumed the reins of power, fully account for the profoundly Christian character of St. Louis, both in word and deed. Queen Blanche was a sincere believer and a pious woman, and she was very anxious to secure the moral and religious welfare of her son. We cannot doubt this, because it is proved by numerous facts, by many documents of the period, and by the testimony of the King himself. On the day of his birth, the 25th of April, 1215, when the feeble new-made mother noticed that the bells of the church of Poissy did not ring as usual, and was told they had been stopped that she might take repose, Blanche immediately commanded that she herself should be moved to a distance if necessary, but that nothing should hinder

[1] Faure, 'Histoire de Saint Louis,' vol. i. p. 38.

the summoning of the faithful to prayer. She herself took charge of the early education of her boy 'as being the future ruler of so great a kingdom, and her own favourite child.' As soon as he entered his fourteenth year, she gave him a strict and careful preceptor, 'who followed him about everywhere, even in his amusements, by wood or stream, so that he might always be teaching him, and who even sometimes used to beat him—which he bore with patience,' say the contemporary chronicles. Later still, when the King related to his intimate friends his recollections of his mother: 'Madame used to say,' he often repeated, 'that if I were sick unto death, and could only be cured by committing some mortal sin, she would let me die rather than utterly offend my Creator.'[1]

A guardianship so careful, firm, and righteous, joined to rare skill in the difficult task of ruling France during a long minority, could not fail to secure to Queen Blanche great influence over her son's character and actions; an influence so great and so lasting that we are sometimes tempted to be surprised at it, and to fancy that Louis, when he was not only a king but a great king, was too weak and too dependent as a son. He had the deepest respect for his mother, great confidence in her political ability, and very lively gratitude for her invaluable energy and maternal devotion. But mother and son were so unlike, both by nature and instinct, that there could be no spontaneous and familiar intercourse between them; none of that communion which is the truest bond of

[1] 'Vie de Saint Louis,' by the Confessor of Queen Marguerite, in Bouquet's 'Recueil des Historiens des Gaules et de la France;' Tillemout, 'Vie de Saint Louis,' &c. &c.

two human souls, because it adds the charm of mutual sympathy to the strong power of affection.

Blanche was ambitious, proud, imperious. These qualities appeared in her youth both towards her husband, Louis VIII., and her father-in-law, Philip Augustus. In 1216 she strongly urged the former to accept the English crown, offered him by the barons of England when at war with King John on the question of Magna Charta; and when Philip Augustus prudently refused to assist his son openly in this hazardous enterprise, the Princess Blanche recruited a band of knights who were to uphold the cause of the French prince on the other side of the Channel, and she herself was present at their meeting and at their departure. Ten years later, when the death of Louis VIII. made her Regent of France, she had to battle for ten years more, until her son's majority, with intrigues, plots, insurrections, open wars; and with what was much worse for her, the secret insults and calumnies of the principal vassals of the Crown, who were eager to snatch back from the rule of a woman the power and independence of which Philip Augustus had deprived them. But Queen Blanche resisted them, either with direct, masculine, and most persevering energy, or with the adroit finesse and ingenious fascination of a mere woman. Although forty years of age when her regency began, she was still beautiful, graceful, abounding in attractions, both of manner and conversation; gifted with the power to please, and the will to use that power with a coquetry that was sometimes a little too obvious to be prudent. Her enemies spread the most odious reports concerning her. One of the highest vassals of the kingdom,

Thibaut IV. Count of Champagne, a clever and voluminous poet, a gay and brilliant knight, was declared to be madly in love with her—her slanderers said, not in vain; and added that she had with his aid assassinated the king her husband. In 1230, some of the principal barons of France—the Count of Bretagne, the Count of Boulogne, and the Count of St. Pol—united to attack Count Thibaut and to seize Champagne; whereupon the Queen Regent, with her young son, came to his rescue, and arriving near Troyes, commanded the barons in the King's name to retire. 'If you have any complaint against the Count of Champagne,' said she, 'present it, and I will grant you justice.' 'We will not plead before you,' was their scornful reply. 'We know it is the way of women to fix their choice above all men upon the man who has killed their husband.' Nevertheless, in spite of this cruel insult, the barons left the field.

Five years after, in 1235, the Count of Champagne himself took up arms against his sovereign. But he was compelled to make peace on very hard terms in order to escape an ignominious defeat, and an interview took place between him and the Queen Regent. '"*Par Dieu!*" said Blanche; "Count Thibaut, you ought not to be our adversary. You should remember all the goodness of my son, and how he went to your aid when all the barons of France were against you, and would have burnt your lands to charcoal." The Count looked at the Queen, who was so wise and so fair, till he was quite abashed by her great beauty, and he answered, "By my faith, Madame, my heart and my body and all my domain are at your command. There is nothing you may deign to desire that I will not gladly do, and, if it please God, never will I fight against you or yours." He departed pensively from her presence, and the sweet looks of the Queen, and her beautiful presence, came often to his mind, so that tender and yearning thoughts entered his heart. But when he remembered how noble a lady she was and how good, and of such a great purity that she would never return his love, his tender and yearning thoughts changed to a great sadness. And because these sad thoughts engender melancholy, he was advised by several wise men to study song and poesy. And he made after that time the most beautiful songs and the most delectable and melodious that were ever heard."[1]

I can find nothing in history to justify the accusations of Queen Blanche's enemies. I do not know if the songs of Count Thibaut ever touched her heart; certainly they never influenced her conduct. She continued to oppose the claims and plots of the great vassals of France, whether her foes or her lovers, and to increase the possessions and the power of the Crown in spite of them. Though a sincere believer and a wise, devoted mother, she was essentially a politician, engrossed by the love of power, the claims of her position, and her temporal success. I can find in her no trace of the lofty moral impulses, the sensitive conscience, the enthusiasm and sympathy, which are characteristic of Christian piety, and which guided the whole life of St. Louis. He

---

[1] Jubainville, 'Histoire des Ducs et des Comtes de Champagne,' vol. iv. p. 249; 'Chroniques de St. Denis;' Bouquet's 'Recueil des Historiens des Gaules et de la France,' vol. xxi. p. 111.

derived these noble impulses neither from the teaching nor the example of his mother ; and if we would understand how they existed in him, we must consent to acknowledge one of the mysteries of creation : we must recognise the distinct individuality of each human soul, the separate personality and infinite diversity of disposition given by the Creator in accordance with an unknown and impenetrable design. Enthusiasm, sympathy, and conscientiousness,—these words describe the condition of that man whose whole nature is entirely penetrated and influenced by Christianity; for Christianity says to a man, 'There is none good but one, that is, God,' and so leads him to put his trust and hope in God; it lifts him above the interests and chances of this life, and this is the true and essential character of enthusiasm. Christianity teaches a man to love his neighbours as himself, and thus calls out in him that tender, ready, and universal charity which is justly called sympathy. It gives him a profound conviction of his own moral infirmity, makes him therefore keep watch and guard over his actions, and fills him with doubt lest with all his efforts he should not keep abreast of his duties. In a word, it makes him conscientious. The true Christian, be he great or small, rich or poor, is such a man as this; and Louis IX. was such a man and a king. But neither the general influence of his contemporaries nor the personal influence of his mother could have made him what they themselves were so far from being.

What St. Louis really owed to Queen Blanche, and this was not little, was the authority she gained and kept during her regency over the great vassals, either by force of arms or negotiations, and the predominance which she secured to the Crown, even amidst the fierce contests of the feudal system. She had an instinctive knowledge of what powers and what alliances would strengthen the royal authority against its rivals. When, on the 29th November, 1226, three weeks only after the death of her husband, Louis VIII., her young son was crowned at Rheims, Blanche invited to the ceremony not only the hierarchy and nobility of the kingdom, but the common people of the neighbourhood; she wished to show the royal child to the great vassals, supported and surrounded by the people. Two years afterwards, in 1228, there was an insurrection of the barons assembled at Corbeil, and they proposed to seize the person of the young King, whose progress had been arrested at Montlhéry, on his march to Paris. The Queen Regent summoned around her, besides those lords who remained faithful, the burgesses of Paris and of the country round, who hastened to respond to her call. 'All armed, they started for Montlhéry, where, having found the King, they conducted him to Paris, marching in battle array. From Montlhéry to Paris the road was lined the whole way with armed men and others, who prayed aloud that God would grant the young King a happy and prosperous life, and preserve him from all his enemies. Then the great vassals, hearing of this and not being able to oppose such a mass of the people, withdrew to their own homes, and by the mercy of God, who orders all things according to His will, they dared not attack the King any more during the rest of that year.'[1]

[1] Tillemont, 'Vie de St. Louis,' vol. ii. p. 354.

CHAPTER III.

MAJORITY OF ST. LOUIS—HIS MARRIAGE, AND THE COMMENCEMENT OF HIS GOVERNMENT.

IN 1236, Louis attained his majority and received from his mother's hands the full royal power; a power held in fear and respect, even by the vassals of the Crown, turbulent and aggressive as they still were. But they were also disunited, enfeebled, intimidated, and somewhat fallen into discredit; while for the last ten years they had been invariably baffled in all their plots.

When she had secured his political position, and he was approaching his majority, Queen Blanche began to busy herself with her son's domestic life. She was one of those who like to play the part of Providence towards the objects of their affection; to plan, rule and regulate everything in their destinies. Louis was nineteen years old; handsome, though with that kind of beauty which indicates more moral than physical strength. He had delicate and refined features, a brilliant complexion, and fair hair—shining and abundant—which, through Isabella, his grandmother, he inherited from his ancestors, the Counts of Hainault. He was a man of refined tastes and high spirits; he loved amusement; delighted in games of all sorts and in hunting; was fond of dogs and falcons; took pleasure in rich clothes and magnificent furniture. Nay, a monk is said to have once reproached his mother for having tolerated in the young man some love-fancy which threatened to become an irregular connexion; upon which Queen Blanche determined to have her son married immediately. She found no difficulty in inspiring young Louis with the same creditable wish. Raymond Berenger, Count of Provence, had an eldest daughter, who, according to the chronicles, 'was at that time said to be the noblest, fairest, and best brought up princess in all Europe.' By the advice of his mother and of the wisest counsellors of the kingdom, the young King demanded her in marriage. Her father received the offer with great joy, but was a little troubled at the thought of the large dowry which he was told would be expected with her. However, his most intimate friend and adviser, a Provençal gentleman named Romée de Villeneuve, said : ' Count, let me manage the matter, and do not let the heavy expenses weigh upon your mind. If your eldest daughter makes this royal marriage, the connexion will be so desirable that all the others will marry the better for it, and at less expense.' So Count Raymond followed this advice, and soon recognised its wisdom. He had four daughters, Margaret, Eleanor, Sancia, and Beatrix. After Margaret was Queen of France, Eleanor became Queen of England ; Sancia married the Earl of Cornwall, and was afterwards Queen of the Romans ; and Beatrix was first Countess of Anjou and Provence, and ultimately Queen of Sicily. Princess Margaret of Provence entered France, escorted by a brilliant embassy, which Louis had sent to fetch her; and the marriage was celebrated at Sens on the 27th of May, 1234, in the midst of great public festivities, and public charities likewise.

When he was married and in the enjoyment of domestic happiness Louis renounced of his own accord his former pleasures, both royal and worldly. His entertainments, his hunting, his magnificent ornaments and dress gave place to simpler pleasures and the good works of a Christian life. From that time the active duties of royalty, earnest and scrupulous attention to his religious duties, the tender and vigilant cares of charity, the pure and intense delights of conjugal love, combined with the noble projects of a true knight—a soldier of the Cross—filled up the whole life of this young king, who was humbly striving to become a saint and a hero.

But trouble came to him sometimes in the midst of his felicity. As soon as her son was married, Queen Blanche became jealous of the wife and the happiness which she herself had procured for him—jealous as mother and as queen, who saw a rival both in affection and in sovereignty. This odious sentiment led her on to acts equally undignified, malignant, and unjust.

'The cruelty of Queen Blanche to Queen Margaret was,' says Joinville, 'so great that she would not allow her son to enjoy his wife's companionship during the daytime at all, if she could prevent it. The favourite abode of the King and Queen was at Pontoise, because there the apartments of the King were above those of the Queen, and they had arranged so well that they used to sit and talk on a winding staircase which led from one story to the other, and they had contrived all so cleverly that when the King's guard saw the Queen-mother coming to the apartment of her son the King, they used to knock with their rods against his door, and the King would come running to his own room, that his mother might find him there. Likewise the guard of Queen Margaret learned to apprise their mistress when her mother-in-law was approaching, in order that she might be in her own apartment. Once, when the King was sitting beside the Queen, his wife, who had been in great peril of childbirth, the Queen-mother entered, and saying, " Come away, you can do nothing here," took him by the hand, and carried him off. Whereupon Queen Margaret cried out, " Alas! you will not let me see my lord whether I am living or dying!" and fainted, so that they thought she was dead ; and the King, who believed that she was dead, returned, and after great difficulty she was restored.'

Louis, in this strait, comforted his wife, but yet did not desert his mother. In the noblest of souls and the happiest of lives, there are oftentimes some incurable wounds and some griefs which can only be accepted in silence.

The young King's accession to royal power caused no change in the royal policy, nor in the management of public affairs. There were no innovations dictated by mere vanity ; no change in the acts and words of the sovereign or in the choice of his advisers and the amount of consideration shown to them. The son's reign was but the continuation of the mother's regency. Louis continued to oppose the power of the great vassals in order that he might establish the supremacy of the Crown : he succeeded in subduing Pierre Mauclerc, the turbulent Count of Bretagne ;

won from Thibaut IV. Count of Champagne, the right of suzerainty in the lands of Chartres, Blois, Sancerre, and Châteaudun; and bought from their owner the fertile lands of Mâcon. It was almost invariably by pacific measures, negotiations ably conducted, and treaties scrupulously fulfilled, that he thus extended the domains of the Crown.

Queen Blanche, during her regency, had practised a far-sighted economy which placed large funds at the disposal of her son. Following her example, Louis was economical at ordinary times, but liberal when policy demanded it. The property, and the rights belonging thereto, which he purchased from the Count of Champagne, cost him a sum which would now in English money be as nearly as possible equivalent to £144,000 paid down, and an annual ground-rent of £7,200.[1] The learned language of the political economy of our time—the terms 'sound system of taxation,' 'financial responsibility,' and 'balance of receipts and expenditure'—cannot be applied to the thirteenth century, and to feudal royalty. But we may truly say, that St. Louis, free from all frivolous fancies, and desiring only the well-being of his subjects, managed to maintain order in his royal treasury, and knew both how to economize and how to spend freely for the success of his designs.

I notice here one fact characteristic of both the King and his century. Many of these amicable transactions with his great vassals were almost immediately

---

[1] 40,000 livres Tournois paid down, and a ground-rent of 2,000 livres Tournois, or in modern French money about 3,600,000 francs paid down, and a ground-rent of 180,000 francs.

followed by the departure of the latter on a new crusade. The Christian world had not renounced the hope of freeing Jerusalem and the Holy Sepulchre from the yoke of the Mussulman. The desire to astonish the world by startling acts of penance, and the love of military adventure, still agitated both the highest and lowest ranks of feudal society. Pope Gregory IX. continued to preach a crusade—a double crusade—to Jerusalem for the deliverance of the Holy Sepulchre, to Constantinople for the succour of the recently established Latin Empire, which was already tottering. The King of France found, doubtless, that it was very convenient to extend his dominion thus without war at the expense of his vassals, and to get rid of these turbulent individuals. But to these reasons of general or private interest was certainly added the personal influence of Louis, already passionately absorbed in the thought of the glory and religious salvation which he hoped to win for himself in one of these expeditions.

As early as 1239, some of the principal vassals with whom he had just concluded advantageous treaties—the Counts of Champagne, Bretagne, and Mâcon—started for Palestine at the head of an army of Crusaders, numbering (so it is said) fifteen hundred knights and forty thousand squires. Louis was not content simply with encouraging and promoting this enterprise. 'He desired,' says De Tillemont, 'that Amaury de Montfort, his constable, should in this war serve Jesus Christ in his stead. Therefore he gave him his arms and granted him a daily sum of money, for which Amaury thanked him on his knees. That is, he did him homage after the custom of the time.

The Crusaders were much rejoiced to have this noble lord with them.'

The heavy sickness from which the King suffered five years after, and his pious thankfulness for his cure, are said to have given rise to his resolve to take the Cross. But this is a grave mistake, for from the year 1239, when he saw his chief vassals departing for Palestine with the cross embroidered on their shoulder, the heart of St. Louis had already taken flight towards Jerusalem.

CHAPTER IV.

RELATIONS OF ST. LOUIS WITH HIS VASSALS. HIS FEUDAL CON-
FLICTS. WAR WITH HENRY III. OF ENGLAND.

WHILE awaiting the time when he should be able to gratify his pious hope of becoming a Crusader, Louis diverted himself and feudal France by royal and knightly festivities. He had assigned the province of Poitiers to his second brother Alphonse, but the young prince had not yet received his investiture as a knight, nor had he been put in possession of his domain. In order to perform this double ceremony, the King summoned to Saumur his full court—that is, all his noble vassals, lay and ecclesiastic. There were political motives for this assemblage and for the place of its meeting. The monarch of France displayed all his power and all his magnificence on the confines of Poitiers, and in the centre of a district formerly possessed by the kings of England.

'The King,' says Joinville, who was present, 'gave this feast in the halls at Saumur, which the great King Henry of England[1] had erected, it was said, for his own banquets. This edifice is built after the fashion of cloisters belonging to the White Monks' (monks of the Cistercian order), 'but I doubt if any cloisters could ever have been nearly so large. And I

[1] Henry II. son of Geoffrey Plantagenet, Count of Anjou.

will tell you why I think so: in that aisle of the hall at Saumur where the King banqueted, surrounded by all his knights and officers, who occupied a great deal of space, there was a table where twenty bishops and archbishops were feasted. And beyond the bishops and archbishops there was another table at which was the Queen-mother, Blanche: this was at the further end of the cloisters, and not where the King was eating. In waiting upon Queen Blanche were the Count of Boulogne, afterwards King of Portugal; the good Count of St. Pol, and a German, aged about eighteen, who was said to be the son of the holy Elizabeth of Thuringia. On this account it was said that Queen Blanche used to kiss him on the forehead, out of religious devotion, because she thought his mother must many times have kissed him there. At the furthermost part of the cloister, moreover, there were kitchens, butteries, pantries, and other offices; from this part bread, meat, and wine were served out to the King and Queen. In the other aisles and in the open space in the centre of the cloisters there feasted such a harvest of good knights that I could not attempt to number them, and the people who looked on said they had never seen such a number of surcoats and other vestments of cloth of gold at any banquet as there were there, and they say that above three thousand knights and cavaliers were present.'

From the festivities at Saumur, Louis went to Poitiers, where the new-made Count, his brother Alphonse, was to receive in his presence the homage of the neighbouring lords who had become his vassals. But ill news came to disturb their pleasures; a confidential letter was received, addressed, not to the

King but to his mother, who was regarded by many faithful subjects as the true sovereign of the kingdom, and who doubtless still had her own confidential and secret agents. An inhabitant of La Rochelle wrote to tell Queen Blanche of the existence of a conspiracy among various powerful lords of La Marche, La Saintonge, L'Angoumois, and still further districts, who proposed to refuse homage to the Count of Poitiers, and thus to rebel against the King himself. This unpleasant warning was as true as it was circumstantial. Hughes de Lusignan, Count of La Marche, the principal vassal of the new Count of Poitiers, if he had not originated was certainly the leader of the plot. His wife, Isabella of Angoulême, widow of the late King John of England, and mother of the reigning sovereign, Henry III., was indignant at the idea of becoming a vassal to a prince who was himself the vassal of the King of France, and furious at finding herself, once a queen and still the widow and mother of a king, placed in rank below a mere Countess of Poitiers. When her husband, the Count of La Marche, returned to Angoulême, he found his lady melting from wrath into tears, and from tears rising back again into wrath.

'"Did you not perceive," said she, "that when in order to gratify your king and queen I waited three days at Poitiers, and then appeared before them in their chamber, the King was seated on one side of the bed, and the Queen with the Countess of Chartres and her sister the Abbess at the other, and they never summoned me to sit beside them. They did it designedly, to disgrace me before all these people. And neither on my entrance nor my departure did they so much as rise from their seats; putting me to shame, as you must have seen yourself. I can scarcely speak of it, so overcome am I with grief and shame. I shall die of it; it is even worse than the loss of our lands, of which they have so disgracefully robbed us. But at least, by God's grace, they shall repent of this, or I may see them miserable in their turn, and deprived of their own lands, as I am of mine. And for this end, I, for my part, will strive whilst I have life, even though it should cost me all that is mine."

'"The Count," adds Queen Blanche's secret correspondent, "who is a good man as you know, seeing the Countess in tears, said to her, deeply moved, 'Madame, give your commands, and I will do all that I can: be sure of that.' 'If you do not,' said she, 'you shall never enter my presence more, and I will never see you again.' Whereupon the Count, with many oaths, swore that he would do everything his wife desired."'[1]

He was as good as his word. In late autumn of the same year 1241, 'the new Count of Poitiers, holding his court for the first time, did not fail to summon all the nobles who were his vassals; and as the chief among them, the Count and Countess of La Marche. They went to Poitiers. But four days before Christmas, when all the guests had assembled, the Count of La Marche was seen advancing towards the prince mounted on his war steed, his wife behind him on a pillion, escorted by a troop of men-at-arms also on horseback, their cross-bows in their hands, as if ready

---

[1] This letter, the original of which is in the Bibliothèque Impériale at Paris, was discovered and published by M. Léopold Delisle, with a learned commentary, in the 'Bibliothèque de l'Ecole des Chartres.'

for battle. Everybody waited eagerly for what was going to happen. Then the Count of La Marche, addressing the Count of Poitiers in a loud voice, said, "In a forgetful and weak moment I did once think of paying thee homage, but I now swear with a resolute heart that thy liege servant I will never be. Unjustly thou callest thyself my lord: unworthily hast thou stolen these lands from my son-in-law, Count Richard, while he was faithfully fighting for God in the Holy Land, where by his prudence and tender mercy he delivered many captives." After this insulting speech, the Count of La Marche caused his men-at-arms to disperse roughly all those who were in his way; rushed, as a last insult, and set fire to the quarters which his host had assigned him, and, followed by all his people, quitted Poitiers at full gallop.'

This meant war without doubt: and in early spring of the following year it broke out. But King Louis was found well prepared and fully resolved to carry it on. However, with all his determination, he lacked neither justice nor prudence; he respected popular opinion and wished for the approval of those whom he must needs call upon to compromise themselves with him and for him. He called together the vassals of the Crown. 'What think you?' asked he. 'What ought to be done to a vassal who wishes to hold his lands independent of any liege lord, and who refuses the faithful homage which has been paid time out of mind by him and his forefathers?'

They answered that the lord of the soil ought then to resume this fief as his own property.

By my royal name,' said the King, 'this Count of La Marche pretends to hold lands after such a fashion—lands which have been a fief of France ever since the time of the brave King Clovis, who took all Aquitaine from unbelieving Alaric, King of the Goths, and conquered the whole country up to the Pyrenees.' The vassals promised their king active help against his foe.

The Count of La Marche began the contest. He had powerful allies, but the chief of them, his stepson, Henry III. of England, and his neighbour, Raimond III. Count of Toulouse, were tardy in their movements. Provoked by the devastations committed on his lands, Louis suddenly took the field. He had made great preparations, had provided large stores of provisions, means of transport and encampment, and machinery for carrying on a siege. Four thousand knights and twenty thousand men-at-arms followed him. The provincial militia joined: in short, as it neared the enemy's country, the King's army swelled apace, says the old chronicler, 'like rivers when they approach the sea.' Many fortresses in La Saintonge and L'Angoumois were carried by assault. Furious and desperate with her ill success, the Countess Isabelle of La Marche tried another form of warfare: she gave two of her serfs a poison which they undertook to mix either with the food or wine of the King and his brothers. But when they reached the royal camp, the two poor wretches were discovered, taken, and hanged.

At length the King of England landed at Royan, at the mouth of the Gironde. His Parliament, disliking this war, had refused him any assistance in it; but he brought with him seven of his principal vassals, three hundred knights, and, above all, the treasure which he had succeeded in amassing: 'thirty hogsheads full of esterlings,' says Matthew Paris, 'enough to pay a whole army of Poitevins and Gascons.'

A truce had subsisted for some time between France and England. Henry sent messengers to Louis, informing him that this truce was now broken, since he considered it his duty to defend his stepfather, the Count of La Marche, by force of arms. Louis replied, that on his part he had scrupulously respected the truce, and had no thought of breaking it; but that he considered himself quite at liberty to punish a rebellious vassal. So the war began with ardour on both sides; and this young king, docile son of so capable a mother, soon showed himself to be an unsuspected hero.

Near two towns in Saintonge, Taillebourg and Saintes, on a bridge which commanded the approach to the one and before the walls of the other, Louis fought two battles, where his brilliant personal valour and the enthusiastic devotion of his troops decided the victory and caused the surrender of both places.

'At sight of the numerous banners above which the Oriflamme was floating in front of Taillebourg, and of the multitude of tents pitched close together so as to look like one great populous city, Henry III. turned quickly round to the Count of La Marche. " My father," said he, " is that what you promised me ? Is this the countless army which you engaged yourself to raise for me ; while my sole care should be to provide the money ? " " I never said that," replied the Count. " Yea, truly," observed the Earl Richard of Cornwall, brother of Henry III. "I have in my possession a letter in your own hand upon this point."

And when the Count of La Marche energetically denied having either signed or sent such a letter, the English king reminded him with some bitterness of his many messages and anxious solicitations for help. " I swear these were never with my knowledge," said the Count. " Blame your mother, who is my wife. *Par la gorge de Dieu*, it has all been managed without my knowledge."'

Henry III. was not alone in his disgust at the war into which his mother had thus drawn him. The greater part of his English knights quitted him, and asked of Louis permission to travel home to England through France. Some persons about the court objected to this. 'Let them depart,' said Louis. 'I only wish I could get rid of all my foes thus peacefully.' And when he heard his courtiers making a mock of Henry III. who, deserted by the English and pillaged by the Gascons, had taken refuge in Bordeaux, 'Cease,' said he. 'I forbid you either to ridicule him, or to cause him to hate me for your folly. His charity and piety will save him from all danger and all disgrace.'

When the Count of La Marche himself begged for peace, it was granted by the King with all the prudence of a far-seeing politician, and the pitying kindliness of a Christian. He only exacted that the conquered lands should remain the property of the Crown, and, under the suzerainty of the Crown, should belong to the Count of Poitiers; and that with regard to the rest of his estates, the Count of La Marche, his wife, and children should come and ask them as a grant from the mere will of the King. To this the Count added, as a pledge of his future fidelity, that he would maintain in three of his castles a royal garrison at his own expense.

His submission being thus fully made, the Count was brought into the presence of the King with his wife and children, 'where' (it is chronicled) 'they fell upon their knees and broke into sobs and tears, and began to cry aloud, "Most courteous sire, take away thy anger and displeasure from us, and have pity on us, for we have sinned grievously and haughtily against thee. Sire, according to the multitude of thy great mercies, pardon us our misdeeds!" At which the King, who could not contain himself at the sight, bade them rise, and forgave the Count frankly all the evil he had done.'

As long as the war lasted, Louis had conducted it vigorously and heroically; but he was at the same time a true and generous knight towards his adversaries, full of respect for the laws of chivalry and for feudal honour. His brother Alphonse had been grievously wounded at the siege of Fontenay, and when, after a brave resistance, the place was taken, the son of the Count of La Marche was among the prisoners. Some persons counselled the King to inflict cruel punishments upon the vanquished, in order to avenge the wound which Count Alphonse had received and the obstinate defence of the town. 'No,' said he, 'how can a son merit death for having simply obeyed his father, or vassals for having faithfully served their lord?' Later on, 'Hertold, lord of Mirebeau—a strong castle in Poitou—and vassal of Henry III., seeing the rapid success of the French king, and finding himself unable to resist him, went to seek the King of England at Blaye, where he had taken refuge. "My

Lord King," said he, "your excellence may perceive that fortune is against us. What shall I do? Can you help me in such great danger, or deliver me if I am besieged? Or shall I, like my neighbours, be overwhelmed by a general disaster and forced to yield to the hated French yoke, which my ancestors resisted for so long?" "Hertold," replied the English king, with a dejected aspect, "thou seest that I can hardly deliver even myself from danger. Our Lord and Saviour Jesus Christ was betrayed by His disciple Judas: who then can be secure? The Count of La Marche, whom I looked upon and honoured as my father, has given you all a pernicious example. I leant on a broken reed, and it has pierced me. Thou alone, in consulting me thus, thou hast acted with honour. The lands which thou holdest as my vassal, I will gladly give thee as thy own possessions. Freely therefore do that which seems to thee best." Hertold quitted, weeping, the presence of the English sovereign; and went to the King of France, before whom he presented himself with dishevelled hair and reddened eyes. "My Lord King," said he, "God has in His anger poured out upon me so many misfortunes, that I am constrained, much against my own will, to take refuge under your merciful protection. Abandoned and alone, I throw myself in great sorrow before your royal excellence, begging you to accept and receive my castles, and the homage of my service." To which the King of France replied with a gracious air, "Friend, I know that thou hast been with the King of England, and all that thou hast said to him. Thou alone hast acted faithfully. I receive thee heartily, and will protect thee and thy possessions. Men like thee are those of whom I most approve, and the merciful heart should never be closed against them." Therefore Hertold gave up to the King of France the noble Castle of Mirebeau, with all its lands, and it was immediately restored by Louis, after the Count had taken an oath of fidelity to him. After this example, the whole country, with the exception of Montauban and a few other places, passed into the possession of the French.'[1]

A prince who knew so well how to conquer and how to treat his vanquished enemies might have been tempted to abuse both victory and clemency, and to seek exclusively his own aggrandizement, but Louis was too entirely a Christian for this. Unless war was a necessity or a duty, this valiant and distinguished knight, from the very equity and goodness of his soul, preferred peace to war. The success of his campaign in 1242 did not lead him to make this the first step in a career of glory and conquests; his chief aim was rather to consolidate his victories by securing the benefits of peace to Western Europe, obtaining it for his enemies as well as for himself. He negotiated successively with the Count of La Marche, the King of England, the Count of Toulouse, the King of Arragon, and the divers princes and great feudal lords who had been more or less openly engaged in this war. The latest and most appreciative of his biographers, M. Félix Faure, says that, in January 1243, 'the Treaty of Lorris marked the end of all the feudal troubles so long as the reign of St. Louis lasted. He never again drew his sword save against the Mussulmans, those enemies of the faith and of Christian civilization.'

[1] Matthew Paris.

CHAPTER V.

ATTITUDE OF ST. LOUIS IN THE STRUGGLE BETWEEN THE GERMAN
EMPIRE AND THE PAPACY.

IF ambition had been the ruling passion of King Louis, he might have fostered the dissensions of his neighbours to his own advantage, for he had many opportunities of interfering in their affairs when his influence would have had considerable weight. The whole of Christendom was agitated at this time by the great struggle between the secular and sacerdotal powers, represented by Frederick II. and the two Popes Gregory IX. and Innocent IV. The Emperor and the Pope claimed the right of entire control over each other's actions, and asserted their power of determining each other's destiny.

Louis IX. had only just attained his majority when, in 1237, he received an invitation from Frederick II. to meet him at Vancouleurs, and come to an understanding as to the course which the lay sovereigns ought to pursue with regard to the claims of the Holy See. The King of France had good reason for distrusting the Emperor of Germany. Frederick II. had not long previously married the sister of Henry III. of England, and had on several occasions shown an inclination to help his brother-in-law of England to regain his French provinces. Louis did not decline the meeting at Vancouleurs, but he took the precaution of commanding that an escort of 2,000 knights should accompany him thither. When Frederick heard of this he adjourned the interview to the following year, and there was then no further mention of it. Louis, after this, tried to induce the two sovereigns to restore peace to Christendom, but he failed, and thenceforward maintained an attitude of strict neutrality towards them.

The Pope had very recently pronounced a sentence of excommunication against the Emperor, and had declared him to be deposed from his throne. And now, in order to enlist Louis on his own side, the Holy Father suggested the possibility of the election of the Count of Artois (brother of Louis) as Emperor of Germany, and promised to assist the Count not only with influence but with money.

Louis consulted the barons of the kingdom. 'If the crimes of the Emperor,' they said, 'make it necessary that he should be deposed, his sentence can be pronounced by a General Council only.'

Louis acquainted the Emperor with the proposal which he had received from Rome and the answer which he intended to make to it, and also informed him of the religious offences which the Pope alleged against him as a justification of the sentence of excommunication. 'We do not intend,' said the French envoys to Frederick, 'to attack you without lawful grounds. As to any advantages which the imperial crown may bring, we think that our sovereign, the King of France, who is raised to the throne by the hereditary nobility of his royal blood, is high above an Emperor who owes his elevation to an election which may be refused. Count Robert thinks it honour enough to be the brother of our King.'

The Emperor did not protest against these words; for though they were haughty enough, they were at the same time reassuring.

The Pope convoked a General Council. The Emperor, who foresaw the result of a meeting of his enemies, declared that he would oppose it by force of arms. On the 3d of May, 1241, his fleet attacked and completely defeated the Genoese fleet, which had on board the prelates who were summoned to the Council at Rome. Legates, archbishops, bishops, abbots, delegates from the chapters, more than a hundred eminent ecclesiastics, were seized, thrown into the holds of the victorious vessels, and conveyed to Naples, where the Emperor kept them imprisoned in the castle of San Salvatore. Many French ecclesiastics were among those who suffered from this act of violence. Louis peremptorily demanded their liberty: Frederick refused it, not without a touch of irony: 'Let not your royal Majesty be astonished,' he wrote to Louis, 'if Cæsar keeps in tribulation the prelates of France who came to cause Cæsar tribulation.'

Again Louis remonstrated, this time haughtily and with threats: 'Hitherto,' he said, 'we have had a sure trust that, owing to the reciprocal affection, established for so long a time, no cause either of hatred or variance could arise between the empire and our kingdom; for all the kings of blessed memory, our predecessors, showed themselves eager to contribute to the honour and glory of the empire, and we, who by the grace of God have succeeded them, were animated by the same sentiments. Therefore this is a thing that surprises us greatly. We are deeply moved, and not without reason. You have no cause, no pretext even, of offence against us, and yet you have seized the prelates of our kingdom on the sea. They were on their way to the Apostolic seat, to which they are bound both by faith and obedience, so that they dare not disobey its commands, and yet you detain them in prison. We are more deeply wounded than your Majesty may probably suppose. Their letters have clearly shown us that they entertained no designs against your imperial Majesty, nor would they have taken any share in the less legitimate steps which the sovereign Pontiff may have contemplated. Since, then, their captivity is owing to no fault of their own, your Majesty must restore their rightful liberty to the prelates of our realm. By doing this you will put an end to all estrangement on our part, for be assured that we look upon their detention as a wrong done to our own self. Our royal power must be strangely diminished and debased if we could patiently endure such treatment. Turn your eyes upon the past, and remember how, as every one knows, we repulsed the offers of the Bishop of Palestrina and the other legates of the Church when they endeavoured to obtain our co-operation against you. They could obtain no help in our kingdom against your Majesty. We pray you, therefore, in your imperial prudence, to pause and reflect, and we counsel you to weigh what we have written in the balance of your royal judgment; do not listen only to the promptings of power and to your own will, and so reject our demand, for the kingdom of France is not so exhausted or so weak that you may venture to prick us with your spurs.'

The threat uttered by Louis was not without effect. The Emperor hesitated a little longer, and then set the French prelates at liberty.

Gregory IX. died, and under the pontificate of Innocent IV. the struggle between the Papal See and the Empire became more and more fierce. The two parties and the two adversaries divided the whole of Christendom; sovereigns and peoples were to be found first in one camp and then in the other, now estranged by the Pope's acts of violence and now by those of the Emperor. Doubt and indecision at length affected even the clergy. In 1245, Frederick II. was excommunicated for the third time, and at Paris the Curé of St. Germain de l'Auxerrois announced the sentence in the following words :—

'Listen, all of you! I am commanded to pronounce a solemn sentence of excommunication— tapers lighted and bells tolling—against the Emperor Frederick. I do not know the reason of this. I know there is a fierce quarrel, and that inexorable hatred has grown up between him and another. I know that one of them is doing injustice to the other. But which of them? And to which?—I cannot tell. Therefore, so far as it is in my power, I hereby excommunicate, and declare to be excommunicated, that one who has done wrong to the other; and I absolve him who suffers the wrong—a wrong which embitters the whole Christian world.'[1]

In the midst of this conflict of passions, and at a time of such great perplexity in the minds of men, the conduct of Louis remained unchanged. He took the part of neither one adversary nor the other; he

[1] Matthew Paris, ed. 1644, p. 442.

preserved the most scrupulous neutrality in his relations with the Empire and the Papal See, and laboured hard to establish peace.

In the thirteenth century the principles of national law, especially that of the right of intervention on the part of one government in the struggles either of the sovereigns or the subjects of its neighbours, had not been as systematically laid down and defined as they are now. But the good sense and moral rectitude of St. Louis led him to follow the right path, and no temptation, not even his own fervent piety, ever induced him to swerve from it. It was his constant care not to allow either the State or Church of France to take any part in the struggle between the Papacy and the Empire, and he strove to uphold the dignity of his crown and the well-being of his subjects by using his influence to secure the establishment of a just and peaceful policy throughout Christendom.

CHAPTER VI.

CHRISTIAN EUROPE AND MAHOMETAN ASIA IN THE THIRTEENTH CENTURY.

A JUST and peaceful policy throughout Christendom was the great need of Christianity in the thirteenth century, for it had to struggle with two enemies, and was exposed to two very formidable dangers.

The Crusaders had inaugurated a fierce and bitter struggle with the Mahometans in Asia; and towards the middle of the thirteenth century, in the very heat of the conflict, and from the depths of Asia itself, a barbarous and almost pagan people—the Mongol Tartars—spread like a foul flood over Eastern Europe. They swept over Russia, Poland, Hungary, Bohemia, and Germany, ravaging and threatening with total destruction every province through which they passed. M. Abel Rémusat has studied all the documents relating to these terrible invasions, which he describes with the accuracy of a scholar. He writes as follows:—

'According to the laws established by their first great chief Tchinggis Khan, the Mongols were commanded to show mercy to those princes and nations that gave proof of their submission by surrendering their towns and consenting to pay tribute. All others were given up to the fury of the soldiers, and massacred without distinction of age or sex, the very animals being often included in an indiscriminate slaughter. It was impossible to negotiate with the Tartars in their early invasions; men had either to submit or die, and countless pyramids of human bones, which they erected on the sites of ruined cities, testified to the danger of resistance. These ghastly monuments were to be seen long afterwards, and were the terror of our travellers who passed through the regions which the Tartars had swept over and made desolate.'

The chronicles of the thirteenth century describe the Tartars as—'A terrible race rushing down from the mountains of the North; an impious multitude who fear nothing, believe nothing, and worship nothing but their king—him they call the great King of kings and Lord of lords; men, or rather brutes, who are relentless; monsters having nothing human about them; greedy for blood, and drinking it with delight; tearing and devouring the raw flesh of animals, of dogs—nay, even of human beings; having an enormous head on a misshapen body, huge chests, large arms and short strong legs; clothed in the skins of cattle, and armed with iron lances; untiring warriors, unequalled archers, and of astounding courage, riding on great and strong horses which are so swift that they can go three days' journey in one day, and require no other food than leaves and the bark of trees. These horses they mount by means of three stirrups suspended one from the other, for they need this ladder on account of the shortness of their legs; crossing the broadest and most rapid rivers without delay or difficulty by means of boats made of ox-hide which they carry about with them : and for the matter of that, it gives them no more trouble to swim than to eat.'[1]

The name and description of these barbarians, the report of their devastations, and the terror which they inspired, were soon spread throughout Christendom. The princes of Eastern Europe wrote to their relatives and allies in the West, warning them of the danger which threatened them, relating their own troubles, and imploring help against the common enemy.

'What must be done in so sad a case?' said Queen Blanche to her son the King of France. Louis answered, the chronicles say, 'with mournful voice, and yet not without a certain divine inspiration.' 'My mother,' he said, 'there is one heavenly consolation in which we may find support. If these Tartars, as we call them, come here, either we shall send them back to Tartarus, the place from whence they come, or they will send us up to Paradise.'

M. Abel Rémusat says : 'This play upon the words Tartarus (the infernal regions) and Tartar, which is here attributed to St. Louis, is found in almost all the documents of the period, and it is just possible that it affords the true explanation of the change made in the word Tatars by all the nations of the West. These tribes are called Tatari in the Russian chronicles, Tattari by Christophorus Manlius, and

---

[1] M. Félix Faure has also very ably collected the characteristic features of the Mongol portraits, and put them together so as to form a striking picture. He has taken his materials from the chronicles of the time, and especially from the works of Matthew Paris and Albéric des Trois Fontaines.

Tatari or Tattari in a letter written by Ives of Narbonne to Giraud, Archbishop of Bordeaux. But, as a rule, we find that they were called Tartars from the very first, and " Tartari, imo Tartarei"—Tartars from the depths of Tartarus—as the Emperor Frederick called them, became a favourite expression. There was certainly a very general impression that these Mongols were either demons sent to chastise mankind, or men who had dealings with demons.'[1]

Another incident of less importance for Europe had, however, a more personal interest for Louis, and had already turned all the ardent piety of his inquiring spirit more and more towards the East. In the summer of 1237 he was at Compiègne, celebrating the marriage of his brother Robert, whom he had invested as knight and endowed with the province of Artois for an appanage. In the midst of the festivities people remarked with surprise that four strangers were present, men of foreign race and unfamiliar appearance, whom the King seemed to treat with great consideration. These, say the chronicles, were emissaries from the Old Man of the Mountain, the chief of an Arab sect and tribe which had sprung up in the midst of the religious, political, and warlike agitations of Islamism. This tribe had established itself in the mountains of Anti-Lebanon, between Antioch and Damascus, and its members had been known in the East for more than a century under the name of Assassins. It is said that they owed this name to the blind fanaticism with which they executed the orders of their sheikh (a word which means both chief and

---

[1] Mémoires de l'Académie des Inscriptions et Belles Lettres, tome vi. p. 408.

old man), who insured their passionate devotion to himself by all kinds of material indulgences, and made use of them to get rid of his enemies, near and far, Christian and Saracen. In 1190 they assassinated Conrad, Marquis of Montserrat, then about to ascend the throne of Jerusalem, and the great Saladin himself, in spite of all his victories over the Christians, had twice nearly fallen a victim to their blows.

The fame of the young King's piety and valour had reached Syria, and it was said that Louis was about to start for the East at the head of a new crusade, and to re-establish the kingdom of Jerusalem. This report caused the Old Man of the Mountain to send two of his fanatical followers to France, with orders to kill the future enemy of their country. But, on the receipt of further information, he renounced the design, and sent other two of his followers to France to prevent the execution of the murder. In this they succeeded: they not only warned Louis of his danger, but had time to return and meet the first emissaries of their master, with whom they went back to Compiègne. 'Louis, who had taken every precaution against their attempt, received them well,' say the chronicles, 'and sent them home to the Old Man of the Mountain with rich gifts.'

Voltaire ridicules the whole story with that levity and shallow common sense which so often led him to place blind confidence in his own scepticism, and made him ready to reject as absurd fables any facts which he could not easily explain. 'The great Prince of the Assassins,' says he, 'fearing lest the King of France, Louis IX., of whom he had never heard, should journey to the East at the head of a new crusade, and snatch away his dominions, sent two noble adherents from his court in the caverns of Anti-Lebanon to assassinate the King in Paris. But next day he was told what an amiable and generous prince this was; so he sent two other nobles by sea to countermand the assassination.'[1]

But, in order to disprove the records of the thirteenth century, something more is necessary than merely to burlesque them in the language of the eighteenth. The chronicles of the time give numerous and detailed accounts of these early transactions between the Old Man of the Mountain and St. Louis. The accounts agree with all the documents of the time which refer to the relations existing between the East and West after the commencement of the Crusades. They are confirmed by other and almost contemporaneous testimony, which shows the Old Man of the Mountain, four years later, asking the help of St. Louis against the Mongol Tartars, from whose invasions Western Asia suffered as much as Eastern Europe. Without thinking of any difference of race or religion, the foes of yesterday eagerly sought each other's help against the common enemy of to-day. Such a complication of nations, princes, and events would give rise to many improbable and contradictory facts, and the true history of the period lies hidden under the many legends which exaggerate and disfigure it.

Another apprehension and another temptation were added about this time to those which already attracted the thoughts and heart of Louis to the East. The dangers of the Latin empire of Constantinople increased daily. It was assailed alike by Greek, Mus-

[1] Œuvres de Voltaire, tome xxvii. Edit. de Beuchot.

sulman, and Tartar. In 1236 the young Emperor Baldwin II. resolved to solicit in person the help of the princes of the West, more especially of the young King of France, who was already renowned for his piety and his chivalrous zeal.

Baldwin was the possessor of a treasure which fascinated the imagination of the Christians of those days —the crown of thorns worn by Christ during His passion. He had pledged it at Venice as a security for a considerable loan from the Venetians, and he now offered to make it over to Louis in return for efficient help either in men or money. Louis accepted the offer with rapture. Not long before he had been greatly alarmed at the reported loss of another precious relic, one of the nails said to have fastened the body of our Lord to the cross. It had been deposited in the Abbey of St. Denis, and disappeared one day during a religious ceremony. When it was found, Louis said: 'I would rather that the earth had opened and swallowed up one of the chief cities of my kingdom than have lost it.'

He took every care to avoid the disgrace which would attend any kind of traffic in so sacred a matter, and ultimately obtained the crown of thorns for a sum which, including all expenses, would equal about 54,000*l.* of our money.[1]

[1] 12,000 livres Parisis, about 1,350,000 francs in modern French money. The French *livre* (like the English *pound*) was formerly a pound's *weight* of silver. Charlemagne ordained that a silver sou should be precisely the twentieth part of twelve ounces of silver, and in this way twenty sous came to be looked upon as a livre. Both weight and value have been very greatly reduced in the course of time. Again, the weight of the livre, and consequently its value, varied in different parts of France. The *livre Parisis* was the livre of Paris, the *livre Tournois* (p. 19) the livre of Tours, &c.

We cannot, in the present day, sympathise with the eager credulity which Christian faith does not require and sound criticism entirely condemns; but we ought to and we can understand it in an age when men contemplated every fact and every tradition of the Gospel with a deep, poetic faith, and when the belief that they were in the presence of any fragment or relic of sacred times was sufficient to call forth emotion and reverence as deep as their faith.

It is to such feelings that we owe one of the most perfect and graceful monuments of the Middle Ages, the Sainte Chapelle, built by Louis between 1245 and 1248, to contain the precious relics which he had accumulated. The architect, Pierre de Montreuil, comprehended and glorified the piety of the King in a marvellous manner, and no doubt his own genius was kindled by the same strong religious feeling which animated St. Louis.

CHAPTER VII.

ORIGIN OF THE PASSION FELT BY ST. LOUIS FOR THE CRUSADES.
HIS SICKNESS IN 1244. HIS VOW. HIS DEPARTURE ON HIS
FIRST CRUSADE IN 1248.

AT the close of the year 1244, in the midst of all these European troubles, and when his sympathy with them was so great, Louis fell ill at Pontoise and was soon in extreme danger. The alarm and grief of his realm reached the highest point. Bishops, abbots, priests, barons, knights, citizens, and peasants hurried, some to Pontoise and some to their churches, to learn 'how it would please the Lord to deal with the King.' Louis himself thought that his last hour was come. He caused all the members of his household to be summoned, thanked them for their services to himself, bade them serve God faithfully, and 'did all that a good Christian ought to do' in sight of death. His mother, wife, brothers, and all those who were about him, prayed for him incessantly; 'his mother more than all the others,' say the chronicles, 'and she added to her prayers great austerities.'

At one time the King lay motionless and without sign of breath, so that those around him thought he was dead. 'One of the ladies watching him,' says Joinville, 'wished to cover his face, saying that he was dead; but another lady on the opposite side of the bed would not allow it, for she said that the soul had not yet left the body. The King heard these ladies speaking, and, by the grace of our Lord, he began to breathe again; he stretched out his arms and legs, and said in a voice as hollow as that of one who has risen from the grave, "The dayspring from on high hath visited me, and by the grace of God recalled me from among the dead."'

No sooner had he regained consciousness and the power of speech, than he sent for William of Auvergne, Bishop of Paris, and Peter of Cuisy, Bishop of Meaux, in whose diocese he then was, and asked them to affix the holy cross to his shoulder, as a sign that he should journey beyond the seas to the Holy Land. The two bishops tried to dissuade him from this idea, and the two queens, Blanche and Margaret, implored him on their knees to wait until he was well, and after that to do whatsoever he would. But he persisted, and said that he would touch no food until he had received the cross, and at length the Bishop of Paris yielded and bestowed it upon him. The King received his cross with the deepest emotion; 'he kissed it, and laid it down very gently upon his breast.'

'When the Queen, his mother, knew that he had taken the cross,' says Joinville, 'she showed as much sorrow, according to his own account, as if she had seen him lying dead.'[1]

More than three years passed away before Louis

---

[1] Joinville, chap. xxiv.; 'Vie de St. Louis, par le Confesseur de la Reine Marguerite,' in Bouquet's 'Recueil des Historiens des Gaules et de la France,' vol. xx. pp. 66, 67 ; Tillemont, 'Vie de St. Louis,' vol. iii.; Faure, 'Histoire de St. Louis,' vol. i.

was able to fulfil the engagement to which he had thus pledged himself. We might almost say that he was pledged to himself and by himself alone, and against the will of nearly every one about him.

The Crusades still possessed great fascination for the public mind, and were still the object of religious and chivalric enthusiasm; but, at the same time, they were dreaded and discouraged from a political point of view, and there were many men of very considerable standing, both among the clergy and laity, who would not have dared to say so, but who had no desire whatever to take part in a new crusade. Under the influence of this state of public feeling, not the less seriously entertained because it shrank from showing itself openly, Louis continued for the next three years to busy himself with the affairs of France and Europe. He tried to mediate in his neighbours' quarrels, and attempted to bring about a reconciliation between the Pope and the Emperor, as if it had been the one object of his life. His mother and the wisest of his advisers had once for a short time entertained some hope of being able to induce him to abandon his enterprise. The Bishop of Paris, the same who in the crisis of his illness and at his urgent request had given him the Crusader's cross, one day said to him: 'My lord the King, bethink you that when you received the cross, when suddenly and without due consideration you made this portentous vow, you were very feeble, and, to confess the truth, of clouded mind; your words, therefore, had not the weight of royal authority and verity. Our lord the Pope knows the requirements of your kingdom and the weakness of your bodily health, and he will very willingly grant you a dispensation. Consider how many dangers threaten us: the power of the schismatic Frederick, the snares of the rich King Henry of England, the treason of the Poitevins, only just crushed out, and the subtle disputes of the Albigenses. Germany is agitated; Italy has no peace. The Holy Land is difficult of access; you may never reach it, and, if you do, you leave behind you the implacable hatred for each other of the Pope and the Emperor.'

Queen Blanche made an appeal of a different kind. She reminded her son of the good counsel she had always given him, and told him that a son who obeyed and trusted his mother was well pleasing in the sight of God. She promised that if he would be content to give up his project, the Holy Land should not suffer, for more troops should be sent thither than he would have marched at the head of. The King listened attentively to all that was said, and was deeply moved by it. Then he answered:

'You tell me that I was not in the possession of all my faculties when I took the cross. Therefore, since it is your wish I renounce the cross, I restore it to you.' And with his own hands he unfastened the cross from his shoulder: 'There, my lord bishop, I place the cross with which I was invested in your hands again.'

All present were full of joy, and began to congratulate each other, when, with a sudden change of countenance and of manner, the King said: 'My friends, at this present time I am assuredly in possession of my reason and of all my senses. I am neither weak in health nor of clouded mind.

I now ask to have my cross given back to me. He who knows all things knows that not one morsel of food shall enter my lips until it is once again affixed to my shoulder.' 'These words plainly showed that the finger of God was in this matter, and therefore no one ventured to raise a single objection to the will of the King.'[1]

Louis proclaimed his resolve openly, and urged forward the preparations for a new crusade. He announced that he would start after Pentecost in the following year, 1248.

His brothers first, and then the majority of his vassals, knights as well as great barons, also took the cross. The enthusiasm of Louis was contagious, and many were kindled by it, whilst others for very shame could not forsake their king and lord, who was so noble a prince and so faithful a Christian. On Friday, the 12th of June, 1248, the King went to St. Denis, and there received the oriflamme, and then the pilgrim's wallet and staff. After this, he returned to Paris, and went barefooted to Notre Dame to hear mass, followed by a great crowd of people. Queen Margaret was to accompany him to the East, and she went through the same farewell ceremonies, sometimes with and sometimes after her husband. Queen Blanche waited for her son at Corbeil, and Louis there took leave of her, having first appointed her Regent of France, and granted her the fullest powers during his absence. Some say, however, that she accompanied him as far as Cluny.

'O my fair son, my fair and gentle son!' she said when he bade her adieu. 'O my most tender

[1] Matthew Paris, p. 407.

son, my heart tells me that I shall never see thee
more!' And one account adds that, in spite of her
high spirit and great courage, she fainted twice when
she saw her son finally depart.

The King went on his way, and at Lyons received
the benediction of the Pope Innocent IV.; he there
put a stop to the brigandage of the wicked lord of
one of the castles on the banks of the Rhone, and at
length reached Aiguesmortes, in Provence, as some
say in July, according to others in the beginning
of August. He was to set sail from thence, and
had requested all the Crusaders who intended to
cross the sea with him to meet him there. He took
up his abode in a very humble house, which, as it
was the King's residence, was dignified by the name
of 'palace;' it would not accommodate his own suite
and the retinue of his brothers, tents were therefore erected for them outside the town, and in the
neighbouring hamlets. A great number of Crusaders,
vassals or allies of the King of France, arrived in
rapid succession, and these had separate camps distinguished by their standards. There were thirty-
eight large ships in the port hard by, and a whole
host of vessels of transport. The preparations of the
fleet were completed on the 20th of August, and on
Tuesday, the 25th, Louis went to the humble church,
Notre Dame des Sablons, to invoke the protection
of God for his enterprise, and on the same day he
embarked. A young writer of the present age, who
has collected local details full of interest with regard
to this solemn event, says:—

'It was left entirely to the master-mariners to
decide when the wind would be favourable for setting

sail, and on Friday the 28th, after careful deliberation, they were all agreed. They then summoned the pilot. "Are you ready?" said they. "Yes, masters," he answered. One of them stepped up to the King of France: "Sire, call up your parsons and priests, for the weather is fair and fine." Chaplains, monks, and bishops came on deck, and the same master-mariners called out, "Sing, good fathers; sing, in the name of God!" Whereupon they chant the "Veni Creator," which is taken up in vessel after vessel, until it is heard from one end of the fleet to the other. This pious canticle ended, the pilots call out to the sailors, "Hoist your sails in God's name!" And first from one ship and then from another you hear the captain calling, "Weigh your anchor, for you are too near, and may do us harm."

'Before long the wind filled our sails, and bore us out of sight of the land; we saw nothing but sky and sea, and every day the wind carried us farther away from the places of our birth. And I think this will show you that a man must be very foolhardy if he will run into such danger with other people's goods, or when he is in a state of mortal sin, for he goes to bed at night in a place which may be at the bottom of the sea the next morning.'[1]

Thus thought and wrote the companion and historian of St. Louis, the Sire de Joinville, when, a few days after the King had left Aiguesmortes, he sailed from Marseilles to join him at Cyprus, the general rendezvous of the Crusaders.

[1] Topin, 'Aiguesmortes' (1865); Joinville, chap. xxviii.

CHAPTER VIII.

ST. LOUIS IN EGYPT.

1249—1250.

I AM not now writing the history of St. Louis, and of his heroic and unfortunate crusade. What I desire at this time specially to do is to show the man and the Christian in this king. The world is a stage on which we may see much that impresses us, but not much that we can imitate; great events abound, but noble and virtuous lives are rare, and therefore in every age they possess the charm of novelty, and afford the most salutary spectacle that can be presented to mankind.

Louis arrived at the island of Cyprus on the 12th of September, 1248. He did not expect to stay long there; he hoped to set sail without delay for Egypt, where he proposed to commence the struggle against the Mussulmans. At that time the Christian world believed that in order to deliver the Holy Land from the hands of the infidel, the first blow at Islamism must be struck in Egypt, its stronghold. Louis had appointed Cyprus merely as a meeting-place for the Crusaders who had set out from so many different parts; he had concentrated vast stores of all kinds in the island, provisions, arms, and implements of war, provided at his expense and by his care; but his intention was to convey them immediately to the shores of the Nile. At Cyprus, however, the difficulties and dangers of the expedition began to show themselves. These may have originated either in the social condition and manners of the period, or in the faults of individual men. Many of the crusading princes—nobles who were impatient of control and soldiers from choice—arrived tardily and at long intervals. The King of Cyprus, Henry of Lusignan, and his Cypriot vassals received the Crusaders kindly, and even promised to join the expedition, but they had not received due notice of it, and were not prepared to set out at once. They were glad to prolong the stay of the crusading army, which furnished the court with an opportunity for indulging in the festivities in which chivalry delighted, and proved a source of unexpected profit to the inhabitants of the island. The leader of the crusade, Louis, showed more perseverance in his religious zeal than tenacity of purpose in his practical aims, and he inspired admiration more readily than he exercised power over those with whom he was brought into contact. His opinion as to the wisdom of proceeding at once to Egypt did not guide the council of war, consisting of the principal leaders of the army; they decided on passing the winter in the island of Cyprus; and during those seven months of enforced idleness, the improvidence of the Crusaders, their ignorance of the places, people, and facts of every kind which they were rushing to meet, their blind self-confidence, their obstinate rivalry, their moral disorders and military insubordination, daily aggravated the already enormous difficulties of the enterprise. Louis spent his whole time amongst them in making peace, adjusting quarrels, repressing licence, reconciling the Templars and the Hospitallers. He received envoys from the King of Armenia, the Khan of Tartary, and many other princes of the East, Christian and Pagan, who came, not to offer support in the crusade, but by their intrigues to draw the Crusaders into their own quarrels, and to obtain help in promoting their own private interests.

'The Empress of Constantinople[1] sent me word,' says Joinville, 'that she had arrived at Baffe,[2] a city of Cyprus, and that I must needs go and seek her, I and Monseigneur Erard de Brienne. When we arrived we found that her vessel had dragged its anchors in a storm, and drifted over to Acre, and that she had nothing out of the whole of her luggage except the mantle she was wearing and a surcoat.[3] We escorted her to Limisso, where the King, the Queen, and all the nobles received her with great honour. On the morrow I sent her a piece of cloth for a garment, and some taffetas to line it with. She had come to ask the King's help for her lord, and she managed so well that she carried back two hundred letters and more from me and other friends she had there. In these letters we were bound by oath, if the King or the legate would send three hundred knights to Constantinople after the return of the King from the crusade, we were then bound, I say, by our oath, to go thither also. And when

---

[1] Marie de Brienne, wife of the Latin Emperor Baldwin II.
[2] The ancient Paphos.
[3] A garment worn by ladies over their petticoat and tight-fitting jacket.

we were about to return, in order to fulfil this oath, I appealed to the King before the Count of Eu, whose letter I still have, saying that if he would send three hundred knights I would go and fulfil my oath. And the King answered that he had not the wherewithal, and that great as his treasure was he had poured it out to the very dregs.'[1]

In fact Louis had exhausted his means not only in paying the expenses of the expedition, but in providing money for the Christians scattered in the East, and for the Crusaders who accompanied him. This is a point on which Joinville could speak from experience : 'When I arrived in Cyprus,' says he, ' I found that, after my shipping expenses were paid, I had only 240 livres Tournois[2] left. On this account some of my knights sent me word that, if I did not provide myself with money, they would leave me. But God, who has never failed me, provided for me in a wonderful manner, for the King, who was at Nicosia, sent to seek me, and put 800 livres into my coffers, and then I had more than I knew what to do with.'[3]

At last they left Cyprus, but not without trouble, for a violent storm stranded a hundred and fifty vessels on the coast of Syria. They arrived in sight of Egypt and of Damietta. The principal Crusaders met on board the King's ship, the *Montjoie*. One of those present, Guy, a knight in the suite of the Comte de Melun, wrote to one of his friends, a student in Paris, and said that the King spoke as follows:

' My friends good and true ! If we are inseparable in our love we shall be invincible. We could not have

---

[1] Joinville, c. xxx.   [2] See page 49.   [3] Joinville, c. xxix.

reached this place so quickly without the approval of God. Let us therefore land and take possession of it in all confidence. I am not the King of France; I am not the Holy Church. It is all of you who are both King of France and Holy Church. I am but a man, whose life will fade away like that of all other men when it pleases God. Whatever may be the result of our enterprise, it must be for our good. If we are defeated, we shall ascend to heaven as martyrs; if we conquer, the glory of the Lord will be exalted, and the renown of all France, still more of the whole of Christendom, will be increased. It would be madness to suppose that God, who is all-wise, has raised me up in vain. In our cause He will see His own cause, His great cause. Let us fight for Christ, and Christ will triumph in us, not for us, but for the honour and glory of His blessed name.'

The disembarkation was then decided upon, and commenced on the following day. Large numbers of Saracens were seen upon the shore. The boat which carried the oriflamme was one of the first to reach the land. 'When the King heard that the standard of St. Denis had touched the shore, he walked along his ship with mighty strides, and, in spite of the dissuasions of the legate who was with him, he leaped into the sea to follow it, although the water was up to his shoulders, and he made his way through it to his people who were on the shore, with his shield before his breast, his helmet on his head, and lance in hand. When he had landed he saw the Saracens, and asked who they were. He was told that they were Saracens; whereupon he couched his lance, held his shield before him, and would have made a course against them at once had not some of his more prudent followers prevented it.'[1]

The knights were no less impetuous than their king. As soon as the Crusaders were encamped on the shore, one of the knights, Gautier d'Autrèche, issued all armed from his tent, 'put spurs to his horse,' says Joinville, 'and galloped off against the Turks; but before reaching them he was thrown, and the horse trod upon him. Four Turks attacked him as he lay upon the ground, and as they rode past struck him heavy blows with their maces. The Constable of France and some of the King's troops rescued him, and carried him back to his tent. Late at night we went to see him, for he was a man of high repute and of great valour. His chamberlain came to meet us, and begged us to walk softly so as not to awaken his master. We found him lying upon a coverlid of miniver, and we went up to him very softly and saw that he was dead. When the King heard of it, he said that he would not have a thousand such knights even if he could, for they would all take their own way as this one had done, and pay no heed to his commands.'

Louis remembered at that moment that he was a king and must be obeyed, but he himself was the first to give way to transports of blind unreflecting valour, and the very devotion to his cause made him continually forget, not only the difficulty of success, but the first conditions of it. The whole campaign in Egypt was a series of heroic and irrational actions. At first the boldness of the Crusaders' attack and their brilliant courage struck terror to the hearts of the

[1] Joinville, chap. xxxv.; Matthew Paris.

Mussulmans. They abandoned Damietta notwithstanding its great strength and importance, and the Crusaders took possession of it without difficulty. When the Turkish commander, Fakr Eddin, appeared before the Sultan of Egypt, who was very ill and at the point of death: 'Could you not have held out even for an hour?' said the monarch. 'Was there not one man amongst you who would give his life for the place?' When he saw the Crusaders established in Damietta he tried to dislodge them, by proposing to the King that on the day after St. John the Baptist's day, which was near at hand, there should be a general engagement in a place to be agreed on by both sides, so that the East and West might fairly try the fortune of war, and those to whom fate gave the victory might have great glory, while the vanquished should retreat with due humility. 'Our lord the King answered, "I do not defy the enemy of Christ more on one day than on another; I do not fix any time when I shall rest; but I defy him now and always, to-morrow and all the days of my life, unless he takes pity upon his own soul and believes on our Lord Jesus Christ, who wishes that all men should be saved, and opens His compassionate heart to all those who turn to Him."'

The Sultan still prolonged his attempts at negotiation, and sent to ask the King, 'Why have you brought ploughs, spades, and other implements wherewith to cultivate a land which is ours? I could have given you quite enough wheat for the time that you will be here.' As if to say ironically, 'You are young and delicate, and will not remain here long.' To which the King answered, 'I made a vow and took an oath to come hither, and as far as it was in my power I fixed a time for my arrival, but I have neither made a vow nor taken an oath to return, nor have I fixed any time for my departure. That is why I brought agricultural implements with me.'

There were the same delays and loss of time in Damietta as there had been in Cyprus. The army waited for the arrival of new Crusaders, and whilst waiting they quarrelled over the booty taken in the city, consuming and wasting it without forethought; they fell into all kinds of excesses, which Louis saw and mourned over, but had not the power to repress. 'The barons began to give sumptuous banquets,' says Joinville, 'with great profusion of dishes, and the common soldiers gave themselves up to low debauchery; and it was for this reason that, when we returned from captivity, the King dismissed nearly all his attendants. When I asked him why he had taken such a step, he told me that he knew for certain that the men whom he had dismissed had kept places of ill fame within a stone's throw of his own tent, and that at a time when the army was enduring greater hardships and misery than it had ever known.'

At length, on the 20th of November, after five months of inactivity in Damietta, the army resumed its march: it had received important reinforcements from Europe; among others it had been joined by Alphonse, Count of Poitiers, one of the brothers of the King, and his suite; there was also a strong force of English crusaders just returned from Palestine, whither they had gone at first. Queen Margaret and many pilgrims were left at Damietta under the charge of five hundred chosen knights. There was no port at Damietta, and therefore many prudent leaders urged the seizure of Alexandria, so as to obtain a seaport before proceeding further; but, in opposition to their advice, it was decided that the army should march direct upon *Babylon*, that suburb of Cairo now known as 'Old Cairo,' which in their ignorance the majority of the Crusaders believed to be the true Babylon, and in which they hoped to find vast treasures and to avenge the ancient wrongs of the Hebrew captives. 'It is the head of the whole kingdom of Egypt,' said the Count of Artois, the impetuous brother of the King, 'and he who would destroy the serpent entirely must crush its head.' But the Mussulmans had now had time to recover from their first panic. They had reassembled their forces and prepared a vigorous resistance at all points; every day, at every step, the Crusaders were exposed to sudden attacks, and were assailed by instruments of war hitherto unknown to them. Louis was grievously disquieted. 'Every time,' says Joinville, 'that our holy king heard that the Saracens were throwing Greek fire, he would cast himself upon his couch and stretch out his hands towards the crucifix, saying, "Dear Lord God, take care of my people, keep them for me!"' But his people would not take care of themselves, and the wisest counsels could not influence them so much as the impulsive ardour of the Count of Artois. On the 8th of February, 1250, twenty leagues from Damietta, at a place called Mansourah (or the City of Victory), which stands on the right bank of the Nile, the battle began. There was at first a promise of brilliant success for the Christians, but dissension arose between the Count of Artois and William of Sonnac, the Grand Master of the Templars: the latter wished to wait until the King and the bulk of the army came up, so that they might push their victory to the uttermost. 'At all events,' he said, 'it is to the Templars that the King has assigned the front rank on the march, and Count Robert's place is behind them.' Whilst this dispute was going on, an old tutor of the prince, called Foucault de Merle, who was deaf, and understood nothing that was being said, seized the bridle of Robert's horse and urged him onward, shouting, 'Forward, forward!' Robert turned to the Grand Master, and said that if he was afraid he could stay behind. 'Neither I nor my brethren are afraid,' answered William of Sonnac, 'we will not stay behind, we will go with you, but I greatly doubt whether any of us will ever return.' William Longsword, Earl of Salisbury, the chief of the English crusaders, also put forward a few objections, but the Count of Artois replied to them with insults. 'Count Robert,' said William, 'I shall face danger and death without any fear, and we shall soon be in a place where you will not venture to come near my horse's tail.'

A messenger now arrived, saying that the King commanded his brother to wait for him. But Robert did not heed this, and galloped forward so as to be the first to enter Mansourah, followed by all those who had attempted to dissuade him. The Saracens, thinking that the whole Christian army was upon them, fled from the place; soon, however, they began to rally, especially the Mamelukes, a force consisting of Turkish slaves, and the chief strength of the

Egyptian army; they rushed back into Mansourah and attacked the Christians, who were now broken up into small groups and scattered in all directions. The Count of Artois fell, covered with many wounds, and with him more than three hundred knights, his followers; the same number of English knights, with their leader, William Longsword, as also two hundred and eighty Templars, paid with their lives for the intemperate zeal of the French prince.

The King hastened to the support of his brother, but before he reached him or knew his fate he was himself surrounded by a host of Saracens, and he and his suite were engaged in a fresh and exciting scene of action. 'Never,' says Joinville, 'have I beheld so noble a knight; he was seen above all the rest, for he was taller by the whole head and shoulders; he had a gilded helmet on his head and a long German sword in his hand.' The combat grew so fierce that Louis was for a moment separated from his companions, and on the point of being taken prisoner by six Saracens, who had already seized his horse's bridle; he freed himself by some tremendous sword strokes, and was immediately surrounded by his knights, who had rushed to his rescue in alarm and fury. 'It is said,' writes Joinville, 'we should all have been lost on that day if the King had not been there in person.'

The Saracens began to give way: one of the knights of Malta, Henry of Ronnay, approached the King. Louis asked him if he had news of the Count of Artois, his brother; the knight answered that he had great news, for he was certain that the Count of Artois was in Paradise. 'Ah, sire!' he added, 'be of good comfort, for never King of France attained to such honours as you have done; you have crossed a dangerous river to meet your enemies, and have defeated them and put them to flight. You have captured their engines of war and their tents, and this night you will sleep in their quarters.' 'And the King answered, "that we ought to praise God for all His good gifts," and great tears fell from his eyes.'

All those who were engaged in this great struggle were as deeply affected as the King, but they did not all show such pious sorrow. In the heat of the tumult, 'Seneschal,' said the Comte of Soissons to Joinville, 'let these curs howl on, but, *par la Coiffe-Dieu*—his usual oath—we shall yet tell of this day in the ladies' bowers.'

Although the Crusaders held possession of the field of battle, they did not occupy it as victors: their losses had been heavy and memorable; the enemy hovered on all sides of them, and increased in number and audacity from hour to hour. On Friday, the 11th of February, three days after the battle of Mansourah, the King's camp was attacked by a swarm of Saracens, mounted and on foot. 'When they approached our army they began to throw bolts and darts, and to hurl stones according to their custom, and they fell so thick and fast that many of those present said they had never seen a heavier hail-storm. It was easy to see that these men had no fear of death, and held their lives cheap. When some were tired, others, fresh and eager, took their places. To me they did not seem like men, but more like savage wild beasts.'

The Crusaders defended themselves heroically,— sometimes entrenched behind their palisades, at others rushing forth to scatter their assailants. Louis was always to be found at the point of greatest danger. 'He was never of sad countenance, nor timorous, nor dismayed, and his face showed very clearly that there was neither fear nor perturbation in his heart.'

The Saracens were driven back at all points; and at the close of the day, when his nobles were gathered around him, the King said : 'We owe hearty thanks to our Lord for what He has done for us twice during this week; such great honour, that on Tuesday, the day before Lent, we drove the infidels from their camp, which we now occupy, and on the Friday following, the day just ended, we have defended ourselves against them, although we were on foot, whilst they were mounted.'[1]

But the most exalted virtues cannot compensate for the want of prudence and forethought, and neither great valour nor devout trust in God can remedy the defects of an ill-timed and badly-planned enterprise. When Louis rushed into his crusade he had not duly considered his own position and his strength, nor had he taken into account the difficulties and chances of the enterprise. He was not a victorious barbarian like Tchinggis Khan, overrunning and laying waste the whole world at the head of a wandering nation. Nor was he an adventurer-king like Richard Cœur-de-Lion, engrossed by his own pleasure and glory. In the middle of the thirteenth century the Crusades were no longer the objects of popular and universal interest throughout Christendom as they had been at the end of the eleventh. They had lost the seduction of novelty and the illusion of success.

[1] Faure, vol. i. p. 561 ; Joinville, chap. liv.

The crusades of Louis le Jeune and Philippe-Auguste had both failed; the Christian kingdom had disappeared from Jerusalem, and at Constantinople the Latin Empire was falling into ruin. When Louis left Damietta to conquer Egypt he was at the head of from 30,000 to 40,000 men, knights and soldiers, but a campaign of two months and two battles had sufficed to reduce this army to such an extent that from the 11th of February, 1250, king and nobles hoped for no more than to defend themselves against their enemies. Sickness and want of provisions soon augmented the difficulties of their situation; each day the Christian camp was more and more encumbered by the starving, the dying, and the dead: the necessity of retreat was evident to all. There was now a new Sultan, Malek-Moaddam, with whom Louis opened negotiations, offering to evacuate Egypt and give up Damietta provided that the kingdom of Jerusalem was restored to the Christians, and his army allowed to retreat unmolested. The Sultan seemed inclined to entertain this proposal, and asked what security the King would give him for the surrender of Damietta. Louis offered one of his brothers as a hostage. The Mussulman demanded the King himself. With one voice the whole army protested: 'We would rather,' said Geoffrey of Sargines, 'have been all slain or taken prisoners than have endured the reproach of having left our King in pawn.' The Sultan broke off all negotiations; and on the 5th of April, 1250, the Crusaders decided on a retreat.

It was at this time that all the virtues of the Christian were shown in their noblest and most attractive form in the King. Before the departure of the army, and whilst disease and famine were ravaging the camp, he went about to visit, to console, and to tend the sufferers; his presence and his words exercised a subtle influence over the sick and desponding. One day he had sent his chaplain Guillaume de Chartres to visit one of his personal attendants, a very worthy and humble man, named Gaugelme, who was at the point of death. As the chaplain was leaving—'I am waiting until my lord our holy King comes,' said the dying man: 'I cannot leave this world until I have seen him and spoken to him; then I shall die.' So the King went to see his servant, and spoke to him with much affection, and consoled him. He had only just left him, and had not reached his own tent, when he was told that Gaugelme was dead.

When the 5th of April arrived, the day fixed for the retreat, Louis himself was ill and very weak. He was urged to embark in one of the boats which was to sail slowly down the Nile carrying the wounded and those who were dangerously ill; but he refused peremptorily, saying, 'I will not be separated from my people in the hour of danger.' He remained on shore, and when the time came for starting he fainted several times from exhaustion. 'They called to us as we were sailing down the river,' says Joinville, 'to say that we must wait for the King.' But Louis persisted in his resolve; he was one of the last to leave the camp, mounted on a small Arab horse covered with silk housings; he accompanied the rear-guard, watched over by Geoffrey of Sargines, who was by his side, and 'defended me against the Saracens,' said Louis himself to Joinville, 'like a good servant who drives off the flies from his master's winecup.'

But the courage of the King and the devotion of his faithful followers could not even enable them to make good their retreat. About four leagues from the camp which they had just left, in a village situated on a slight eminence where it was still possible to attempt a defence, the rear-guard of the Crusaders, pressed, harassed, surrounded by Saracen troops, was compelled to halt. Louis could no longer sit upon his horse. 'They carried him into a house,' says Joinville, 'and laid him down almost dead, and a citizen's wife from Paris took his head upon her knees; they did not believe that he would last until evening.' With his consent one of his faithful followers went out to parley with one of the Mussulman chiefs: a truce was about to be concluded, and the Mussulman was in the act of taking the ring off his finger as a pledge that he would keep it; 'but meantime,' says Joinville, 'a very great misfortune befell us, for a vile traitor of a sergeant, whose name was Marcel, began shouting out to our people, " Sir knights, give up your arms, the King commands it; do not cause your King to be slain." And so, believing that the King had commanded it, they gave up their swords to the Saracens.' Being made prisoners, the King and all the rear-guard were now taken back to Mansourah. The King was put on board a boat; his two brothers, the Counts of Poitiers and Anjou, with all the other Crusaders, were bound with cords, and followed in a great troop marching on foot along the banks of the river.

The vanguard and all the rest of the army—those who, like Joinville, were sailing down the Nile, and those who travelled by land—soon met with the same fate. 'We thought it better,' says Joinville, ' to surrender to the Sultan's galleys, because then we had a chance of keeping together, than to surrender to the Saracens on the shore, who would have separated us, and sold us to the Bedouins. An old quartermaster said, "Sire, I can't swallow this advice." I asked him what he would like better, and he said, " To my mind it would be much better if we were all slain, for then we should go to Paradise." But we did not agree with him.'

 All the prisoners were collected at Mansourah— more than ten thousand in number, says Joinville. And here the King met with fresh trials, and we have again to record his heroic Christian deeds. He was a prisoner, and was at first loaded with chains; he was so ill and weak that he could not stand: his teeth chattered, his face was pallid and covered with sores, and he was so thin that his bones seemed as if they would start through his skin. All his clothes were lost, and he had nothing but just one green surtout which a poor fellow in his service stripped off and gave to him; he had but one attendant left, a man named Ysambert, who cooked for him, dressed and undressed him, even carried him about, and this man says that never did he see the King angry or cast down, or complaining: on the contrary, he bore his own sufferings and the adversity of his followers with great patience, and prayed without ceasing. His fervent and unwearied piety excited the respect of the Mussulmans, and one of them brought him his Breviary, which had been lost at his capture. Louis received it with great joy, and at once resumed his observance of the services of the Catholic Church. The Sultan, Malek-Moaddam, freed him from his fetters and put an end to all his privations; he even treated him with a certain magnanimity; but at the same time he asked as the price of a truce and his liberty the immediate surrender of Damietta, a heavy ransom, and the restitution of several places in Palestine still held by the Christians. The Sultan would have liked to treat separately with all the principal Crusaders, in the hope of setting them at variance, and he therefore addressed the same demands to all of them. Louis forbade his followers to enter into any private negotiations, saying that it was for him alone to make terms for all of them, and that he would pay for all. The Sultan sent word to the Christian chiefs that he would have them beheaded if they refused his demands; but they all obeyed the King's injunction. Louis on his side answered that the places which he was called upon to surrender were not his; some of them belonged to foreign princes, who alone had any right to dispose of them, and others to the religious orders, Templars and Hospitallers, who had taken an oath never to surrender them for the ransom of any one, let him be whom he might.

The Sultan was surprised and annoyed. He threatened to put the King to the torture, or send him to the Grand Khalif of Bagdad, who would keep him in prison for the rest of his life. 'I am your prisoner,' said Louis; 'you can do with me as you will.'

'We are greatly astonished,' said the Mussulman. 'You say that you are our prisoner, and we had indeed thought so; but you treat us as if we were held captives by you.' The Sultan understood that he had to deal with a man of indomitable will, and the negotiations were therefore restricted to arrangements for the ransom and the surrender of Damietta. Louis was asked 500,000 livres[1] (about £405,280 of our money) as the price of his liberty. 'I will gladly pay 500,000 livres as the ransom of my followers,' said he, 'and I will restore Damietta in return for my own liberty, for I am not a man who can be redeemed with gold.'

'By my faith,' said the Sultan, when he heard this, 'the Frank is a fine fellow not to higgle over such a sum of money. Go back, and tell him that I will give him 100,000 livres to help him pay the ransom.'

The negotiations were concluded on this basis: victors and vanquished left Mansourah, and travelling some by land and others down the river Nile, they arrived within a few leagues of Damietta. There, for the first time, the King and the Sultan had an interview; they decided on the manner in which the convention should be carried out, and appointed the 7th of May for the surrender of Damietta.

But on the 2d of May there was a great tumult in the Mussulman camp. Hurried movements and confused cries indicated some serious outbreak; Louis and his nobles waited anxiously, not knowing what was going on, or what the result would be to themselves. Suddenly several Mussulmans, Emirs of the Mamelukes, entered the King's tent, sword in hand, with an excited but not threatening aspect: they had just killed the Sultan Malek-Moaddam; he had

---

[1] It is probable that the livre spoken of is the livre Tournois, and, according to M. de Wailly, this would be a sum of about 10,132,000 francs in modern French money.

incensed them, and they had been plotting against him for a long time.

'Fear nothing,' they said to Louis, with great deference, 'and, gentlemen, do not be alarmed. You need not be astonished at what has just taken place; there was no help for it. Fulfil your part of the treaty that has been made, and you shall soon be free.'

Then one of the Mameluke conspirators, Faress-Eddin-Octaï, who had just helped to kill the Sultan with his own hands, and to tear out his heart, entered the tent, sword in hand: 'What will you give me?' he said to the King, 'I have killed your enemy, who would have put you to death if he had lived;' and he then abruptly demanded that Louis should make him a knight. It was a very honourable title in the eyes of Orientals, and Saladin himself had been willing to receive it at the hands of one of his Christian prisoners. Louis answered nothing; several Crusaders around him urged him to gratify the wish of the Emir, with whom the decision of their fate now rested.

'I will never make a knight of an infidel,' said Louis. 'Let the Emir become a Christian, then I will take him back to France with me, and enrich him, and make him a knight.' At this the Mameluke withdrew in silence.

It has been said that the Mussulman conspirators, being puzzled in the choice of a new sovereign, and filled with admiration for the piety and resolution of Louis, which were equally indomitable, entertained the notion of making him their sultan. 'Do you think that I ought to have accepted the kingdom of Babylon[1] if it had been offered me?' he once asked

[1] See page 66, line 6.

of Joinville. '"I answered," says Joinville, "that if he had he would have done a very foolish thing, seeing that they had just murdered their lord." Nevertheless, he said that he would not have refused it. And you must know that the project only failed because they said that the King was the haughtiest Christian ever known.'

After three days of excitement and uncertainty in both camps, during which the Christians were at one moment threatened with a general massacre and the next treated with the greatest consideration, the negotiations were resumed and concluded, the terms being almost the same as those agreed upon by the King and the late Sultan. On the 5th of May, Louis with his nobles and the Mameluke chiefs had arrived before the walls of Damietta. There fresh dangers awaited them: some of the Saracens wanted to take possession of the town by force, and made an unsuccessful attempt to scale the walls; the Crusaders whom Louis had left to defend it, and at their head Queen Margaret, who had only just given birth to a son, hesitated to give the town back into the hands of the infidels. At every new difficulty and delay the Emir Faress-Eddin-Octaï, he whom Louis had refused to make a knight, said to the messengers who passed between them, 'Tell the King from me that, so long as he is in our hands, he must not show in any way that this annoys him, or he is a dead man.' At length all the difficulties were removed, and the conditions agreed upon for the payment of the ransom and setting the Christian prisoners at liberty were ful-

---

[1] Guillaume de Chartres; Bouquet's 'Recueil des Historiens des Gaules et de la France,' vol. xx. p. 31; Joinville, chap. lxxii.

filled. On the morning of the 7th of May, 1250, Geoffrey of Sargines restored the keys to the Emirs; the Saracens rushed into the town in great disorder, and committed all kinds of acts of violence.

While the King was waiting on board his ship for the completion of the payment of the ransom for his brother the Count of Poitiers, a Saracen came up to him very well clad and a goodly man as to his person, and presented him with some jars of curdled milk and flowers of divers kinds, telling him that they were from the children of the Nazar[1] of the former Sultan of Babylon. He spoke in French, and the King asked him where he had learnt it; upon which he answered that he had formerly been a Christian. Then the King said, 'Depart from me, for I will not speak another word to you.'

At length Louis saw a galley approaching in which he recognised his brother: 'Light up! light up!' he shouted to his sailors. It was the signal agreed upon for their departure, and leaving the shores of Egypt the whole Christian fleet set sail for the Holy Land.

[1] Farmer-general—Inspector.

CHAPTER IX.

ST. LOUIS IN PALESTINE AND SYRIA.

INDEPENDENTLY of the heavy losses which he had incurred during his stay in Egypt, the forces of the King were still further diminished when he set sail for the Holy Land by the desertion of some of the principal leaders who had accompanied him. The Count of Soissons, of Bretagne, and many others, who were either sick, disheartened or penniless, renounced the crusade and set out for Europe. When on the 14th of May he arrived at St. Jean d'Acre—a remnant of the kingdom of Jerusalem still belonging to the Christians—Louis had no difficulty in discovering that many of those who had accompanied him so far now wished to leave him. He had at all times shown great consideration for the opinion and wishes of his subjects—a very rare virtue in monarchs—and he preferred the acquiescence of free men to the obedience of slaves. He called them together in council, and said :—

'My Lords! The Queen my mother has entreated and commanded me, so far as it is in her power, to return to France, as my kingdom is in great danger, for I have neither peace nor truce with the King of England. On the other hand, the people of this country to whom I have spoken tell me that this land is lost if I leave it, for all those who are in Acre will follow me, since none dare remain in it with so small a force. I beg you, therefore, to take this matter into consideration ; and because this question is of such grave importance, I give you until this day week to deliberate, and then you will answer as it seemeth good to you.'

'On the following Sunday,' says Joinville, 'we presented ourselves before the King, who then asked his brothers and other lords what advice they gave him, whether to go or stay. They all answered that they had deputed Guy of Mauvoisin to convey their opinion to the King. The King commanded him to proceed with that which he had undertaken to do, and he spoke as follows: "Sire, my lords, your brothers and the other nobles here present, have carefully considered your position, and they see that you cannot remain in this country with honour either to yourself or your kingdom. For of the knights who accompanied you, and who joined you in Cyprus, numbering in all two thousand eight hundred, there are not now a hundred in this town. Therefore, sire, they advise you to go back at once to France and provide yourself with men and money, so that you may quickly return to this country and avenge yourself on the enemies of God who held you in prison." The King would not rest content with the opinion expressed by Guy of Mauvoisin, but questioned the Count of Anjou, the Count of Poitiers, and many other nobles who were seated behind them, and they all agreed with him who had spoken for them. . . . I was the fourteenth in rank, and sat opposite the legate,' continues Joinville ; 'he asked me what I thought, and I said that, if the King could manage to carry on the campaign for a year, he would gain great honour by remaining. And the legate said angrily, "How is it possible for the King to carry on the campaign with such a handful of troops?" I answered with equal warmth, for I thought he had said it to annoy me, "Sir, since you wish it, I will tell you. It is said —I do not know if it is true—that the King has not yet spent any of his own money, but only the money of the clergy. Let the King therefore now expend the royal treasure, and send to seek for knights in the Morea and over the sea. When they hear of the high pay which the King offers, knights will come to him from all quarters, and then he will be able to carry on the campaign for a year if it pleases God, and by staying he will deliver the poor prisoners who were taken captive when they were serving God and the King, and who will never be set free at all if the King goes away." There was not one present who had not dear friends in prison; therefore no one answered, but all began to weep. The legate next questioned William of Beaumont, who was at that time Marshal of France, and he answered that I had spoken well. "And I will tell you why," said he. But his uncle, the good knight Jean of Beaumont, who was very anxious to return to France, stopped him most rudely, crying out, "Now, long tongue! what do you want? Sit down and be quiet." The King said, "My lord Jean, that was not well done: let him speak." "Certes, sire, I will not let him;" and the Marshal was forced to be silent. No one else agreed with me except the lord of Chatenay. Then the King said, "My lords, I have listened with attention to all that you have to say, and I will answer you on this day week, and inform you what it is my pleasure to do."

'When we had left the presence of the King I was attacked on all sides. "The King is mad, Sieur de Joinville, if he takes your advice rather than that of the whole kingdom of France." The tables were laid soon after this, and the King bade me sit near him during the repast, in the place where I always sat when his brothers were not present. He did not speak one word to me while the meal lasted, which was not his wont, for he always showed me great attention at that time. I verily believed that he was angry with me for saying that he had not employed his own money, when he had really expended such very large sums. Whilst the King was at prayers after the repast, I went away to a grated window which was in a recess near the head of the King's bed, and put my arms through the bars, and then folded them outside the window; and I stood there leaning against the window, and thinking that if the King returned to France I would go to the Prince of Antioch (who was a kind of relation, and had sent to seek me) until there was another crusade, by the help of which the prisoners might be set free. . . .

'At that moment the King came up, and leant on my shoulder, and placed his two hands on my head. I thought it was Philip of Nemours, who had annoyed me the whole day on account of my advice to the King, so I said, "Leave me in peace, Monseigneur Philippe!" Now it chanced that, as he was trying to turn my head towards him, the King's hand slipped down over my face, and then I knew that it was the

King, because of an emerald which he wore on his finger. And he said, "Be still; I want to ask how you, who are so young, could be so bold as to venture to advise me to stay, in opposition to all the greatest and wisest men of France, who counselled me to go?" "Sire," I answered, "if I had an evil thought in my heart, I would never, at whatever cost, advise you to carry it out." "Do you say," he continued, "that I shall do an ill deed if I leave this land?" "Yes, sire, I do believe it, so help me God in time of need!" And he said, "If I stay, will you stay?" I replied, "Yes, if I can; either at my own expense or at that of some one else." "Now be of good cheer," he said; "for I am right well pleased with what you have said; but tell no one of it all this week."

'On the following Sunday we met again in the presence of the King, and when he saw that we were all assembled, he said, "My lords, I thank all those who advised me to return to France, and I also return many thanks to those who advised me to stay here. Now I have considered this matter, and if I stay here I do not see that there is any danger of the loss of my kingdom, for the Queen Regent has plenty of men who will defend it. And I have thought much, also, of what the knights in this country say, that if I depart Jerusalem is lost, for no one will dare to stay after I am gone. I have determined, therefore, that I will not at any cost leave the kingdom of Jerusalem which I came to conquer and to keep. And now I am firmly resolved to stay here for the present, and therefore I ask the great lords who are here, as well as all good knights who are willing to stay with me, to come and speak to me freely, and I will give you such ample supplies that the fault shall not be with me if you do not remain." Many who heard these words were put to shame by them, and many wept.'[1]

Having resolved to stay in the East, Louis hastened the departure of his two brothers, the Count of Anjou and the Count of Poitiers, together with those Crusaders who wished to renounce the expedition; and he sent them to France, bearing a long letter addressed 'to his dear and faithful prelates, nobles, knights, citizens, burgesses, and the whole people of the kingdom of France.' It contained an admirably candid account of all that he had done and what had befallen him in Egypt, from the capture of Damietta to the time that he had set sail for Acre, and a pressing exhortation to send the reinforcements which he wanted in order to obtain the freedom of all the Christians still kept in captivity by the Mussulmans, and to insure the safety of all the towns and possessions still held by Christians in Palestine and Syria. I do not hesitate to affirm that never, in any age or in any country, has a sovereign laid before his people his actions and motives, his aims, his failure, his success and his needs, with more unflinching frankness, with so much modest dignity, and such deep religious feeling.[2]

To such an extent did Louis carry his conscientious scruples and virtuous inflexibility, that, after the departure of his brothers, 'he called together all the

---

Joinville, chap. lxxxii. &c.

[2] My account of this remarkable document is taken from the text given in the supplements to the edition of Joinville published by Ducange (1668), pp. 384—388.

officers of his household, exhorted them to lead sober and chaste lives, and said that, if any were afraid of failing in this duty, he was prepared to grant leave for their return to the West. Not one asked for this permission. But some time after St. Louis found that there were sixteen or seventeen who had not lived as they ought to have done; he dismissed them from his household, and would not pardon them for three or four months, until Easter of the following year.'[1]

We have no very definite or reliable information as to the numerical strength of the army after the desertion of the King's brothers, but there can be little doubt that it was unequal to the double task which Louis had set before him—the liberation of the Christian captives held by the Saracens, and the security of the Christians in Palestine and Syria. In his own heart Louis always brooded over another project which he did not openly proclaim; this was to snatch the Holy Sepulchre from the Mussulmans and once more establish the kingdom of Jerusalem:—his was one of those ardent natures which hope against hope. Twice he seemed on the point of realizing this dream: in 1250, Malek Hasser, the Sultan of Aleppo and Damascus, who was then at war with the Mameluke Emirs of Egypt, offered to restore the kingdom of Jerusalem if he would enter into active alliance with him against his enemies. The temptation was strong; but, on leaving Damietta, Louis had concluded a ten years' truce with the Emirs, who on their side had undertaken to set free all their Christian captives. The agreement was at that time being carried

[1] Tillemont, vol. iii. p. 392.

out. Louis would not break his word to the Mussulmans, nor would he leave the Christians, whom he had promised to deliver, in captivity, and very probably exposed to a frightful massacre. He made answer to the Sultan of Damascus that he would call upon the Egyptian Emirs to fulfil their engagement without any further delay, and that, if they refused, he would willingly make war upon them. The Emirs did not refuse; they even set free a considerable number of the captives, but they still retained some thousands. Louis waited, negotiating slowly both with the Sultan of Damascus and the Egyptian Emirs. In 1252 the latter, being hard pressed by the enemy, applied in their turn to the King, offering to restore the ancient kingdom of Jerusalem with the exception of four places, to set free all their Christian captives, and to excuse the payment of the 200,000 livres still owing for the ransom. Louis accepted the offer, and a treaty was concluded at Cæsarea; but at the very time when it should have been carried out the Egyptian Emirs and the Sultan of Damascus changed their minds, forgot their differences, and united to attack the remnant of crusading Christians.

Louis had not been dismayed by danger or discouraged by reverses, nor could he be daunted by disappointment: he at once threw his whole energy into a consideration of the position of the Christians in Syria and Palestine; he made every effort both to insure their present safety and also to train and prepare them as a basis of support in future crusades. He resolved to spend in the fortification of their towns the 200,000 livres which he was now prevented from devoting to the ransom of Christian prisoners in

Egypt, and preparations were at once begun for putting St. Jean d'Acre, Jaffa, Cæsarea, and Sidon in a state of defence; he visited them constantly, and in case of need protected them against the attacks of the Saracens with such forces as he had,—the Crusaders who had not deserted him, the Templars and Hospitallers, and the Christian population of the East. He had sent a great number of workmen to fortify Sidon; the Saracens surprised them, and massacred nearly all of them,—two or three thousand, say the chronicles. The King resolved to avenge them, and to pay them a solemn act of homage; after making a raid upon the towns and lands of the Mussulmans in the vicinity, he arrived before Sidon.

'The corpses of the Christian workmen had been left unburied on the ground, and emitted a pestilential stench. The King did not content himself with giving orders that they should receive Christian burial, nor even with superintending their interment; he put his own hands to the work, touching the ghastly remains with the greatest reverence, and helping to place them in sacks which had been prepared for the purpose. "Let us go," he would say in the morning to his attendants, "let us help to bury those martyrs who have suffered death for the sake of our Lord. And do not be weary in well-doing, for they have endured far greater things than this will cost us." And when he saw his knights shrink with disgust from the task, " Do not loathe these poor bodies," he said, "for these men are martyrs and in Paradise."'[1]

---

[1] M. Faure, who gives this account, has collected his material from scattered notices in Joinville, the Confesseur de la Reine Marguerite, Guillaume de Nangis, Guillaume de Chartres, &c.

Asiatic and European, Mussulman and Christian, the inhabitants of Syria and of the neighbouring countries, all beheld this manifestation of faith, piety, loyalty, persevering courage, and sympathetic goodness with surprise and respectful admiration. The King's name and his person became the object of curiosity and reverence. 'A great troop of pilgrims from Upper Armenia,' says Joinville, 'on their way to Jerusalem, came to me, and begged that I would show them the saintly King. I went to the King, and found him sitting in a tent on the bare sand, without carpet or cushion under him. I said, "Sire, there is a great crowd of pilgrims here, and they have begged me to show them the royal saint; for my own part I have no desire to kiss your bones just yet." The King laughed heartily, and bade me bring them to his presence, which I did. And when they had seen the King, they commended him to God; and the King did the same by them.'

The Mussulmans were sometimes rough and threatening, but Louis speedily made them respectful. The Old Man of the Mountain, who was accustomed to inspire fear in all around him, one day sent a messenger to express his astonishment that the King had not yet, 'in order to keep him as a friend, offered him rich presents, as is done yearly by the Emperor of Germany, the King of Hungary, the Sultan of Babylon, and others.' Louis received the messenger coldly, and told him to return in the afternoon. He did so, and found the King sitting in state, having on his right hand the Grand Master of the Templars, and on his left the Grand Master of the Hospitallers, the two Orders for which the Old Man of the Mountain showed most consideration; 'knowing well,' says Joinville, 'that if he had caused one of the chiefs of either Order to be killed by his assassins he would be replaced by another equally good.' The King had deputed the two Grand Masters to answer for him; they told the messenger 'that his master must be very foolhardy to venture to send such an insolent message to the King, and that if it had not been for the great respect they felt for the King to whom the messenger had been sent, they would have had him thrown into the filthy sea of Acre in spite of his master. And we command you,' added they, 'to return to your lord, and to come back within a fortnight, bringing such letters and jewels from your prince that King Louis shall be contented with him and with you.'

The Old Man of the Mountain did not venture to resist this summons: his messenger returned a fortnight later bringing presents, to which Louis responded by sending back 'a great abundance of jewels, scarlet cloth, cups of gold, and silver bridles.'

The position of St. Louis was precarious and full of peril, and yet he contrived to inaugurate and maintain friendly relations with the non-Christian races that did not make war on him. It was during his sojourn in Syria that he sent the monk Rubruquis, whose quaint account is still extant, on a mission to Mangou, Khan of the Mongol Tartars.

Louis was influenced not only by political motives, but by the hope of attracting these barbarians to Christianity, and he displayed the credulity of blind zeal in giving credit to the slightest rumour of any readiness on their part to receive the Christian faith. More than once Mussulmans from Egypt or Syria were so deeply touched by his piety and many virtues that they had gone to him, begging to be made Christians. 'He received them with great joy,' says his confessor, Geoffrey of Beaulieu, 'and had them baptized and carefully instructed in the faith of Christ. He supported them entirely at his own expense, took them with him to France, and provided means of subsistence for them, their wives and children.' But this was not all; in 1270, by his will, he enjoined his successor to continue 'to all the converts, great and small, whom we brought from over the sea with us, the supplies which we set apart for them.'[1] The ardent piety and royal generosity of the King impressed even his greatest enemies, and extorted from them expressions of esteem, and almost of sympathy. Whilst he was at Jaffa the Sultan of Damascus sent him word that, if he wished, he might make a pilgrimage to Jerusalem, and that he should do so in perfect safety. 'The King held a great council,' says Joinville, 'and no one advised him to go. They pointed out to him that if he, who was the greatest of Christian kings, visited Jerusalem as a simple pilgrim, without delivering the city from the hands of the enemies of God, all other kings and pilgrims who followed in his steps would be contented to perform their pilgrimage in the same manner as the King of France had done, and would trouble themselves no further about the deliverance of Jerusalem.'

They also cited in support of the advice a great example: in 1192, sixty years earlier, an illustrious Crusader, less holy but quite as brave as himself,

[1] Bouquet's 'Recueil des Historiens des Gaules et de la France,' vol. xx. p. 16; Duchesne, vol. v. p. 430.

Richard Cœur-de-Lion, King of England, discovered that he was quite close to the Holy City. One of his knights cried out, 'Come, sire, come hither, and I will show you Jerusalem.' When Richard heard that, he covered his eyes and wept, and cried to our Lord, 'Ah! Lord God, I pray Thee not to let me even see Thy Holy City, since I am not able to deliver it out of the hands of Thine enemies.'

In the beginning of the year 1253 Louis was still in Syria, undertaking many expeditions, devoting himself to the Christian cause, and working for it with more perseverance than success, when at Sidon he received news which caused him the greatest sorrow and anxiety. Queen Blanche, his mother, had resumed her regency during his absence, and he now heard of her death at Paris, the 27th November, 1252. The Pope's legate, the Archbishop of Tyre, and Geoffrey of Beaulieu, the King's confessor, endeavoured to break the sad tidings to him as gently as possible; they went with him into a small private chapel adjoining his chamber, and all sat down near the altar. At their first words Louis uttered a great cry, and, bursting into tears, fell on his knees before the altar. 'So great was his grief,' says Joinville, 'that for two days he could see no one. After that he sent one of his attendants to seek me. When I entered the room in which he was sitting all alone, he stretched out his arms, and said, "Ah, Seneschal, I have lost my mother!"'

His loss was indeed a heavy one, both as son and as king. Even those contemporary writers who are least favourable to her acknowledge that Queen Blanche was 'the most discreet woman of her time, singularly acute and sagacious, with a man's courage, but the attractions and keen perceptions of her sex; magnanimous in her nature, a woman of indomitable energy; sovereign mistress of all the affairs of the century; guardian and protector of France; best to be compared to Semiramis, the greatest among women.'

During her son's minority, and from the time of his departure for the East, she had given him constant proofs of enthusiastic but not blind devotion, and had been very useful to him in spite of being slightly tyrannical. Several of the chroniclers assert that the absence of her son from 1248 to 1252, her anxiety on his account, and the duties which she undertook to perform for him, shortened her life. She died at the age of sixty-five; a few days before her death she bade farewell to the world, took the veil and made her vows as a nun of the Abbey of Maubuisson, which she had founded ten years previously and in which she was buried.

Queen Margaret shared her husband's grief. 'Madame Marie de Vertus,' says Joinville, 'a very excellent and pious woman, came to tell me that the Queen was in great affliction, and begged me to go to her and comfort her. When I entered I found her weeping, and I said that he had spoken truly who said that no faith was to be placed in women, " for she was the woman whom you hated above all others, and yet you show all this sorrow for her." She replied that she did not weep for the death of Queen Blanche, but for the King's grief, and for her daughter Isabella,[1] who had been left in France under the care

[1] Afterwards Queen of Navarre.

of her grandmother, and would now fall to the charge of men.'

Louis had a sincere love for his wife, and it was well merited, for during the whole crusade both in Egypt and Syria Queen Margaret had displayed both the constancy and courage of her affection. And yet when she rejoined the King at Sidon, in 1253, on hearing of her arrival, Louis asked his seneschal if the Queen and the children were well, and Joinville remarks: 'During the five years I had been with him he had never spoken of the Queen or of his children either to me or any one else. It seemed to me not a right thing thus to be a stranger to his own wife and children.'

But let the degree of affection in the royal household have been what it might, there can be no doubt that his mother Queen Blanche was the woman whom the King most admired, whom he most trusted, and who was treated by him with the greatest respect and consideration.

CHAPTER X.

RETURN OF ST. LOUIS TO FRANCE. HIS DOMESTIC POLICY.

ON the death of the Regent, all the letters which Louis received from France urged his immediate return. The Christians of Syria gave the King the same advice. 'The King,' they said, 'has done everything for us that he can do here; he will now serve us much better if he sends us help from France.' Louis decided on his departure, and embarked at Acre on the 24th of April, 1254. 'He told me that it was the same day of the month as that on which he was born,' says Joinville, 'and I told him he might well say that he had been born again now that he had escaped from that land of peril.'

Thirteen vessels, large and small, composed the King's fleet. As they drew near the isle of Cyprus, the King's ship struck on a sandbank in the night, and seemed in danger of becoming a wreck. The terror of those on board was very great. Queen Margaret was there with the three young children to whom she had given birth in the East. 'The nurses went to her and said: "Madame, what shall we do with your children? Shall we wake them and take them up?" The Queen, despairing of life in this world either for herself or her children, said: "You will not wake them nor take them up; you will let them go to God in their sleep." The King was entreated to leave the ship and go on board another; he summoned the master-mariners, and said, "Suppose the vessel was yours, and was laden with merchandise; I ask you, upon your honour, if you would abandon it?" And they all answered No, because they would rather run the risk of being drowned than pay 4,000 livres or more for a new ship. "Then why do you advise me to leave the ship?" "Because," they answered, "the stakes are not equal; for no amount of gold or silver can equal the worth of your life, nor of the lives of your wife and children who are on board, and for that reason we urge you not to put yourself and them in danger." Then the King said: "Sirs, I have heard your opinion, and that of my own people, and now in my turn I will give you mine, which is this. If I abandon this ship, there are five hundred persons who will remain in the isle of Cyprus for fear of bodily peril (for there is not one of them who does not love his life as well as I love mine), and who, peradventure, will never return to their own land. Therefore I prefer to place myself, my wife, and my children in the hands of God rather than cause so great an injury to so many persons as are on board."'

I do not think that history affords any other example of a king so mindful of the fate and interests of strangers in the midst of such great danger to him and his. However, the royal vessel got off the shoal, and went on its way; on the 8th of July, after sailing for ten weeks more, the King and all his fleet reached the port of Hyères in Provence, which then belonged to the Empire and not to France. For two days Louis refused to disembark, as he was most anxious on his return to set foot for the first time on the soil of his own land at Aiguesmortes, from whence he had set out six years previously. But at length he yielded to the entreaties of the Queen and of all those with him, landed at Hyères, journeyed slowly through France, and arrived at Vincennes on the 5th of September, 1254. On Sunday, the 6th, he went to St. Denis to thank God for having protected him during his long pilgrimage, and on the following day he made his royal entry into Paris. 'The burgesses and all others in the city went to meet him, decked and dressed in their best, each one according to his means. Other cities had received their king with delight, but Paris showed greater joy than any. For many days there were bonfires, with dances and other public entertainments, which however were put an end to sooner than the people desired; for St. Louis was much troubled at the great expense, the dances, and the frivolities in which they were indulging, and so he went away to Vincennes, in order to put a stop to the whole thing.'[1]

I find in Joinville an anecdote relating to just this period of the King's life which is too characteristic to be passed over in silence.

'Whilst the King was staying at Hyères,' he says, 'in order to procure horses to take him into France, the Abbot of Cluny made him a present of two palfreys which were worth quite 500 livres, one for himself and the other for the Queen. When the abbot had made this present, he said: " Sire, I will come

---

[1] Joinville, chap. cxxi.—cxxiii.; Bouquet's 'Recueil des Historiens des Gaules et de la France,' vol. xx. p. 70; Tillemont, vol. iv. pp. 31—45.

to-morrow to speak of things which concern me." On the morrow the abbot returned; the King listened very attentively, and for a very long time. When the abbot had taken leave, I went to the King and said: "Sire, if you will allow me, I wish to ask you whether you have not listened more graciously to the Abbot of Cluny because he gave you those two palfreys yesterday?" The King reflected for some time, and then said, "Yes, truly." "Sire," I said, "do you know why I put this question to you?" "Why?" he asked me. "Because," I answered, "I warn you and advise you to forbid your sworn councillors, when you come to France, to take anything from those who have to plead before them, for rest assured that, if they receive anything, they will listen more patiently and attentively to those who give, as you have done to the Abbot of Cluny." Then the King summoned his council, and repeated what I had said, and they told him I had given him good advice.'

It was in this frame of mind—humble, conscientious, free from egotism, with ready sympathies, and animated not only by reverence for truth and justice, but by love for them—that Louis returned to France, and resumed the government of his kingdom after an absence of six years, during which his efforts on behalf of Christianity had been as heroic as they were unavailing. Those who were nearest to him, and knew him best, were astonished not only at what he had remained, but also at what he had become during his long and severe trial.

'When happily the King had returned to France, with what piety he conducted himself towards God, with what justice towards his subjects, how compassionately towards the afflicted, with what humility in all that concerned himself, and how zealously he endeavoured, according to his strength, to grow in grace,—these things can be attested by those who watched his life closely, and knew how sensitive was his conscience. Persons of most intelligence and discernment think that as gold is more precious than silver, so the life and conduct of the King, after his return from the Holy Land, were devout and regenerate, and of higher excellence than his old manner of life, although even in his youth he was always good and pure, and worthy of great esteem.'

Thus speaks Geoffrey of Beaulieu, the King's confessor, in a brief and simple chronicle—the brevity, in fact, almost amounting to dryness, but the work of a man who was well acquainted with his subject.[1]

These words of his confessor are fully confirmed by the King's subsequent career, by the laws which he enacted, by his domestic policy and relations with foreign Powers, in short by every act in the reign of St. Louis during the fifteen years which elapsed between the return from his first and his departure on his second crusade. His idea of government differed from that of many sovereigns. He did not desire to establish a deliberate and inflexible policy, recognising only one special aim, and pursuing it by means which may be more or less justifiable and more or less successful, but which must always be accompanied by a large share of crime in the rulers, of iniquity in their actions, and of suffering to the country at large. Before the time of St. Louis this

[1] Bouquet's 'Recueil des Historiens des Gaules et de la France,' vol. xx. p. 18.

had been the policy of his grandfather Philip Augustus, and after him it was more especially that of his grandson Philip le Bel. Both one and the other of these able monarchs laboured ceaselessly to extend the dominion and power of the Crown, to subjugate not only their neighbours but their vassals. Their aim was to destroy the feudal system by force and fraud, and to substitute for it an absolute monarchy; by liberality, as well as usurpation, to place the royal authority high above the power and rights of the nobles and the people.

St. Louis neither desired nor attempted anything of the kind; he did not make war upon the feudal system either openly or covertly, but loyally accepted its general principles which he found embodied in the facts and spirit of the age. Whilst he repressed with great firmness all the attempts of his vassals to throw off their allegiance to him and make themselves independent of the Crown, he respected their rights, was scrupulously mindful of his promises, and exacted no more than was really due to him. He had granted a charter to the heirs of the Countess Mahaut of Boulogne, promising them the county of Dammartin, of which he meanwhile retained possession. At her death, one of her heirs, Renaud, Seigneur de Trie, brought the charter to the King, and claimed fulfilment of the promise. But the seal was broken; and at that time the seal was held to be the only proof that a document was genuine. All that remained of the King's effigy consisted of part of the legs and the stool for the royal feet.

'The King showed it to all of us who were of his council,' says Joinville, 'and asked us to help him in coming to a decision. We all said, without a single exception, that he was in no way bound to execute the charter. Then he asked John Sarrazin, his chamberlain, to hand him a document for which he had asked, and when he received it he said, " Sirs, this is the seal which I used before I crossed the sea, and you can plainly perceive from it that the impression on the broken seal is similar to that on the seal which is entire; therefore I cannot, with a clear conscience, keep back the county." He then called Renaud de Trie, and said, "I make over the county to you."'

Many of his vassals were also vassals of the King of England, and this gave rise to many subtle and difficult questions as to the extent of the service they owed to both kings. These conflicts between custom and duty were very displeasing to Louis.

'At the beginning of the year 1244, he commanded all those nobles who held fiefs in English territory to appear before him in Paris, and addressed them as follows : " As it is impossible for any man living in my kingdom and having possessions in England to serve two masters rightly, you must therefore either attach yourselves altogether to me, or inseparably to the King of England." After saying this, he left them entire freedom of choice.'[1]

[He thus endeavoured to promote justice and peace in the heart of feudal society, instead of cultivating those germs of difficulty and constantly recurring occasions for dissension which he might have used to increase his own power.]

---

[1] Faure, 'Histoire de St. Louis,' voL i. p. 401.

CHAPTER XI.

FOREIGN POLICY OF ST. LOUIS.

IN his relations with neighbouring sovereigns Louis showed the same loyalty and endeavour to promote peace which we have noticed in his domestic policy.

'Some members of his council,' says Joinville, 'told him that he did not act wisely in not allowing these foreigners to make war upon one another; for if he left them to impoverish themselves they would not be so likely to run a-muck at him as if they were very rich. To this the King answered that these words were not well spoken, "for," said he, "if the neighbouring princes see that I leave them to fight, they may well take counsel together, and say, 'The King has some evil design in allowing us to attack each other.' And then, out of the hatred they would bear me, they would all run a-muck against me, and I might lose everything, without taking into account that I should earn the enmity of God, who has said, ' Blessed are the peace-makers.'"'

So great was his fame as a true friend of peace and an equitable arbitrator in the contests between princes and people, that his intervention and his decisions were often asked for and accepted, in disputes beset with great difficulty and danger. In spite of his brilliant victories in 1242, over Henry III. of England at Taillebourg and Saintes, Louis saw, after his return from the East, that there was no solid peace between England and France, and that at any moment the possessions which he had acquired by these victories might again give rise to new wars, which would be injurious to both, and possibly disastrous to one people or the other. He conceived the idea of establishing this very desirable peace upon a sound basis, by founding it on a transaction which both sides should acknowledge to be equitable. He succeeded in this by restoring to the King of England some of those possessions which he had lost in the war of 1242, and by obtaining from him in return, 'both in his own name and in the names of his sons and of their heirs, a formal renunciation of all the rights to which they could lay claim in the Duchy of Normandy, the counties of Anjou, Maine, Touraine, and Poitou; a resignation of the homage paid for Berry, Bretagne, Auvergne, Marche, Angoumois, and in general a cession of all the possessions which he and his ancestors had ever held on the continent of Europe, with the exception of those which the King of France restored to him by this treaty, and of those which he still held in Gascoigne.' For all these the King of England undertook to pay homage to the King of France in the character of Peer of France and Duke of Aquitaine, and to fulfil strictly all the duties of his fiefs.

When Louis informed the members of his council of this transaction, 'they were strongly opposed to it,' says Joinville. 'It seems to us, sire,' they said, 'that if you believe you have no right to the posessions which you and your ancestors have conquered from the King of England, you do not make fitting restitution to the said king unless you restore them all to him ; and if you believe that you have a right to them, you throw away all those that you give up to him.'

'Sirs,' answered Louis, 'I am certain that the ancestors of the King of England very justly lost the possessions which I keep ; and the land which I give him I do not give it to him and his heirs because they have a right to it, but in order to create love between his children and mine, who are cousins-german. And it seems to me that what I give to him I use right well, for he was not formerly my vassal, and now he comes to do me homage.'

And, in truth, Henry did go to Paris in order to take with him the treaty which he had signed, and to perform the ceremony of homage.

'Louis received him like a brother, but spared him nothing of a ceremony which, according to feudal notions, was no more humiliating than the name of "vassal," which the greatest lords bore proudly. It took place on Thursday, the 4th of December, 1259, in the royal meadow before the palace, and in that part which we now call the Place Dauphiné. There were great crowds of prelates, barons, and other distinguished persons of the two courts and of both nations. The King of England, kneeling and bareheaded, without mantle, belt, sword or spurs, put his joined hands into those of his suzerain the King of France, and said : "Sire, henceforth I am your man, to serve you in word and deed, and I swear and promise to be faithful and loyal and to maintain your right to the utmost of my power, and to do justice at your behest or the behest of your deputy, to the best of my judgment."

'The King then kissed him on the mouth, and raised him up.'[1]

Three years later Louis gave, not only to the King of England, but to the whole English nation, a striking proof of his prudence, justice, and good faith. A fierce civil war had broken out between Henry and his barons, in which both sides were defending their own rights, whilst neither respected the rights of their adversaries, and England endured alternately the tyranny of the King and the tyranny of the nobles.

Both sides had agreed to submit their differences to the arbitration of the King of France, and on the 23d of January, 1246, Louis pronounced a solemn judgment in favour of the English king, at the same time upholding the Magna Charta and the traditional liberties of the people; his decision closed with these conciliatory words:

'It is also our desire that the King of England and his barons shall mutually forgive each other, and that they shall forget any resentment which may still exist between them, and which has arisen in consequence of the circumstances now submitted to our arbitration; and that from henceforth they shall respectively abstain from any annoyance or injury on account of these circumstances.'

But when opinions and interests are violently opposed and passions fully roused, the wisest decrees and most prudent counsel that man can utter do not suffice to re-establish peace; the lessons taught by experience are often absolutely necessary, and the

[1] Joinville, chap. xiv. ; Faure, vol. ii. p. 151.

opponents will not submit until one or the other, and perhaps both, are exhausted in the struggle, and feel the absolute necessity either of making some concession or accepting their defeat. The conciliatory arbitration of the King of France did not put a stop to the civil war in England ; but Louis did not seek in any way to take advantage of it in order to increase his own possessions and power at the expense of his neighbours : he stood aloof from their quarrels, and his unsuccessful mediation was followed by an honest neutrality.

Five centuries later the great historian Hume wrote the following encomium :—' Whenever this prince interposed in English affairs, it was always with an intention of composing the differences between the King and his nobility; he recommended to both parties every peaceable and reconciling measure; and he used all his authority with the Earl of Leicester, his native subject, to bend him to compliance with Henry.'[1]

Louis pursued the same course towards all neighbouring states, great and small, strong and weak. In Flanders, Piedmont, Provence, Arragon, everywhere and on every occasion, his chief aim was to promote peace and to uphold both the laws of the land and the rights of the people. He was at the same time energetic and circumspect, always ready to use the influence which naturally belongs to a king of France, but he never allowed France to be compromised by the difficulties and quarrels of other nations; nor would he tolerate the use of his country's name and weight to serve the ends of any mere personal ambition, not

[1] Hume, vol. ii. p. 38.

even if these ends would have promoted his own interest or that of his family. He gave a very decided refusal to the offer of the crown of Sicily for one of his sons. The Pope (Urban IV.) claimed the disposal of it, and urgently desired Louis to take it. When the crown was accepted by his brother Charles Count of Anjou, Louis, who had no power to prevent his receiving it, showed his displeasure openly and would give no sanction to the act.

The sovereign Pontiff wrote oftentimes to the King, entreating him to help his brother, who was already in Italy. He described the arrival of the Count of Anjou in Rome, without money, without horses: he conjured the King 'in the name of their brotherly love, in the name of Holy Church, his mother, or rather in the name of Him who repays a hundredfold all that is lent to Him.' But in vain; Louis contributed neither his son, his money, nor his men. He disapproved of the enterprise; for although Pope Innocent IV. had excommunicated and deposed the Emperor Frederick II.[1] in the presence of the Council of Lyons but without its approbation, Louis considered that the House of Suabia—of which Conradin was the last and only representative—had an indisputable right to the crown of Sicily, and he refused to be a party to any action which might weaken its claims.

But prudence does not always suffice to prevent a government, whether monarchy or republic, from rushing into a fruitless and disastrous enterprise and dragging a whole nation after it; political honesty and respect for right and justice give a far more essential

[1] On the 17th of July, 1245.

and much safer guarantee against the commission of similar crimes than mere prudence. Louis IX. was not a prudent monarch by disposition or nature; his conduct with regard to the Crusades shows how far it was possible for him to be led astray by irresistible impulse and rash enthusiasm; but when there was a right to be respected, a duty to be fulfilled, in his relations with his people and with other sovereigns, he was cautious and circumspect. The nobility of his nature made him more prudent than his descendant Louis XI. two centuries later, in spite of the much-vaunted and undoubted ability of that monarch.

CHAPTER XII.

THE KING'S LEGISLATIVE AND ADMINISTRATIVE POWER.

SOMETHING higher than prudence, higher even than virtue is required, if a monarch—a man to whom the government of men has been committed—is to accomplish his entire task and actually to deserve the title of 'Very Christian.' He must know the 'enthusiasm of humanity'; his heart and brain must be in sympathy with the vast number of human beings over whose fate he exercises so great an influence.

More than any king who has ever lived, St. Louis seems to have been actuated by this generous sympathy and fellow-feeling with his subjects. He loved his people and he loved mankind spontaneously, and because he could not help it; he took the tenderest and deepest interest in their destiny, their happiness, their sorrows. He was dangerously ill in 1259, and desired to give his last and most earnest advice to his son, Prince Louis, who died the year following. He said: 'Fair son, I pray you to teach the people of your kingdom to love you; for verily I would rather that a Scotchman should come from Scotland and govern the people of this realm loyally and well, than that you should govern them badly.'

To govern wisely, to watch over the interests of all classes in his kingdom, to secure strict and ready justice to all his subjects, these things were sources of continued and anxious solicitude to St. Louis. M. Félix Faure, in the history to which I have alluded, enumerates all the journeys which the King undertook in his own country between 1254 and 1270, in order to make himself acquainted with the facts and details of his government; and he also gives an account of all the 'Parlements' which Louis held during the same period for the better administration of justice: these two tables show how unceasing was his activity. Joinville's account of the simple and kindly manner in which St. Louis would himself listen to the grievances of his subjects, and administer justice, has been often quoted, but I cannot resist the temptation of repeating it.

'Now many a time it befell,' he says, 'that in summer, after mass, the King would go and sit down in the wood at Vincennes with his back to an oak, and would make us all sit round him. And all those who had any grievance came to speak to him without hindrance from any ushers or such folk. And then with his own lips he would question them. "Is there any one here who has a suit to bring before me?" And all those who wished to appeal to him would stand forward; then he would say, "Be silent, all of you, and your cases shall be dispatched one after the other." Upon that he would call Monseigneur Pierre de Fontanes and Monseigneur Geoffroy de Villette,[1] and would say to one of them, "Dispose of this case for me." When he saw anything to correct in the words of those who spoke for him, or in the words of those who spoke for others, with his own lips he

[1] Two eminent jurists and councillors of St. Louis.

would correct it. Sometimes, in summer, I have seen him come into the garden at Paris to administer justice to his people, and he would be dressed in a camlet coat[1] and a surcoat of tiretaine[2] without sleeves, a coat of black taffetas on his shoulders, his hair very carefully combed and without coif, and a hat with white peacock's feathers on his head. Carpets were spread that we might sit around him, and all the people who brought suits before him stood round about, and he would have their cases dispatched in the manner I have described before, as he used to do in the wood at Vincennes.'

The active benevolence of St. Louis extended beyond this paternal interest in the private affairs of his people; he gave quite as much attention and interest to those measures which were required by the social conditions of the age and the general welfare of his kingdom. Among the twenty-six ordinances, edicts, and official letters of his reign contained in the first volume of the 'Recueil des Ordonnances des Rois de France,' seven at least were acts of great legislative and administrative importance. These decrees all bear the same character, and whatever may have been their result, their aim was never to extend the power of the Crown or to serve some special interest of royalty when it was struggling with other social forces; they were intended to effect great social and moral reforms, were directed against the violence, the disorder and the abuses

---

[1] The 'cotte,' or coat, was the principal vestment at that time; the 'surcoat' was worn over it.

[2] 'Tiretaine,' a coarse woollen material, grey, still manufactured in France.

of feudal society, and aimed at the extension of justice and peace in the nation, but they did not seek to destroy the existing conditions of society, or to control them exclusively in the interest either of the King or of any one class of citizens.

Many other of the King's ordinances and decrees have been published, either in the later volumes of the work already alluded to or in similar collections. M. Daunou, in an article on St. Louis which he has prepared for the continuation of 'L'Histoire Littéraire de France, par des Membres de l'Institut,' vol. xix. has alluded to a great many inedited documents to be found in different archives. The great collection of legislative enactments known as the 'Établissements' of St. Louis, which seems to be a kind of general but confused code of laws of the period, is probably a work of jurisprudence of later date than this reign; but in it we see the same endeavour to secure practical and moral reform, and note the same absence of attempt to promote any private interests whatsoever. There is a spirit of such true piety in the paragraph which serves as a preface to this work, that it might have been dictated by St. Louis himself. I reproduce it here, with only such modifications in the language as may be necessary to render it intelligible.

'Louis, by the grace of God King of France, to all good Christians dwelling in the kingdom and under the suzerainty of France, and to all others present and to come, greeting in the name of our Lord Jesus Christ.

'Seeing that malice and fraud are so prevalent in the human race that some men often do wrong and injury and all kinds of evil to their fellows against

the will and the law of God, and that there are
many who have neither fear nor dread of the terrible
day of judgment of the Lord Jesus Christ; and
seeing that we wish all our subjects to live in peace
and loyalty, and each one to beware of doing any
ill to his neighbour for fear of bodily chastisement
and loss of worldly goods; seeing that we desire
also to punish and repress malefactors by means of
the law and by a rigorous execution of justice, and
by turning for help to God, who is a true and just
Judge above all others: We have therefore ordained
these enactments, and we require that justice shall be
administered in accordance with them in all lay courts
throughout the kingdom and suzerainty of France.'

At the head of one of his essays Montaigne wrote,
'This is an honest book.' We may say of the measures
and decrees of St. Louis that they were acts of honest
legislation, altogether devoid of egotistical ambition,
of party spirit, or the desire of inventing a system;
they were inspired solely by an instinctive respect for
the common rights of all men, and by love of the
public good.

Another act, known as the Pragmatic Sanction, is
also given[1] as the work of St. Louis, under date of March
1268. Its object is first to assert the rights, liberties,
and canonical rules of the Church of France; then
to forbid 'the exactions and very heavy pecuniary
dues imposed, or which may at any future time be
imposed, upon the said Church by the Court of
Rome, by which our kingdom has been miserably im-
poverished, unless they arise from a reasonable, pious
and very urgent necessity, from some unavoidable

[1] Recueil des Ordonnances des Rois de France, vol. i. p. 97.

cause, and are imposed with our spontaneous and express consent, together with that of the Church of our kingdom.'

The authenticity of this document was eagerly maintained in the seventeenth century by Bossuet,[1] and has been asserted in our own days by M. Daunou,[2] but many and weighty reasons have been urged in opposition to it, which M. Faure sums up in the following words:—

'It is not mentioned by any writer of the period, or in any contemporaneous document; in the correspondence between Louis and the sovereign Pontiffs of his reign it is never once alluded to, although analogous subjects were discussed, and the importance of this would have given it precedence over all the others. It was not until two hundred years after the date assigned to it (in the remonstrances presented to Louis XI. by the 'Parlement' of Paris when, on his accession to the throne, he violated the Pragmatic Sanction of his father, Charles VII.) that the Pragmatic Sanction of St. Louis was for the first time alluded to and quoted. The authority of his name was then invoked in aid of legislative measures to which the promoters wished to give the appearance of ancient and venerable institutions. It is impossible to understand why Philip le Bel—the grandson of Louis—did not quote this document in his disputes with Boniface VIII. Why did not Charles VI. succeed, if it existed when he tried to put a stop to the exactions of the Court of Rome? Nay, how was it that Charles VII., when he promulgated his Prag-

[1] In his defence of the declaration of the clergy of France in 1682, chap. ix. [2] L'Histoire Littéraire de France, vol. xvi. p. 75.

matic Sanction, did not rest it upon an authority and example so highly revered as that of his sainted ancestor?'

I do not intend to discuss this unimportant problem of historical criticism, but I wish to call attention to the fact that, even if the authenticity of the document is open to doubt, there is nothing in the 'Pragmatic Sanction of St. Louis' which is not in entire harmony with all that we know of the character and actions of that prince. In his relation to the Papacy he was the respectful, affectionate and faithful son of the Church, but he took good care to maintain the independence of his crown in temporal affairs, and his own right of supervision, and sometimes even of intervention, in spiritual matters. I have already called attention to his cautious and reserved attitude in the great quarrel between the Papacy and the Empire, and to the firmness with which he resisted the violent measures of Gregory IX. and Innocent IV. against the Emperor Frederick II. He carried his notions as to the entire independence of his authority and judgment beyond political matters, and into questions that were purely religious. The Bishop of Auxerre one day said to him, in the name of several prelates: 'Sire, the archbishops and bishops here present desire me to tell you that Christianity is perishing in your hands.' The King made the sign of the cross, and said, 'Now tell me how that may be.' 'Sire,' said the bishop, 'it is because people now-a-days think so little of excommunication that those who are excommunicated are not afraid of dying before they have obtained absolution, and rendered satisfaction to Holy Church. Therefore these prelates require of you, sire, for the love of God, and because you ought so to do, that you command your serjeants and bailiffs, by the seizure of their goods, to compel all those who have been excommunicated for a year and a day to obtain absolution.' And the King replied that he was quite willing to command that this should be done when he had received proof that they were in the wrong. The bishop said that the prelates would not on any account consent to this, and that they did not acknowledge the King's jurisdiction in ecclesiastical matters; and the King said that he would not consent on any other condition, for that it would be against God and against reason if he were to compel those who were excommunicated to seek absolution when not they, but the clergy, were in the wrong.

'For example,' said the King, 'take the case of the Count of Bretagne, who for seven years was at law with the prelates of Bretagne, and all that time was excommunicated, and at the end of it he proved his case, and the Pope condemned them all. Now, if I had constrained the Count to obtain absolution at the end of the first year, I should have sinned against God and against him.' Thereupon the prelates were forced to submit, and I have not heard that any similar demand has ever since been made.[1]

[1] Joinville, chap. xiii. p. 43.

CHAPTER XIII.

CHRISTIANITY OF ST. LOUIS IN HIS PRIVATE AND SOCIAL LIFE, A WELL AS IN HIS ⸱PUBLIC CAREER AND POLITICAL RELATIONS.

I NOW come to that which is perhaps the most striking and original feature in the character of St. Louis. He was engrossed by religion,—I may say that piety was his ruling passion; and yet his naturally clear and upright judgment in secular and social affairs was scarcely ever disturbed by his religious views. He was not content with the mere forms and appearances of a thing or a person, but must go straight to the very heart of every fact, seeking truth and justice underneath all human conditions, social relations, and royal customs.

Tillemont, the most thorough and minutely accurate of his historians, analyses the life of Louis as the best method of describing it.

'We will study him,' he says, 'first as a simple individual, with no other care than that of his own soul; then as a father, the head of a family, having the charge of a wife, children, and servants; and last of all as a king, to whom has been confided the guidance of a whole people, and who has to conduct himself as a Christian prince both toward his own subjects and the nations around.'

I am certain that this was precisely the order in

which St. Louis himself viewed his duties, and I shall preserve a certain harmony and conformity with that which was passing in his own thoughts, if I close this sketch by relating some of those incidents in which the innermost recesses of so noble a nature are spontaneously and truthfully revealed.

'He called me one day,' says Joinville, 'and said, "You are a man of such a light nature that I do not dare to speak to you of things relating to God, and I have called these monks who are here because I wish to ask you a question." Now the demand was this:

'" Seneschal, what is God?"

'" Sire," I answered, " so good a thing that better cannot be."

'" Truly," said he, "that is well spoken, for the answer you have given is written down in the book which I hold in my hand. Now I wish to ask," he continued, " which you would prefer to be, a leper or to have committed a mortal sin?" And I, who never told him a lie, I answered I would rather commit thirty mortal sins than be a leper. When the monks had gone, he called me to him alone, made me sit down at his feet, and said, " How could you tell me what you did yesterday?" And I answered that I should say the same thing over again. Then he said, "You spoke rashly and foolishly, for there is no leper so hideous as he who is in a state of mortal sin. When a man dies he is set free from the leprosy of the body, but when a man dies who has committed a mortal sin, he does not know, nor can he be quite sure, that his repentance has been such as to secure the forgiveness of God. And for this reason he ought to be greatly afraid lest this leprosy of sin should last as long as God is in heaven. Therefore I entreat you, as urgently as I can, for the love of God and the love of me, to teach your heart to choose rather that any ill should happen to your body, by leprosy or any other disease, than that mortal sin should attack your soul."

'Another day he asked me,' says Joinville, 'if I wished to be honoured in this world and to go to Paradise when I died; and I said, " *Yes.*" Then he said, "Beware, then, of doing or saying anything wittingly which, if all the world knew, you would be ashamed to own, and would hesitate to acknowledge, I did this, I said that."'

Tillemont says, 'Even in his early youth he had a great dislike to profane oaths in conversation; he contented himself with affirming a thing in the simplest and plainest terms, without introducing the name of God, or of the saints or evangelists, or using a single word which could diminish the respect due to things sacred, whatever cause he might have for anger. When he wished to affirm a thing very strongly, he would say, "Truly it is so," or "Truly it is not so." In order to avoid using other oaths he used at one time to say, "*By my name!*" but hearing that a religious person found fault with this expression, he never after made use of it.'[1]

M. Faure says: 'It was with the utmost sincerity that he placed the name of Christian high above his title as king. One day, at the Castle of Poissy, the place of his birth, he said to those around him: "In this castle God granted me the greatest blessing and the greatest honour I ever received in this world."

[1] Tillemont, vol. v. p. 371.

'Every one tried to find out, but no one could guess this honour: his words seemed to point rather to the town of Rheims, where he had been crowned, than to Poissy. At last he said, with a smile, " I was baptized here." He always retained a feeling of affection and gratitude for Poissy, as if it had been his native land. In the letters which he wrote as friend to friend when he wished to discard even the shadow of royal dignity, he was in the habit of styling himself " Louis of Poissy," or " Louis, lord of Poissy."'[1]

I have already spoken of his relation to the two queens, his mother and his wife. His position was often one of great difficulty, but his conduct was never short of exemplary. Louis was a model both of conjugal fidelity and filial piety. He had eleven children by Queen Margaret, six boys and five girls. He loved his wife very tenderly and was scarcely ever apart from her, and the noble courage which she displayed during the first crusade certainly made her dearer to him than ever. But he was not blind to her ambition and her want of political capacity. When he was preparing for his second crusade, he did not confide the regency of France to Queen Margaret in his absence; nay more, before he left the kingdom he took care to regulate her expenses and to restrain her power; he forbade her to receive any presents for herself or her children, to interfere with the administration of justice, or to choose any attendant for herself or her family without the consent of the Council of Regency. He had good reasons for acting in this manner, for about this time Queen Margaret, eager to hold the same position in

[1] Faure, vol. ii. p. 559.

the state that Queen Blanche had done, was making provision for herself in case of her husband's death. She had induced her son Philip, heir to the throne and at that time only sixteen years old, to take oath that he would remain under her tutelage until he was thirty, that he would have no advisers of whom she did not approve, reveal to her all the designs which were formed against her, enter into no alliance with his uncle, Charles of Anjou, and keep this oath which she administered to him a secret. Louis was probably informed of this strange transaction by his young son himself, and Philip took care to ask Pope Urban IV. to absolve him from his oath. But the King foresaw the tendencies of Queen Margaret, and therefore adopted measures to protect the crown and the kingdom.

The education of his children, their future position and well-being, engrossed the attention of the King as entirely, and were subjects of as keen an interest, as if he had been a father with no other task than the care of his children. 'After supper they followed him to his apartment, where he made them sit around him for a time whilst he instructed them in their duty; he then sent them to bed. He would direct their attention particularly to the good and bad actions of princes. He used to visit them in their own apartment when he had any leisure, inquire as to their progress, and, like a second Tobias, give them excellent instruction. . . . . On Maunday Thursday, he and his children used to wash the feet of thirteen poor persons, give them large alms, and afterwards wait upon them whilst they dined. The King, together with his son-in-law King Thibault, whom he loved and looked upon as his own son, carried the first poor man to the hospital of Compiègne, and his two eldest sons, Louis and Philippe, carried the second. They were accustomed to act with him in all things, showing him great reverence, and he desired that they and Thibault also should obey him implicitly in everything that he commanded.'

He was very anxious that his three children born in the East during the Crusade—Jean Tristan, Pierre, and Blanche—and even his eldest daughter Isabella, should enter the monastic life, which he looked upon as the most likely to insure their salvation; he frequently exhorted them to take this step, writing letters of the greatest tenderness and piety, especially to his daughter Isabella; but, as they did not show any taste for it, he did not attempt to force their inclinations. Thenceforward, he busied himself in making suitable marriages for them, and establishing them according to their rank; at the same time he gave them the most judicious advice as to their conduct and actions in the world upon which they were entering. When he was before Tunis and found that he was sick unto death, he gave the instructions which he had written out in French with his own hand to his eldest son, Philip. They are models of virtue, wisdom, and paternal tenderness, worthy of a king and a Christian.[1]

I proceed now from the family of St. Louis to the royal household, and pass on from his children to his

---

[1] There are several versions of these instructions, differing in form but identical in spirit. They are contained in Bouquet's 'Recueil des Historiens des Gaules et de la France,' vol. xx. pp. 84, 300, and 459; Tillemont, vol. v. pp. 166 and 180—383; Faure, vol. ii. pp. 582—593.

servants. In the relation between master and servant we miss the strongest tie—that of blood, and lose that intensely personal and yet disinterested feeling which parents feel when they live again in their children: kindly feeling and custom, much weaker motives, form the bond between master and servant, and give a moral tone to the relation. Now, in St. Louis, the kindliness of his nature was so great that it resembled affection, and called out affection in the hearts of those to whom it was shown.

He could not pardon any breach of morality in his servants, but he passed over in silence all the small faults of which they were guilty, and in such cases treated them not only with gentleness but with that consideration which calls out self-respect, and raises a man in his own eyes, let his position in life be what it may. 'Louis visited his servants when they were sick, and he never failed to pray for them himself and to entreat the prayers of others also, when they were dead. A mass for the dead was chanted for them daily, at which he was always present.'

He took into his household an old servant of his grandfather's, Philip Augustus, dismissed by that king because one day his fire crackled and Jean, who had charge of it, had not been able to make it burn quietly. Now from time to time Louis used to suffer from an inflammation of the right leg. That part between the calf and the ankle would swell, grow very red and cause him great pain. One day when he had an attack of this kind and was lying down, he wished to examine the part affected. Jean held a lighted candle close to the King, and so awkwardly that a drop of boiling grease fell on the bad leg. The King started up from his bed and cried out, 'Oh, Jean, Jean, my grandfather sent you away for a much less thing!' and this exclamation was the only reproof which Jean received for his clumsiness.

Far from the King's household, not engaged in his service, and without any personal claim upon him, there was a large class of persons who nevertheless held an important place in his thoughts and whom he was always ready to help. They were the poor, the infirm, the sick, and all who were destitute and in misery. All the chronicles of the time and the historians of his reign praise his charity as much as his piety, and the philosophers of the eighteenth century almost overlooked his love of relics in consideration of his benevolence. The benevolence of St. Louis was not of that vicarious kind which contents itself with making laws and instituting charities; he was not satisfied merely to build and endow hospitals, infirmaries, and asylums, such as the Hôtel Dieu (or hospital) at Pontoise, those of Vernon and Compiègne, and the Maison des Quinze-Vingt for the blind; it was benevolence shown in his own person, by his own actions, and it taught him that no deed of mercy was beneath the dignity of a king.

Wherever the King might be, a hundred and twenty poor persons received daily two loaves each, a quart of wine, meat or fish enough for a good meal, and a silver penny. Mothers had an extra loaf for each child. Besides these hundred and twenty who received outdoor relief, thirteen others were daily admitted to the palace, and had their meals with the officers of the royal household. Three of them dined at the same time as the King, in the same apartment, and quite near to him.

'Many a time,' says Joinville, 'I have seen him cut their bread for them, and pour out their drink. One day he asked me if I washed the feet of the poor on Maunday Thursday. "Sire," I answered, "what, the feet of those dirty wretches! No, indeed, I shall never wash them." "Truly," replied the King, "you have spoken ill; for you ought not to despise that which God intended for our instruction. I pray you, therefore, first of all for the love of God, and then by your love towards me, that you make a habit of washing their feet."'

Sometimes, when the King had a little spare time, he would say, 'Let us go and visit the poor of such a place, and give them a feast to their liking.'

Once when he went to Château Neuf on the Loire, a poor old woman, who was standing at the palace door with a loaf in her hand, said, 'Good King, it is this bread, thy charity, upon which my poor husband lives, who is lying at home very ill.' The King took the loaf, saying, 'The bread is hard enough,' and went with her to the house to see the sick man.

One Maunday Thursday, at Compiègne, he was going to all the churches, walking barefooted from one to the other, as he was wont to do, and distributing alms to all the poor whom he met when he saw a leper on the other side of a muddy pool in the street. The leper did not dare to approach the King, but he was trying to attract his attention; Louis immediately crossed over to him, gave him some money, and then took his hand and kissed it. 'All present,' says the chronicle, 'were astonished, and made the sign of the cross when they witnessed the pious temerity of the King, who was not afraid to press his lips to a hand which no other person would have dared to touch.'

In acts like these there is infinitely more than the kindness and generosity of a noble nature; they show that fervour of Christian sympathy which at the sight of human suffering, either of body or mind, knows no fear, shuns no anxiety, feels no repugnance, and has no thought beyond alleviating pain and administering comfort.

And the man who felt and acted thus was no monk, no monarch absorbed by his religious duties, and exclusively addicted to charitable works and devout observances; he was a knight, a warrior, a politician, a true king, as earnest in the performance of the duties of his position as in doing deeds of charity. [He obtained the reverence and admiration of his intimate friends as well as of strangers, sometimes by the fervour of his mystic piety and his monkish austerities, sometimes by his administrative ability, his freedom from intolerance and prejudice, and the noble independence of his attitude even towards those representatives of Christian faith and the Christian Church with whom he was in full sympathy.

'The King himself was considered the wisest member of his whole council; when grave difficulties arose or great questions had to be discussed, no one showed more insight or was able to estimate them more justly; and in addition to a clear and vigorous intellect he possessed the power of expressing his thoughts with such a measured grace that he was a most perfect and agreeable speaker.'

'He was very cheerful,' says Joinville; 'and when we were in private with him, after dinner, he used to sit at the foot of his bed, and if the Franciscans and Dominicans told him of a book which they thought he would like to hear, he would answer, "No, you shan't read to me now, for there is no book so good after eating as a talk *ad libitum;* that is, let each one say what he likes." But, for all this, he was very fond of books and learning.

'He sometimes listened to the sermons and discussions in the University, but he took care also to seek the truth himself in the Word of God and the traditions of the Church. When he was in the East he heard that a Saracen sultan had collected a great number of books for the use of the philosophers of his sect; he was ashamed to think that the Christians were less zealous to learn the truth than the infidels were to teach themselves lies. Therefore, on his return to France, he commanded that search should be made in the abbeys for all the genuine works of St. Augustine, St. Ambrose, St. Jerome, St. Gregory, and other orthodox teachers, and, having caused them all to be copied, he had them laid up in the treasure-house of the Sainte-Chapelle. He read them whenever he had any spare time, and gladly lent them to those who could make any use of them either for themselves or others. Sometimes towards the close of the afternoon he would send for persons of well-known piety, and converse with them of God, and also of the Bible stories and the lives of the saints or fathers of the Church.'

He had a special friendship for Robert of Sorbon the founder of the Sorbonne, and not only afforded him every facility and gave him all the necessary help for establishing his learned college, but also made him one of his chaplains, and often invited him to sit near him at dinner in order that he might have the pleasure of hearing him converse.

'One day it happened,' says Joinville, 'that Master Robert of Sorbon was sitting by my side at dinner-time, and we were talking together in a low voice. The King reproved us, saying, "Speak aloud, or your companions will think that you are speaking ill of them. If you are talking of anything at dinner-time that can give us pleasure, speak so that we can hear you; if not, be silent."'

Another day, when they had met in the King's presence, Robert of Sorbon reproached Joinville for being 'more magnificently attired than the King, for,' said he, 'you dress yourself in furs and green cloth, which the King does not do.' Joinville defended himself very warmly, and turned the tables on Master Robert, attacking him for the smartness of his clothes. The King took the part of the learned doctor, but when he had left them, 'My lord the King,' continues Joinville, 'called Monseigneur Philip, his son, and King Thibault, and sat down at the door of his oratory; placing his hand on the ground, he said, "Come and sit close to me, that no one may hear us." Then he said he had called us that he might confess to me that he had been wrong in defending Master Robert. "But," he said, "I saw he was so taken aback that he had need of my help. For all that, do not think too much of what I said in defence of Master Robert; for, as the Seneschal has said, you ought to dress well and suitably: your wives will love you the better for it, and your people will also think more of you. For," said this wise king, "we ought so to choose both our apparel and our dress, that the old men of this age may not say we do too much, nor the young ones that we do too little."'

In his own costume and manner of life nothing could be more simple than St. Louis. 'After he returned from beyond the sea,' says Joinville, ' he never wore furs, either miniver or squirrel, nor scarlet cloth, neither did he use gilded spurs or stirrups; his vestments were of camlet or of pers'—a dark blue cloth—'and the linings of his coverlets and garments were of doeskin or hareskin.'

He dressed and undressed himself almost without attendants, rose in the morning and went to bed at night, dispensing altogether with royal etiquette. 'But,' adds Joinville, 'the daily expenses of his household were very great; he behaved with great generosity and liberality in the "Parlements" and at the assemblies of the barons and knights; the service of his court also was conducted with great courtesy, liberally and without stint; far more so than had been the case for a long time at the court of his ancestors.'

CHAPTER XIV.

THE CRUSADE THE RULING PASSION OF ST. LOUIS. IN SPITE OF STRENUOUS OPPOSITION, HE DECIDES ON A SECOND CRUSADE (1270). HIS ARRIVAL AND DEATH BEFORE TUNIS (25TH AUGUST, 1270).

UNQUESTIONABLY the life of St. Louis was no mere empty royal life. Its varied interests and great labours might have employed the most active mind, and satisfied the most exacting conscience; but although the soul of the King was serene and calm, his imagination was incessantly excited, and he suffered om a kind of pious fever,—a fever very different ı its aim, but also similar in kind, to that which consumes those great potentates whose restless nature is always discontented, who cherish some vast project quite apart from the ordinary course of events until its accomplishment becomes their fixed idea and ruling passion. As Alexander and Napoleon continually formed new plans, or, to speak more accurately, new dreams, of conquest and dominion, so Louis, in his Christian ambition, always pictured to himself the return to Jerusalem, the deliverance of the Holy Sepulchre and the victory of Christianity over Islamism in the East. It was all in vain that during his first crusade he discovered the immense difficulty, not to say the impossibility of the enterprise, and found that his utmost efforts could not ensure success: the crusade always remained his passion, as the one and only method of realizing his fondest hope and fulfilling his most sacred duty. During the first years after his return from Syria to France—that is, from 1254 to 1260—it does not appear that he spoke of his scheme even to his most intimate and confidential friends. But I am convinced that it was never out of his thoughts, and that he always hoped favourable circumstance would recall him to his interrupted work.

There was no lack of difficulties in the East: the Christians of Palestine and Syria were exposed to perils and losses which increased daily; they were losing their bravest warriors, the Templars and Hospitallers, by incessant warfare; their strong places were falling to ruin; the soldiers of the Cross were defeated now by the Tartars of Tchinggis Khan, now by the Mamelukes of Egypt; the Latin Empire of Constantinople was disappearing; and the Greek Church had again obtained possession of St. Sophia. The most lamentable accounts, the most urgent entreaties daily reached the Christians of the West; and Pope Urban IV. made a special appeal to the King of France. Geoffrey of Sargines, the heroic and faithful representative whom Louis had left in St. Jean d'Acre at the head of a small garrison, wrote to tell him that all was lost unless they received immediate succour.

In 1261 Louis held a 'Parlement' at Paris, and although he did not then speak of a new crusade, he took measures which revealed his intentions and thoughts. Fasts and prayers were appointed on behalf of the Christians of the East; all extravagant expenses, shows, and tournaments were forbidden; and frequent and important military exercises were appointed.

In 1263 the crusade was preached throughout France. Taxes were levied in aid of it which even the clergy had to pay. Princes and barons undertook to join in the expedition; some even went so far as to set out. Louis congratulated himself, and showed his pleasure and approval without openly declaring his own intention. In 1267 a 'Parlement' was convoked at Paris. The King very discreetly broached the subject of a crusade first of all to some of his barons, in order to make sure of their approval. Then suddenly, after the precious relics from the Sainte-Chapelle had been exposed to the gaze of the assembly, he opened the proceedings by an earnest exhortation to all present 'to avenge the ancient wrongs of our Lord and Saviour in the Holy Land, and to regain the heritage of Christendom so long—for our sins—in the possession of the infidel.' The following year another 'Parlement' met at Paris, and there, on the 9th of February, 1268, the King made a vow to set out in May of 1270.

Great was the surprise of many of his subjects, and their anxiety was even greater than their surprise. The country was tranquil and prosperous to an extent that had been unparalleled for a long period; there was peace without, and law and order within; feudal quarrels were becoming rare, and were promptly settled; the royal authority was felt everywhere, and was accompanied by a more orderly administration and greater certainty of justice; the King possessed the confidence as well as the respect of his whole people, and he was respected and obeyed by all his agents. 'Why should we risk,' they said, 'these advantages in a costly and distant enterprise where success is more than doubtful?' Either from good sense or from displeasure at the taxes imposed upon them, many ecclesiastics as well as laymen were unfavourable to the crusade. Pope Clement IV., who had succeeded Urban IV., 'hesitated for some time about urging St. Louis to this enterprise; indeed, it seems that in a letter which he wrote towards the close of September 1266, he rather dissuaded him from it. He was, however, annoyed at having written this letter almost as soon as he had dispatched it, and said just the reverse in a letter which he wrote with his own hand, and at first thought of sending immediately; but, hesitating still, he withheld it.... He ended by making up his mind to encourage the King in his pious design; but when he learnt that Louis was taking three sons with him to the crusade, the eldest twenty-two, and the two others seventeen and eighteen years old, he could not resist writing to the Cardinal of Sainte-Cécile as follows: " It does not seem to us that it would be wise or judicious to allow so many of the King's sons to take the cross, especially the eldest; and, although we have heard many reasons given in favour of the opposite view, yet either we deceive ourselves entirely, or they are devoid of any reason whatsoever."'[1]

Grave anxiety was felt as to the King himself: his health was very much shattered, and it was feared that he himself was no better able to bear the fatigue of the expedition than his country was likely to endure without loss the disadvantage of his absence. Many of his wisest and most faithful advisers openly opposed his scheme. Joinville says: 'It came to pass that the King summoned all his barons to Paris during Lent (1267). I sent my excuses to him on

[1] Tillemont, vol. v. pp. 10—17.

account of a quartan fever which I then had, and begged him graciously to dispense with my attendance. He sent word that he insisted on my going, for he had good physicians at Paris who would soon cure a quartan fever. So I went thither. When I had heard mass at the Madeleine I went to the King's chapel, and found him mounted upon the platform where the relics were, and causing the true cross to be carried down. When the King was descending, two knights who were of his council began to speak together, and one said, "Never believe me, if the King does not now take the cross." And the other answered : "If the King takes the cross, it will be one of the saddest days that ever was in France; for if we do not also take it we shall lose the King's love, and if we take it we shall lose the love of God, because it will not be for His sake that we undertake this crusade."' The King earnestly entreated Joinville to take the cross, but he positively refused to do so. 'I thought,' he says, 'that all those who advised him to undertake that voyage committed a great sin, because France was in such a condition that the whole kingdom was at peace within itself, and at peace with all its neighbours ; and, from the time that he departed, its condition has never ceased to grow worse and worse. Those who advised this voyage in his weak state of health committed a great sin, for he was able neither to ride in a carriage nor on horseback; nay, his debility was so great that he allowed me to carry him in my arms from the house of the Count of Auxerre, where I took leave of him, to the Franciscans. And yet, feeble as he was, if he had remained in France, he might have lived for many years, and done much good.'

But the impulse had been given, not only to the King, but to his family and the whole feudal world; his sons, his brothers, his son-in-law Thibault, King of Navarre, many foreign princes, 'a multitude of counts, barons, and knights,' took the cross; some with eager fervour, others with resignation and after much hesitation. The second crusade of St. Louis was a flame which leaps up at intervals from a dying fire, and throws out bright and fitful gleams.

But, together with tidings which aroused angry alarm, news came from the East which inspired fresh hopes and expectations. The Emperor Michael Palæologus had returned to Constantinople, and he held out to the Pope and all Christendom the hope of reunion between the Greek Church and the Church of Rome; Mohammed Mostanser, the King of Tunis (as he called himself), spoke of becoming a Christian, he and all his subjects, and offered to decide on taking this step if he could be secured against their seditions. Clement IV. was enchanted with the Greek promises. Louis heard of the prospect of the Moslem conversions with rapture; he was in the state of mind of a man who has taken a final resolve which is very dear to him, and who listens with the most astounding credulity to any reasons and hopes which seem to justify his course. 'Ah,' he wrote, 'if I might only hope to be the godfather and the compeer of so great a godson!' At the fête of St. Denis, the 9th of October, 1269, Louis was present in the abbey church, at the baptism of a recently-converted Jew. The Tunis envoys were also there: he called them to him, and said with great emotion, 'Tell the King your master, from me, that I desire the salvation of his soul so ardently that I would consent to be in prison among the Saracens all the days of my life and never see the light of day again, if only your king and his nation might become true Christians.' From henceforward Louis was absorbed by Christian zeal and faith, and was more saint than king.

He set out from Paris on the 16th of March, 1270, having left Queen Margaret, whom he would not allow to accompany him further, in the tower of the Castle at Vincennes. He was weak in health and almost ill, but quite content; and probably out of all those who accompanied him he alone had no anxious forebodings. Again he was to embark from Aiguesmortes. No definite plan for the expedition had yet been decided upon. Should they go first to Egypt, to Palestine, to Constantinople, or to Tunis? Were there any means of transport on which they could rely? There had been negotiations on the subject with the Venetians and the Genoese, but nothing was definitely settled. It was a haphazard expedition, in which men put their trust in Providence, and forgot that Divine Providence does not dispense with human foresight. Louis arrived at Aiguesmortes in the middle of May, and found neither Crusaders nor vessels; all the preparations were made slowly, imperfectly, and without order; every one relied too much upon the King, who relied too much upon every one. At length, on the 2d of July, 1270, the expedition set sail, and actually left Aiguesmortes before any person knew, or the King had told any one, where it was going. Not until he reached Sardinia, after four days' delay at Cagliari, did Louis declare to the leaders of the crusade, who had assembled on board his vessel the *Montjoie*, that he was on his way to Tunis, where their Christian work was to begin.

On the 17th of July, the fleet arrived before Tunis ; and the admiral, Florent de Varennes, without orders from the King, probably even in opposition to instructions which showed less impatience, took immediate possession of the port and of some Tunisian vessels, which offered no resistance. He sent word to the King ' that it was only necessary to support him, and that the disembarkation of the army could take place in perfect safety.' War was thus commenced against the Mussulman prince who had so recently been expected very shortly to become a Christian. Fifteen days later, after several combats devoid of result between the Crusaders and the army of Tunis, all this improvidence, delay, and, to call things by their right name, political and military incapacity, had rapidly brought its inevitable consequences. The reinforcements which his brother Charles, King of Sicily, had promised to Louis, had not arrived ; there was a lack of provisions ; the intense heat of an African summer caused a pestilence which spread so rapidly that before long there was no time to bury the dead, they were thrown one on the other into the trench which surrounded the camp, and before long the whole camp was infected.

On the 3d of August Louis was attacked by the prevailing fever, and was obliged to keep his bed within his tent. He asked news of his son, Jean Tristan, Count of Nevers, who had fallen ill before him, for he had not been told of the death of the young prince, who had expired on board the vessel to which he had been carried in the hope that the sea-air might be beneficial to him. Jean Tristan and the Princess Isabella were the dearest of all his children ; Louis joined his hands when he heard of his death, and sought some relief for his sorrow in silence and prayer. He became rapidly worse, and sent for his son and successor, Prince Philip, took from his Breviary the 'Instructions' which he had written for him in French with his own hand, gave them to him, and exhorted him to observe them scrupulously. He also asked for his daughter Isabella. 'She had been adorned by the most saintly demeanour from her very infancy, and in this the King had taken great delight,' although she had refused to become a nun, which he had wished. She fell weeping at the foot of his bed, and he gave to her husband, Thibault, King of Navarre, some written counsel which he had prepared for her; then he called her to his side and gave into her own hands a paper, which he charged her to deliver to her youngest sister, the Princess Agnes, wife of the Duke of Burgundy. 'Most dear daughter,' he said, 'lay this to heart; many persons go to bed full of vain and sinful thought, and in the morning are found dead. The true way of loving God is to love Him with our whole heart, and He well deserves our love, for He first loved us.' He was too weak to say more.

On the 24th of August, after he had thus taken leave of his children, he was informed that envoys from the Emperor Michael Palæologus had landed at the Cape of Carthage; they were commissioned by their master to beg for the intervention of the King with his brother Charles, King of Sicily, to induce him to refrain from making war on the recently re-established empire of Greece. Louis made a last effort to receive them in his tent in the presence of some of the members of his council, who were most uneasy at the fatigue he was undergoing. 'I promise you, if I live,' he said to the envoys, 'to do that which the Emperor requires of me; meanwhile I exhort you to have patience, and to be of good courage.'

This was his last political act and his final anxiety in the affairs of this world; after this he was absorbed in pious thought and prayer, in reveries concerning his own duties and spiritual experiences, or those interests of Christianity which had been so dear to him all his life. He repeated his usual prayers in a low tone; he was heard to murmur, 'Grant us, we pray Thee, O Lord, to despise for love of Thee the prosperity of this world, and not to fear its reverses.' And also, 'O Lord God, have mercy upon this people who remain here, and lead them back to their own land. Let them not fall into the hands of their enemies, and let them never be forced to deny Thy name.'

On the night of the 24th of August he started up several times in his bed and called out, 'Jerusalem! Jerusalem! we will go to Jerusalem!' At last he ceased to speak, although he showed that he was in full possession of his faculties, and in sympathy with and conscious of the friends who surrounded him, and the priests who brought him religious consolation; by his desire he received extreme unction at the foot of his bed, extended upon a coarse sack covered with ashes, and with the cross before him. On Monday, the 25th of August, 1270, about three o'clock in the afternoon, he expired peacefully. His last words were, 'Father, after the example of the Divine Master, into Thy hands I commit my spirit.'

CHAPTER XV.

PORTRAIT OF ST. LOUIS AS THE IDEAL MAN, CHRISTIAN, AND KING OF THE MIDDLE AGES. HIS PARTICIPATION IN THE TWO GREAT ERRORS OF HIS TIME.

THE world has seen more profound politicians on the throne, greater generals, men of more mighty and brilliant intellect, princes who have exercised a more powerful influence over later generations and events subsequent to their own time; but it has never seen such a king as this St. Louis, never seen a man possessing sovereign power and yet not contracting the vices and passions which attend it, displaying upon the throne in such a high degree every human virtue purified and ennobled by Christian faith. St. Louis did not give any new or permanent impulse to his age; he did not strongly influence the nature or the development of civilization in France; whilst he endeavoured to reform the gravest abuses of the feudal system by the introduction of justice and public order, he did not endeavour to abolish it either by the substitution of a pure monarchy, or by setting class against class in order to raise the royal authority high above all. He was neither an egotist nor a scheming diplomatist; he was, in all sincerity, in harmony with his age and sympathetic alike with the faith, the institutions, the customs, and the tastes of France in the thirteenth century. And yet, both in the thirteenth century and in later times, St. Louis stands apart as a man of profoundly original character, an isolated figure without any peer among his contemporaries or his successors; so far as it was possible in the Middle Ages, he was an ideal man, king, and Christian.

It is reported that in the seventeenth century, during the brilliant reign of Louis XIV. Montecuculli, on learning the death of his illustrious rival, Turenne, said to his officers, 'A man has died to-day who did honour to mankind.' St. Louis did honour to France, to royalty, to humanity, and to Christianity. This was the feeling of his contemporaries, and after six centuries it is still confirmed by the judgment of the historian.

I have shown his sympathy with his age, and his superiority to it; nevertheless he was not free from its great defects. St. Louis was a Christian, and yet he did not recognise the rights of conscience; he was a king, and by his blind infatuation for the Crusades he imposed useless dangers, miseries, and sacrifices upon his people for a fruitless enterprise. It is not my intention to discuss here the leading idea and general influence of the Crusades; originally they were without doubt the spontaneous and universal impulse of Christian Europe towards a noble, disinterested, and moral aim, worthy alike of men's enthusiasm and their devotion. The attacks of Islamism had for a long time compelled Christianity to occupy a defensive position, which was both humiliating and full of peril, and the crusade was an aggressive reaction. As to results, I think that the Crusades have had many that are valuable; and if we take a comprehensive view of events and centuries, we shall see that they rather aided than impeded or changed European civilization. But in the last half of the thirteenth century all the good that they could do had been accomplished, and they had lost that character of spontaneous and general impulse which had been at once their strength and their excuse; people of all classes were beginning to be doubtful and tired of them; not only the Sire de Joinville, but many burgesses and country people had ceased to be attracted by the enterprise or to believe in its success. By his blind infatuation, St. Louis did more than any other man of that period to incur the responsibility of prolonging a movement which was more and more inexpedient and ill-timed, because day by day it became less spontaneous and more impossible of success.

On another subject, of even greater importance than the Crusades, St. Louis was quite as much in error, although his personal responsibility was less because he obeyed the prevailing and emphatic belief of his time with a sincere conviction of its truth. This was the employment of compulsion in matters of religion, and the prohibition by the State of all opinions condemned by the Church.

'The war waged against religious liberty has been for many centuries the great crime of Christian society, and the cause not only of most grievous wrongs, but of all the most formidable reactions to which Christianity has been exposed. We see the culminating point of this most dangerous theory in the thirteenth century, when it was enforced by legislation as well as upheld by the Church. The confused code which bears the name of 'Établissements' or Statutes of St. Louis, and which contains many ordinances belonging to periods both preceding and subsequent to his reign, explicitly condemns to death all heretics, and commands the civil governors to carry out the sentence of the bishops on this point. St. Louis himself asked Pope Alexander IV., in 1255, to extend the Inquisition (which was already established in the ancient domains of the Counts of Toulouse on account of the Albigenses) to the whole kingdom and to place the power which it gave in the hands of the Franciscans and Dominicans. It is true that the bishops were to be consulted before the inquisitors could condemn a heretic to death, but this was more an act of courtesy to the episcopacy than an effectual guarantee for the liberty of the subject; indeed, with the feelings entertained by St. Louis on this subject, liberty, or to speak more correctly, the merest shadow of justice, had reason to hope for more from the church than from the throne.

The extreme rigour of St. Louis against what he called 'that vile oath,' blasphemy (a crime which is indefinite enough except in name), gives perhaps the most striking indication of the state of people's minds, and especially of the King's mind on this subject. Every blasphemer was branded on the lips with a red hot iron. 'One day the King caused a burgess of Paris to be branded in this manner. Violent murmurs arose in the city, and reached the King's ears. He answered by declaring that he would consent to be branded on his own lips and to keep the disgrace of the mark all his life, if only the vice of blasphemy could be banished from his kingdom.' Some time afterwards, when he was executing a work of great public utility, he received numerous expressions of gratitude from the owners of property in Paris. 'I expect a greater recompense from the Lord,' he said, 'for the maledictions which I received after branding that blasphemer, than for the benedictions which I now receive on account of this act of public utility.'

Of all human errors, the most popular are the most dangerous, for they are the most contagious, and those from which the noblest natures find it most difficult to keep themselves free. It is impossible to observe without alarm the aberrations of reason and moral rectitude into which men who were in other respects enlightened and virtuous have been dragged by the leading ideas of their generation. And this alarm is very greatly increased when we discover what iniquity, what suffering, what public and private calamity have been the result of deviations from right which were tolerated by the noblest spirits of the age. On the question of religious liberty, St. Louis is a striking example of the degree to which an upright judgment and scrupulous conscience may be led astray if it falls under the dominion of a popular feeling or idea. In all times of great intellectual fermentation he stands as a solemn warning to those men who prize independence of thought as well as of action, and to whom nothing is so dear as justice and truth.

---

[1] Faure, vol. ii. p. 300; Joinville, chap. cxxxviii.

JOHN CALVIN.

BORN AT NOYON, *July* 10, 1509.
DIED AT GENEVA, *May* 27, 1564.

CHAPTER I.

FINAL JUDGMENT ON GREAT MEN AND GREAT EVENTS MUST BE RESERVED FOR FUTURE GENERATIONS. CHARACTERISTICS OF THE RELIGIOUS REFORM OF THE SIXTEENTH CENTURY.

GREAT events and great men impose a difficult and painful task upon those who wish to understand them thoroughly, and to appreciate their worth. They form the stage upon which all the difficult and striking complications of good and evil, truth and error, virtue and vice, noble and base passions, valuable results and fatal consequences are displayed. They represent the noble impulses and also the disastrous failures, the grandeur, but at the same time the imperfection of human nature and human destiny; and we cannot, therefore, contemplate them without sadness and perplexity.

In modern times, the French Revolution as an event, and the Emperor Napoleon I. as a man, have furnished and continue to furnish us with the absorbing interest of watching such a drama. I say, 'continue to furnish,' for, clearly, so far as either the French revolution or Napoleon is concerned, the drama is not ended, the final catastrophe of the plot is not yet known. In the great stream of events it is the final issue which decides as to the value of the source. There is a reckoning to be held with all great events and all great men,—a balance to be struck between what they have cost humanity, and that for which humanity is indebted to them; but this final account is not closed until late. Is there any one in the present day, who, even with a full knowledge of events, would venture to pass a final judgment on the French revolution and the Emperor Napoleon? Is there any one who could apportion their due share of esteem and reprobation to the great fact and the great man of this century, and whose judgment would be received with general and lasting assent? Could any one decide without hesitation to what extent their influence has been for good or for evil?

The answer to this question is in the hands of the generations to come. It is our successors who determine by a final analysis the good and evil in the works of their precursors; in this they will be guided by the impressions which they themselves receive from these actions, as well as by the principles and examples which have been bequeathed to them. One after the other the generations are called upon to take up their inheritance; one after the other they enter into their work, guided by their own light, their own liberty, and their own responsibility. It is for them to distinguish truth from falsehood, justice from injustice, that which is useful from that which is injurious, the practicable from the chimerical, and, according to right and reason, to accept or reject or modify the decisions and actions of their predecessors. It is only after these prolonged investigations by the intelligence and experience of mankind that the true worth of great events and great men can be determined, and history can pass sentence upon their claims to the gratitude or censure of the human race.

I do not intend, from any considerations of prudence, to take refuge in this obscurity of the future, or to keep back my thoughts and observe silence as to my hopes and fears. In one of the brightest moments of our epoch, forty years ago, when I recommenced my course of lectures on Modern History at the Sorbonne, I expressed my conviction that the youthful generation to which I addressed myself might, without too much self-confidence, use the words which Homer attributes to Sthenelus:—'We thank Heaven that we are better than our forefathers.'

In recent meditations on the union of Christianity and Liberty, and the difficulties which our recollections of the French revolution seem to oppose to the realization of this union, I said, 'Severity is necessary, but justice is due to different periods and to a different state of society. We have learnt as much morality and reason within the last century as we have forgotten, as much and more. Society in France has attained its actual condition by efforts more or less apparent and more or less rapid, but efforts which have never been altogether suspended, in spite of many interruptions and great vicissitudes. France has freed herself in turns from the feudal system, from the selfish ambitions and claims of the great nobles, from the predominance of court influence, and from the despotism, improvidence, and extravagance of absolute power. She has desired national unity, civil equality, and political liberty from the earliest period of her existence. All her great politicians, and the whole nation, in its unconscious but irresistible tendency, have aimed at and desired the same ends. The revolution of 1789 was the most violent and serious explosion of this unceasing national effort. Was it a fatal termination or a fruitful crisis? France then thought that she obtained a great victory, not only for herself, but for all humanity. Did she deceive herself? Have we walked for so many centuries in a good or an evil path, towards success or deception? Are we still making progress, or has our decline already commenced? Many eminent and honest thinkers hold very different opinions on this subject, and some of them utter dark and alarming prophecies, whilst others continue to chant songs of triumph.

'I have some right to say that no one has felt the crimes, faults, errors, and follies of word and deed which blazed out in the French revolution, more keenly than I have done. I have never hesitated to express what I thought of them; and my frankness on this subject may perhaps explain the heat of some of the controversies which I have had to sustain in my political career; my views irritated the prejudices and wounded the self-love of very many. I retract nothing,—neither sentiments nor language,— on that sad phase of our contemporary history.'[1]

[1] *Méditations sur la Religion chrétienne dans ses Rapports avec l'État actuel des Sociétés et des Esprits*, 1868, pp. 15-18.

But, in spite of the many bitter recollections and painful mistakes of that time, I still retain my confidence that this age and my country have more to hope than to fear from the criticism of the future, and that the beneficial results of the French revolution, both for France and the whole world, will far exceed the errors into which it was the means of plunging them and the evils it has inflicted. I am not however at all astonished at the uncertainty and doubt to which this prolonged crisis has given rise; error and evil are still so prominent that the final issue cannot but appear uncertain; and the perils of the good cause —the cause of liberty, morality, and good sense— are still so great that it is impossible to look upon the question as decided, and to rest with confidence in the prospect of future success.

The religious reform which was the revolution of the sixteenth century has already been submitted to the test of time, and of great social and intellectual perils. It brought with it much suffering to the human race, it gave rise to great errors and great crimes, and was developed amidst cruel wars and the most deplorable troubles and disturbances. These facts, which we learn both from its partisans and opponents, cannot be contested, and they form the account which history lays to the charge of the event. But as the Roman Cornelia could point to her sons, so, after three centuries of trial, the Reformation of the sixteenth century can show the nations among which it has prevailed, and which have been formed under its influence—England, Holland, North Germany, the Scandinavian States, the United States of America— calling attention to their moral and social condition, their attitude with regard to reverence for right and reason, and their position so far as success and worldly prosperity are concerned. These, also, are well-known and definite facts. I do not hesitate to affirm that the revolution of the sixteenth century has nothing to fear from the investigations of the nineteenth: the children are an honour to their mother.

There are many different causes for the general and final success of this movement, but I wish now to point to only one of them. The Reformation of the sixteenth century was essentially and from the very first a religious reform; politics occupied a secondary position; they were necessary means, but not its chief aim. It was begun in the name of Christianity and from an impulse given by religion; liberty was only called in as a weapon to help faith. The strength of the movement was derived from its influence on the inner life of the soul, for both leaders and followers were much more engrossed by the future and eternal state of man than by his temporal condition. The reform of the sixteenth century embraced the whole man and his destiny: first his moral state in himself and before God, then his social condition among his fellows. This is the peculiar and great characteristic of the movement, the principal source of the good which it has done, and we must therefore place it by the side of the price which it has cost.

According to the decree of history and the verdict of Bossuet, two men, Luther and Calvin, were the most mighty in their influence and the truest representatives of that great movement and of that period. Luther marched at the head of German religious reform; Calvin took the lead in France. Both these men were at the same time successful innovators, profound theologians, clever politicians, eloquent orators, and great writers. Both were exposed to many attacks and much persecution; both gained great admiration and devotion; and they both struggled greatly, suffered greatly, and greatly triumphed. Not one of the conditions which give a man power in his lifetime, and make his name great in history, was wanting to either of them. They bore, during their lifetime, the whole weight of responsibility which is attached to power and greatness, and for three centuries history has connected it with their names.

The time has come, I think, when we ought to understand them aright, and appreciate them justly, and I wish to make this possible as regards Calvin. It is no part of my design to recount his whole history, and to follow him step by step throughout his stormy career. It is the man himself, the moral and intellectual being, his own thoughts and his own desires, that I wish to study and to depict.

CHAPTER II.

BIRTH AND PARENTAGE OF CALVIN. HIS BROTHER CHARLES. EDUCATION OF CALVIN. HIS CHOICE OF A CAREER.

JOHN CALVIN was born at Noyon in Picardy, on the 10th of July, 1509. He belonged to a family which had originally consisted of simple mechanics, and had only just entered the rank of burgesses. His grandfather was a cooper at Pont-l'Evêque in Normandy; his father, Gerard Chauvin or Cauvin, settled, at some time and from some motives now unknown, at Noyon, where he was a notary in the ecclesiastical court and secretary to the bishop, Charles de Hangest, who treated him with kindness. No ambition is more disinterested than that of a father, but it is none the less keen, and the desire of Gerard Cauvin's heart was that his children should continue to climb the social ladder, of which he was already standing on the first step. At that time the Church offered an opening to all, and a means by which the very lowest might possibly rise very high. The pious wishes of Jeanne Lefranc, wife of Gerard Cauvin, were in harmony with the more worldly desires of her husband: they devoted their two eldest sons, Charles and John Calvin, to the Church.

The great difference in the life and character of these two young men, who followed the same path from the very first, is a sign of the times and of the opposing currents which influenced society.

The elder of the two brothers, Charles Calvin, became a priest, and died in 1536, one of the chaplains of St. Mary's church at Noyon; 'but,' an almost contemporary chronicler says, 'he was easily led astray by the errors which abounded in those days, for he loved the path of liberty, and despised the Church. He uttered blasphemous opinions concerning the sacraments. In spite of many remonstrances he remained shameless, like a man plunged into the depths of iniquity, and persisted in his faults. In 1534 the chapter found it necessary to lament for him as a hopeless and lost soul. He showed himself reprobate in everything, and took care to manifest his indifference to the remedies offered to him for the salvation of his soul. He lifted himself up against God himself, and blasphemed the holy sacrament of the altar. At length, in 1536, he was very ill, and as he had forsaken God, so also at his deathbed did God abandon him as a lost soul. He refused to receive the holy sacraments; on which occasion his body was placed between the four pillars of a gibbet in the place of execution at Noyon.'

One of the modern biographers of John Calvin has concluded from these facts that Charles died a Protestant; but this is a great mistake. Evidently Charles Calvin lived and died a dissolute man and an unbeliever, and at the same time remained chaplain of the Catholic Church in his native town. The sixteenth century abounds in similar instances.

At this very time, from 1534 to 1536, whilst Charles was leading a licentious life and dying miserably at

Noyon, John left his native land in order that he might openly profess and promulgate his austere faith. At Basle he published the first edition of his 'Institutes of the Christian Religion,' the most solid body of doctrine which the reformed Church possesses. After having wandered for some months in Italy to make proselytes, he established himself at Geneva, in order to organize both the reformed Church and reformed society, and to carry on that fierce struggle with libertines and sceptics in which his life was so rapidly consumed.

The family of the Calvins presents a true picture of the period; in the sixteenth century the same thing was going on everywhere, unbelievers and fervent Christians, libertines and men of the most austere lives, were springing up and living side by side. Two contrary winds were blowing over Europe at that period, one carrying with it scepticism and licentiousness, while the other breathed only Christian faith and the severest morality. One of these arose chiefly from the revival of the ancient literature and philosophy of Greece and Rome; the other sprang from the struggles made in the Church itself and in its Councils to arrive at a reform which was at the same time greatly desired and fiercely opposed.

These two impulses and these two paths give a special character to the whole of the sixteenth century. It was at the same time the fascinated worshipper of pagan antiquity and the fervent apostle of Christian reform ; it was full of impulse and of doubt, of unbridled licence and of rigorous puritanism, fruitful alike in learned sceptics and pious reformers, bold in making use of the fact of liberty without admitting it in principle; it was, in short, the age which produced Erasmus and Luther in Germany, and Montaigne and Calvin in France.

The education of Calvin bore the impress of this fluctuation between opposing tendencies and temptations. He was brought up at first by the liberality of the Church, and for its service; at the age of twelve he was nominated to a chapel at Noyon, called the chapel of La Gésine, and went to Paris from 1523 to 1527, to study classics and philosophy in the colleges of La Marche and Montaigu, where he obtained well-deserved distinction by his zeal and assiduity. 'He spoke little,' says a chronicle, 'and only on serious and weighty matters; he was not given to much company, but spent his time alone.' His seriousness, and possibly his severity, had already impressed his fellow-students, who nicknamed him 'The Accusative Case.' The report of his success reached Noyon, and procured for him the post of curé at Marteville, and two years after at Pont-l'Evêque, although he had only received the tonsure, and never took any further steps towards becoming a priest. He himself says that he was 'at that time more attached than any one to the Papal superstitions,' and he scrupulously fulfilled the duties of his position. He sometimes preached at Pont-l'Evêque, to which place he was very glad to have been appointed; 'joyous and proud,' according to one of his biographers, ' that a single essay should have made him a curé.'

The native place of his family seems to have cherished all recollections connected with Calvin. Thirty years after his death, Cardinal Alexander de Medicis, legate of Pope Clement VIII., and at a later period himself pope under the title of Leo XI., was on his way to Vervins, to assist in framing the treaty between France and Spain; he passed near Pont-l'Evêque, and there stopped his whole retinue, 'got down from his litter, and went on foot to see the cottage in which he had been told that John Calvin was born.'

Calvin did not long follow the course prescribed by the Church. 'My father,' he says, 'saw that the study of the law generally enriched those who pursued it, and this hope made him suddenly change his mind with regard to me. And thus it happened that being withdrawn from the study of philosophy in order to learn the law, I compelled myself to work faithfully, so as to obey my father's will. But, all the while, God in his secret providence made me finally turn my head in another direction.'

CHAPTER III.

CALVIN THE LAW STUDENT, AT ORLEANS AND BOURGES.
CALVIN THE REFORMER, IN PARIS.

I AM inclined to think that his father's will was not the only, and possibly not even the principal, guiding motive in Calvin's resolution. From the age of fourteen, when he began his studies in the college of La Marche, at Paris, he had been a pupil of the learned professor Mathurin Cordier, or Corderius, who was afterwards placed by him at the head of the College of Geneva. Robert Olivétan, afterwards one of the translators of the Bible, was a fellow-countryman and relative of whom he saw much when he was at Noyon. These two men were well acquainted with the labours of Luther, and were themselves following the current of the new ideas; and, doubtless, if they had not attracted Calvin towards these ideas, they had at least prepared him to receive them. Be that, however, as it may, in accordance with his father's wish and his own inclination, he abandoned the Church in 1529, and went first to Orleans and then to Bourges to study law. At these two universities there were celebrated professors who taught, not only jurisprudence, but the various branches of history, philosophy and philology, which are cognate to that science. Calvin met there Pierre de l'Estoile,

Petrus Stella, a learned and subtle jurist, who was afterwards President of the Court of Inquiries in the 'Parlement' of Paris; Alciati of Milan, who had been appointed by Francis I. as the most learned doctor of the time in Roman law, and also as one of the most elegant scholars in ancient literature; and Melchior Wolmar, the German, a learned Greek scholar, who read Homer and Demosthenes with his pupils, and who also read with them —but not quite so openly—the Bible. From the earliest times the French jurists had been adversaries, rather than partisans, of the Romish Church, and after the revival of pagan literature the more learned among them frequently prided themselves upon displaying great independence and freedom of thought. The three professors of Orleans and Bourges became the revered masters of Calvin, and Calvin was the favourite pupil of his masters. But he was not long a pupil. 'He profited so greatly in so short a time,' says Beza, 'that he was not considered as a student, but as one of the learned doctors,' and he was often called upon to take the place of his masters in the professorial chair. But neither law nor learning, nor any of the sciences taught by these professors, could satisfy Calvin's soul or his intellect. In speaking of himself at this time, he says:—'My conscience was very far from being in a condition of certain peace. Every time that I looked down into myself or lifted my heart up to God, such a supreme horror took possession of me that there was no purification or expiation which could have cured me; and the more closely I considered my own nature, so much the more was my conscience goaded with fierce stings, so that there remained no other comfort except to deceive myself by forgetting myself. But God, who took pity upon me, conquered my heart and subdued it to docility by a sudden conversion. . . . Having then received some taste and knowledge of true piety, so great a desire was incontinently kindled in me to profit by it, that although I did not entirely renounce all other studies, yet I paid but little attention to them. . . . Before the year was at an end, all those who were yearning for the true doctrine began to look towards me as a teacher, although I myself had only just begun to learn. . . . Being of a shy and solitary nature, I have always loved retirement and tranquillity; I began therefore to seek out some hiding-place, and some means of withdrawing myself from my fellows; but, so far from attaining my desire, it seemed, on the contrary, as if every retreat I chose in a remote spot was at once converted into a public school. In short, although it has always been my chief desire to live in private without being known, yet God has led me hither and thither, and turned me in so many directions by different changes, that he never left me at peace in any place, until, in spite of my own desires, he made me come forward, and brought me into public life.'

All uncertainty had disappeared and anxiety for himself had been removed; Calvin recognised his mission and entered on his vocation with great ardour. In 1531 or 1532, after three years of study he gave up the law, as he had given up the Established Church; he left Bourges, returned to Noyon, resigned his cure at Pont-l'Evêque and his chapel of La Gésine in 1534, sold the small property he inherited on the death of his father, and thenceforward devoted himself entirely to the work of religious reform; a reform which was then in its infancy, and was fiercely opposed. No resolve was ever taken more spontaneously, more conscientiously, or involved a more full and free self-sacrifice and such singleness of aim in the desire to serve, at all costs, the cause which he looked upon as the cause of the highest truth and the law of God.

He took up his abode at Paris with Etienne de la Forge, a wealthy merchant, and an ardent partisan of the Reformation, 'whose memory,' says Calvin, ' ought to be venerated by the faithful as that of a martyred saint of Christ.' He was, in fact, burnt at the stake a few years later. At his house the faithful reformers, who were already fiercely persecuted, were in the habit of meeting in secret. Calvin frequently addressed these meetings; he spoke with a confidence which carried conviction to his hearers, and almost always ended his discourses with the words : ' If God be for us, who can be against us ?' His indefatigable activity and already wide-spread influence soon attracted the attention of enemies as well as friends. ' In the midst of his books and studies, he was,' says Etienne Pasquier, ' of such a restless nature, that he must still be doing the very utmost to promote the advancement of his sect. Our prisons were sometimes crowded with poor misguided men, whom he exhorted, consoled, and strengthened unceasingly by his letters; he never failed to find messengers to whom the prison doors were open in spite of all the efforts of the jailers to keep them out. This was his method of proceeding at first, and it was by such means that little by little he won over part of our France.'

Nevertheless, Calvin still remembered that not long previously he had himself been a Catholic, and at this time he showed a consideration for the institutions and members of his ancient Church, and a moderation both of judgment and language, which gave way, only too soon, to violence and invective. On the 29th of June, 1531, he wrote from Paris to Francis Daniel, one of his fellow-students at Orleans, as follows :—

'I went to the monastery on Sunday to see the nuns, and, according to your wish, to fix the day on which your sister should take the vows. They informed me that, at a meeting held by the sisters, in accordance with a solemn custom, she and some of her companions had been already authorized to take the vows. I sounded your sister's heart, that I might learn if she accepted this yoke meekly, and if her neck had not been broken rather than bent to it. I exhorted her to confide freely in me all that was passing in her soul. I have never seen any one more ready and resolute, and it would be impossible to accomplish her desire too soon. Every time that she heard her vow spoken of one would have said that she was playing with dolls. It was no part of my mission to try and turn her aside from this feeling, but I urged her in a few words not to go beyond her strength, not to expect anything rashly from herself, but to place her whole trust in God, in whom we live and move and have our being.'

A few years later Calvin would not have undertaken such a mission; or, if he had, he would not have acquitted himself with so much delicacy and reserve. His first published work was an appeal for mercy—or, to use the language of the eighteenth century, for toleration—on behalf of the reformers, who were persecuted, banished, imprisoned, and led to the stake. He put forth his protest humbly, in the shape of a commentary on Seneca's treatise, 'De Clementia' (On Mercy); so humbly that many of his biographers, and among others the new editors of his complete works, have considered that he did not intend to defend the persecuted reformers, and that his commentary on Seneca's treatise was simply the work of a moral philosopher and a philologist. It is true that Calvin does not once speak of the reformers and the hardships which they endured, throughout the work; he does not make a single allusion to them which can be laid hold of. Still, I am not the less convinced that, by this publication, he hoped to serve the cause of his brethren, and that, if reform had been triumphant and powerful, his commentary on Seneca's treatise would never have appeared. The very title of the book, and the circumstances under which it was published, are much stronger proofs in favour of this assertion than the doubts concerning it, which would arise from Calvin's reserve of language. The dedication of the work to Charles de Hangest, the Bishop of Noyon, his former patron, confirms me in this opinion. So long as prudence was possible, Calvin was prudent, and anxious to conciliate the established authorities. Very respectfully he placed a eulogy of clemency under the eyes of a Catholic prelate whom he knew to be well-disposed towards himself, and who would, as he hoped, use his valuable influence on behalf of the proscribed reformers.

The Bishop of Noyon was not the only person of whom Calvin thought and to whom he spoke at this time with an almost affectionate deference. On the 4th of April, 1532, he wrote to Erasmus, to whom he sent his book, and reminded him in the most flattering terms of his own recent labours on the works of Seneca, addressing him as 'the honour and the chief delight of the world of letters.' He did not then foresee that three years later, when his friend Bucer introduced him to Erasmus at Basle, after talking to him for some little time, Erasmus would say to Bucer, in a low tone, 'I see rising up within the Church a great scourge against the Church.'

At the same time that Calvin was anxious to conciliate persons of importance he took great pains to secure publicity and success for his book. On the 22d April, 1532, he wrote to his friend Francis Daniel, at Orleans, 'The die is cast: my commentaries on Seneca's treatise "De Clementia" have appeared; but they are printed at my own expense and have cost me more money than you will believe. I am now trying to gather a little of it in again. If you wish to help me in that way I will send you a hundred copies, or as many as you think it well to take. Meanwhile accept the copy which I send you, and do not think that I impose any law upon you in this matter, for I wish you to feel perfectly free in all your dealings with me.'

Calvin was not slow in recognising that in the presence of questions and passions which agitated men's minds more violently from day to day, prudence and conciliation were of very little use, and that, whether for defence or attack, it was necessary to have recourse to more powerful weapons. He was one of those who do not rush to the fore-front of every struggle, but who, at the same time, will not make any sacrifice of their own belief or opinion to avoid a contest, and who enter into it heart and soul when once it becomes inevitable. Before long an incident occurred which gave rise to this necessity. Calvin was very intimate with Nicholas Cop, rector of the University of Paris, who in virtue of his position was to deliver a discourse on All Saints' day, in 1533, at the church of the Mathurins. Calvin offered to compose the sermon, and ' constructed a very different kind of oration,' says Beza, 'from the ordinary one, for he spoke of religious matters with great freedom, and in a liberal tone of which the Sorbonne and the " Parlement" did not at all approve; so much so that the "Parlement" sent to seek Nicholas Cop, and he set out to go to them with his attendants; being warned, however, that they intended to imprison him, he did not go to the palace, but turned back and fled from the kingdom, going to Basle, the native place of his father, William Cop, physician to the king, and a man of great renown.'[1] Calvin also was accused, and Jean Morin, the judge in criminal causes, went to his rooms and examined all his papers, with the intention of arresting him. Calvin had been warned, however; he 'escaped by the window, took refuge in the Faubourg St. Victor, at the dwelling of a vine-dresser, changed his clothes,' and left Paris, scarcely knowing whither he was going.

[1] Beza, *Histoire des Églises réformées de France*, vol. i. p. 14, and *Histoire de la Vie et de la Mort de Calvin*, 1657, p. 14.

CHAPTER IV.

CALVIN A FUGITIVE. PERSECUTION OF THE PROTESTANTS
IN PARIS.

FOR more than a year Calvin led a wandering and unsettled life; he took refuge first of all at the Château d'Hazeville, near Mantes; next at Angoulême, with the canon Louis du Tillet, who cautiously befriended religious reform; and then at Nérac, where Margaret of Valois, Queen of Navarre and sister of Francis I., held her court, and offered a welcome asylum to all more or less openly avowed reformers. Calvin met there the learned Le Fèvre d'Etaples, or Faber Stapulensis, at that time an old man, and one of the first who had sown the seeds of the Reformation in France. Thanks to the friendship which the bishop, William Briçonnet, entertained for him, he had begun the good work in the diocese of Meaux, but had not dared to carry it on, or to call it by its true name. Twelve years previously, one of the boldest and most ardent reformers, William Farel, had been staying with him at Meaux, and one day Le Fèvre said to him, with a burst of prophetic conviction: 'My dear William, God will renew the face of the earth, and you will see it, even you.' When he saw Calvin at Nérac in 1533, he often conversed with him, and had a presentiment of his destiny; he 'looked at this young man with a favourable eye,' says Beza, 'as if he foresaw that he would be the author of the restoration of the Church of France.'

Another guest, who was also Queen Margaret's chaplain at Nérac, Gérard Roussel, had much conversation with Calvin, and endeavoured to persuade him that it was necessary 'to purify the house of God, but not to destroy it.' But Calvin had already abandoned that notion; and subsequent events, as well as reflection, confirmed him more and more in the belief that any such attempt would be fruitless.

Whilst he was thus wandering from one place of refuge to another, sheltered by sincere but timorous friends, the contest on both sides and the passions of both parties were becoming daily more and more violent. Charles V. had just granted some concessions to the German Protestants; Francis I. became, in consequence, more hostile to the Protestants of France, in the hope of thereby winning over the recently elected Pope, Paul III. The excesses of the Anabaptists, and their outburst at Munster in 1534, had given rise to great irritation and alarm at the new doctrines and their abettors; and these feelings, although they were strongest in the Catholic governments, were yet general in all. A very rash and indiscreet manifestation on the part of certain French Protestants furnished their enemies with new weapons, by means of which they influenced both the king and the public. Violent placards against the mass and the doctrine of transubstantiation were printed at Neufchâtel, in Switzerland, and in October, 1534, were posted up by night at all the crossways in Paris, and were even affixed to the chamber-door of Francis I. in the castle of Blois. The king's anger knew no bounds: he determined to make the most ample reparation to the Catholic faith, and at the same time to give a terrible lesson to Protestant audacity. On the 21st of January, 1535, a solemn procession left the church of St. Germain l'Auxerrois; John du Bellay, Bishop of Paris, bore the sacred elements in his hands, whilst the three royal princes of France and the Duke de Vendôme walked on either side, and held the canopy over him; the king followed with a lighted torch in his hand, walking between the Cardinals de Bourbon and de Lorraine. At every oratory which they passed, the king gave his torch to the Cardinal de Lorraine, and then joining his hands, he humbly prostrated himself and implored the forgiveness of God for his people. When the procession was ended, the king stayed to dinner with John du Bellay, and there was afterwards a meeting of the leading members of all the religious orders. The king took his seat upon a kind of throne which had been erected for him. From thence he uttered a discourse which breathed sorrow for his realm, and curses on the authors of an outrage against the faith and the Church. He ended by saying, 'Whatever progress this contagion may have made already, the remedy is still easy, if all of you are animated by the same zeal which is felt by me— if you forget the ties of flesh and blood, remember only that you are Christians, and denounce without pity all those who are partisans or abettors of this heresy. As for me, if my right arm was gangrened, I would cut off my right arm; and if my sons who now hear me were to suffer so great a calamity as to fall into these cursed and detestable opinions, I would give them up, and offer them as a sacrifice to God.'[1] At these words the Constable de Montmorency[2] said to the king, 'Sire, you must begin with your sister.' 'Oh, as for her,' answered the king, 'she loves me so well that she will never believe anything except what I wish.'

On the 29th of January an edict was promulgated which condemned those who harboured heretics, 'Lutherans and others,' to the same penalties as 'the heretics aforesaid,' unless they gave up their guests to justice. An accuser received one-fourth of the victim's goods which were confiscated. A few days before this, on the 13th of January, 1535, Francis I. signed an edict which was still more extraordinary as the work of a king who was a patron of literature: he decreed the abolition of printing because it was the means of propagating heresy, and forbade the printing of any book on pain of death. Six weeks later, however, on the 26th of February, the king was ashamed of such a decree, and delayed its execution indefinitely.[3]

These edicts were preceded and accompanied by numerous punishments. 'The Journal of a Citizen of Paris,' the writer of which was a Catholic of the period, enumerates with a certain satisfaction twenty-four heretics burnt alive in Paris between the 10th of November, 1534, and the 3rd of May, 1535, without taking into account many who were condemned to less cruel sufferings. The trials were now

---

[1] Garnier, continuateur de Vellay et Villaret, *Histoire de France*, vol. xxiv. pp. 536-540.

[2] He was not made Constable of France until 1538.

[3] Garnier, *Histoire de France*, vol. xxiv. p. 140. Henri Martin, *Histoire de France*, vol. viii. p. 223.

conducted with great rapidity. The judge of criminal causes in the Court of the Châtelet, passed summary judgment, and the 'Parlement' confirmed his sentence. At first the victims had been strangled before they were burnt, but before long they were burnt alive, in accordance with the custom of the Spanish Inquisition. Even this was not enough, and those who were condemned to die were suspended by iron chains to a kind of seesaw, which 'swung them high into the air and then lowered them' into the fire until at length the executioner cut the rope and the victim fell into the flames. The records of these trials were burnt together with the victims, in order that the reformers might not be able to obtain any reliable account of their martyrs.

Some Protestant historians, both ancient and modern, have asserted that Francis I. was present on several occasions at these horrible spectacles, and they have specially named as one of them the 21st of January, 1535. Not one of the principal contemporary chronicles, either Catholic or Protestant, confirms this imputation;[1] we find no mention of it in the 'Journal du Bourgeois de Paris,' nor in Beza, nor in Jean Crespin, the compiler of 'The Book of Martyrs from John Huss to those of the year 1534.' Florimond de Ræmond, a chronicler of the sixteenth century, who was for a short time a Protestant, but very speedily returned to the Catholic faith, and in 1572 was counsellor to the 'Parlement' of Bordeaux, asserts that the sight of these tortures was far from producing that satisfaction and approbation in the public mind which was expected from them.

[1] I think M. Michelet and M. Henri Martin were right in rejecting it.

'Everywhere,' he says, 'the fires were lighted; and although on the one hand the justice and severity of the laws restrained not a few and kept them to their duty, yet on the other hand the stubborn resolution of those who were dragged to execution greatly astonished many. For they saw simple, silly women seeking fierce torments in order to make trial of their faith, and going to their death singing psalms, and with no other cry than *Christ, the Saviour;* young maidens walking more gaily to the place of torture than they would have done to the nuptial couch; men rejoicing when they saw the terrible implements and preparations for death, and although half-burnt and roasted, yet immoveable as rocks when the waves of torture dashed over them. These sad and incessant sights excited some disquietude not only in the minds of simple folk, but among those of the higher classes, for they could not persuade themselves that these people had not reason on their side, since they maintained their opinions with so much resolution and at the cost of life. Others had compassion upon them, were grieved to see them so persecuted, and when they beheld the remains of those sufferers, their blackened corpses hanging in vile chains in the public streets, they could not restrain their tears; nay, their very hearts wept as well as their eyes.'

It was in the presence of such facts as these, and under the influence of the horror and terror with which they inspired the reformers, that Calvin resolved to leave his own country and to seek elsewhere safety, liberty, and the possibility of defending a cause which had become all the dearer to him because it was so cruelly persecuted. He was too shrewd not to perceive that he must quickly exhaust the different asylums open to him: Queen Margaret did not wish to go too far in opposition to the king her brother; the canon Louis du Tillet was half afraid that his fine library might be compromised through the use made of it by his guest, who was expounding and preaching in the neighbourhood of Angoulême; Gérard Roussel, the Queen's chaplain, thought Calvin was going too far, and was afraid that if the Reformation succeeded completely, the bishopric of Oléron, which he wanted and at a later period obtained, would be suppressed; Le Fèvre d'Etaples, who had more sympathy with Calvin than any of the others, was seventy-nine years old, and desired that his days might end in peace.

Calvin left Angoulême and Nérac, and stayed for a time at Poitiers, where the friends of religious reform who gathered round him, eager for his words, celebrated for the first time the Lord's Supper according to the evangelical rites, in a cave near the town, which is called to this day Calvin's Cave. He was soon compelled to leave Poitiers, and went to Orleans and thence secretly to Paris, where he saw a man whose name was one day to spread a dark stain over his own, the Spaniard, Michael Servetus, a guilty heretic in his eyes. Calvin offered to meet him at a conference, and discuss with him the doctrine of the Trinity, which the Spaniard had just then openly attacked. Servetus accepted the challenge, but did not appear when the appointed time arrived. Possibly some angry scorn lingered in Calvin's heart, who left Paris and went to Noyon, to take final leave of his family. At length he set out for Strasburg, already one of the strongholds of the Reformation, where he had many friends—among others, the learned Bucer, with whom he had been in constant correspondence. He arrived there probably about the beginning of the year 1535; but he did not settle at Strasburg; he preferred Basle, the place where men of letters, scholars, theologians, and celebrated printers were to be found—Erasmus, Simon Grynæus, and Froben —and where he hoped to find the leisure which he needed in order to produce the great work which he had projected, his " Institutes of the Christian Religion."

CHAPTER V.

CALVIN THE THEOLOGIAN.

THE production of the 'Institutes' was by no means the most difficult or meritorious act of Calvin's life, for a man's superiority and force of character are not manifested in the labour of solitary thought, but in the contests of public and practical life. Geneva was the stage on which we can best see how Calvin comported himself as a man; but the 'Institutes of the Christian Religion' were, and are still, the noblest monument of the greatness of mind and originality of idea which distinguished him in his own century. More than that, I believe this book to be the most valuable and enduring of all his labours; for those churches which are specially known as the reformed Churches of France, Switzerland, Holland, Scotland, and the United States of America, received from Calvin's Institutes the doctrine, organization and discipline which, in spite of sharp trials, grave mistakes, and claims that are incompatible with the progress of liberty, have still, for more than three centuries, been the source of all their strength and vitality.

The preface of the book is, in itself and apart from what follows, very remarkable and very characteristic of the man. Calvin dedicated his work to Francis I., to the persecutor of French reformers during one of the fiercest outbreaks of persecution, and at a time when he himself had been compelled to leave his country in order to live in security, and speak with freedom. 'And do not think,' he says to the king, 'that I endeavour here to plead my own individual defence, in order to obtain permission to return to the land of my birth; for, although I have such an affection for it as it is in human nature to feel, yet, under existing circumstances, I do not suffer any great grief at being absent from it. But I plead the cause of all the faithful, nay the cause of Christ, which is at the present time so completely rent and trampled under foot throughout your kingdom that it seems to be in a very desperate case. And all this has come to pass more through the tyranny of certain Pharisees than by your desire.'

Calvin was the boldest, and at the same time the least revolutionary among the reformers of the sixteenth century; he was devoid of fear, but he had great deference and consideration for authority, even whilst he was openly opposing it. It appears that the original idea of his great work occurred to him in 1534, whilst he was at Angoulême, on a visit to the canon Louis du Tillet. 'But nothing was farther from my thoughts, Sire,' he says in the preface, 'than to write things which should be laid before your Majesty; my intention was only to teach certain rudiments, so that those who were moved by some good impulse from God might be instructed in true piety. And chiefly, by this my labour, I wished to serve our people of France, of whom I saw many hungering and thirsting for Jesus Christ, but very few who had any true knowledge of him.' The idea of the book was therefore, at first, exclusively religious, and it was destined for the use of the followers of the French reformers. But when Calvin was about to publish it, he again becomes prudent and politic; he addresses his book to the King of France, invokes the authority of the persecutor, and endeavours to convince his reason. He shows himself to be a respectful and faithful subject at the same time that he is an independent Christian and a reformer.

The language and conduct of Calvin were certainly not owing to any uncertainty in his convictions, or any feeling of timidity in the presence of royalty; in this preface he often forgets or puts aside the very prudence and policy which induced him to address the king. He places Francis I. in a very difficult position, and hopelessly offends him by the brutal violence and insulting familiarity with which, whilst addressing the king, he speaks of the Catholic Church and of its dignitaries; sometimes he encourages, sometimes threatens the king himself; he undertakes to prove that the reformers are not insurgents, that they do not meditate any plot against the crown or threaten any danger to the state; he goes so far as to promise that, even if the king refuses to do them justice, and if he continues to allow them 'still to be cruelly persecuted by imprisonment, scourging, torture, confiscation, and the stake, yet in our patience we shall possess our souls, and shall wait for the mighty hand of the Lord.' But at the same time Calvin predicts that the Divine wrath will overtake the king if he persists in persecuting the reformers: 'For he is a true king who, in the government of his kingdom, recognises that he is indeed the minister of

God; and, on the contrary, he who does not reign to the end that he may set forth and show the glory of God is not a king but a brigand. They are deceived who expect long prosperity in a kingdom which is not ruled by the sceptre of God; that is to say, by his Holy Word.' From page to page we see this alternation between religious zeal and policy; the author is aiming at a revolution, but all the time we see in the reformer the man who respects law and order.

The question whether the 'Institutes of the Christian Religion' was written first in French or in Latin has been often discussed and is not yet decided. The preface from which I have quoted the preceding passages is in French, and bears date Basle, —'the first day of August, 1535.' I have it now before me in a copy of the French edition which was published at Geneva in 1562; my copy formerly belonged to Sully, and the margin is full of notes in his own handwriting. It is said that no French edition of the work itself bearing date 1535 can now be discovered; the earliest edition known is that which was published at Basle in 1536, in Calvin's own name, and of which both the body of the work and the preface are in Latin. There was no French edition with date and the author's name until 1540. I do not intend at this time to plunge into the controversy that has been excited by the chronological difficulty which envelopes the history of this book; I have studied it carefully, and am inclined to think, with many of Calvin's latest and most learned historians, that the 'Institutes of the Christian Religion' was written originally in French, and published at Basle in 1535, without the author's name, and that it was written first of all and specially for the French nation, and was intended to remove from the mind of Francis I. and the general public, the impressions produced by the recent excesses of the Anabaptists, which their enemies laid to the charge of the reformers also. It is certain that the dedication to Francis I. was written and published first of all in French, and on the first of August, 1535: these facts are beyond dispute. How was it that a preface written in French, and dated 1535, was put at the head of a book written in Latin, and not published until 1536? The book itself, in this first edition, was probably nothing more than the rather hasty and incomplete anonymous work of a young man as yet little known, who had just left France, and was still much more French than, as he became later, European. It was a first work, a sketch rather than such a treatise as the title would lead the reader to expect. Calvin himself points this out in the preface to his 'Commentaries on the Psalms,' in which he gives many important details connected with his own life and works. That which seems to me the most probable solution of the question is still beset with many difficulties, and I will not linger to discuss them. Be this as it may, from 1536 to 1559 Calvin published eight editions of his 'Christian Institutes,' and they were successively revised and enlarged to such a degree as ultimately to form a work which differs from the first known edition both in extent and form, although it is identical in spirit and in all essential points. The edition of 1559 is the last which Calvin prepared for the press, and it has therefore served as the basis for all other editions and for the numerous translations which were made at a later period. It is undoubtedly the true work of Calvin, and contains his latest injunctions respecting the doctrines of the reformed Church, the rules for its internal government and its relation to the state, its position in the commonwealth as well as its faith and Christian discipline.

In order thoroughly to understand the fundamental idea and true aim of Calvin's book we must transport ourselves to the precise period when he first originated and wrote it. Luther, born in 1483, twenty-six years before Calvin, had accomplished, between the years 1517 and 1532, his work of struggle and rupture with the Church of Rome; the Confession of Augsburg had been published;[1] the Protestant princes had entered into the Smalcaldic league;[2] the religious peace of Nuremberg had been concluded and ratified by the Diet of Ratisbon;[3] in fact, when Calvin left France and took refuge at Basle in 1534, the German Reformation was established in central and northern Europe. But the new work was not so far advanced in western Europe, especially in France and the neighbouring countries speaking the French language. In them the war against the Church of Rome had also been eagerly commenced, the demolition of the ancient edifice had been pursued with ardour, but the work was hindered and opposed by the people, and the construction of a new Church had not even been commenced. The reformed Church appeared here and there, but without any bond of unity or organization, and even in its cradle a prey to uncertainty, confusion, and anarchy.

Calvin was so strongly impressed by this fact that

[1] In 1530.   [2] In 1530.   [3] In 1532

it became an object of constant anxiety to him; his intellect was so clear and strong that he could not fail to understand the full extent of the evil which was implied in the wavering, divided, and scattered state of the reformation in France, and he set to work to remedy it. His first act was to produce his 'Institutes of the Christian Religion,' and by so doing he took the most effectual means of creating a religious and social organization for the reformation which was at that time springing up, in and around France.

It is by its doctrines and its institutions, by its faith and its discipline, that a religious society is founded and maintained. The first great work of Calvin was devoted to proclaiming the grounds of the reformed faith, its rules of church government, organization, and discipline, and its rights and duties in connexion with the state. He was occupied during his whole life either in putting into practice the principles which he had imposed upon the Church, or in inducing his followers to carry them out.

As to that which concerns faith, his idea may be traced throughout the whole of the 'Institutes.' He does not put forth new doctrines and purely philosophical notions when he calls upon his contemporaries to join the cause of religious reform. He does not desire to innovate, but to restore, and he opposes the authority of Jesus Christ and the Gospel to that of the Church of Rome and tradition. His own position in this great enterprise was full of difficulty; this was the time of Rabelais, Erasmus, and Montaigne on the one hand, and of the popes Julius II., Leo X., Cardinal Cajetan, and the Dominican Tetzel on the other. In the presence of two opposing parties, both hostile to him, of unbelieving or sceptical freethinkers and of blind adherents of the Papacy, Calvin lived and moved. He had, at the same time, to protest against intellectual licence and ecclesiastical infallibility. He faces both, however, with his opinion clearly defined, his side taken once for all, and his position maintained with all his unbending strength. He has the most entire and ardent belief in the Divine revelation contained in the Bible. For him the Christian religion, as contained in the Old and New Testaments, is a fact at the same time supernatural and historical, an authentic and potent reality, the starting-point of all his thoughts and the law of his whole life. Three of the first chapters of his book bear the following titles :—

'In order to draw near to God the Creator we have need of the Holy Scriptures for our guide and teacher.'

'Human reason furnishes proofs which are quite strong enough to remove all doubts concerning the truth of the Scriptures.'

'The authority of the Scriptures must be sanctioned by the testimony of the Holy Spirit, in order that we may fully believe it; and it is an impious fiction to say that this authority is derived from the judgment of the Church.'[1]

In this circle the mind of Calvin moves. His book is only the development and commentary of the great Christian truths, facts, dogmas, and precepts with which the Holy Scriptures furnish him.

[1] Calvin, *Institution de la Religion chrétienne*, vol. i. chaps. vi. viii. and ix. edition of 1559.

CHAPTER VI.

CALVIN'S BELIEF IN THE PLENARY INSPIRATION OF THE BIBLE.

I CANNOT attempt to follow him in his vast work, to discuss his interpretations of gospel facts and words, and his deductions from them. Calvin's books, his life, and the Church established by him, show that the system which he founded was both strong and compact, wanting neither in logical accuracy nor in practical and available power. For more than three centuries it has embodied the faith and regulated the lives of many millions of Christians in France, Switzerland, Holland, Scotland, England, and America. In spite of its imperfections it is, on the whole, one of the noblest edifices ever erected by the mind of man, and one of the mightiest codes of moral law which has ever guided him. I will only pause here to notice two of Calvin's doctrines, which I look upon as grave errors, opposed, in my opinion, to the true spirit of Christianity, and at the present time out of harmony with the intellectual and social progress of the human race.

The earliest complaints and attacks made by the reformers were called forth by assertions of the authority and infallibility of the pope. Luther was the first and mightiest, as he was also the most impetuous leader of the assault. Calvin followed in the same path; but he looked upon the work of demolition as almost completed, and his own special work was to replace the authority and infallibility of the Church by the authority and infallibility of the sacred monument of divine revelation—that is, to put the Bible in the place of the Pope: everything in the name and in virtue of the Bible, nothing in opposition to or without the Bible. This was Calvin's fixed idea, and the supreme law of the Church which he established.

The extent and success of his work sufficiently prove that he discerned the needs and religious instincts of his age. Calvin's reformed Church at once took up an important position which it has now occupied for three centuries. Catholicism and Protestantism may continue their long struggle, but they cannot underrate each other's strength; they have both survived many reverses; they live on in spite of many faults, and at the present time they are both face to face with the same enemies. Both are now impelled by reason and commanded by necessity to acknowledge their faults and to recognise the cause of their reverses. In so far as the future is in the hands of man, their future depends on the extent to which they have attained the clearness of vision which belongs to long life and experience.

I am a Protestant, and for that very reason I intend to speak exclusively of Calvin's errors and faults as a Protestant reformer.

When he proclaimed the absolute infallibility and universal authority of the Holy Scriptures, he failed to recognise the true object and meaning of the divine revelation which they contain. It is a revelation, which refers to the relation between man and God, the duties of man towards God and towards his fellowmen. This is indicated from the very beginning by the nature of the subjects treated of, and it is confirmed by the Decalogue and the Gospel. I may quote here some of the reflections which I have already published on this subject, for day by day I find that they represent my thoughts more accurately. Like Calvin, 'many pious and learned men uphold the plenary inspiration of the Holy Scriptures; they assert that not only the thoughts but the words in which they are clothed are divinely inspired—every word on every subject, the language as well as the doctrine. This assertion seems to me to indicate a deplorable confusion, giving rise to profound misconceptions as to the meaning and aim of the sacred volume, and causing its authority to be very seriously compromised. God never intended to teach men grammar by a supernatural process, and he no more intended to teach them geology, astronomy, geography, and chronology than grammar. Not on these do the rays of divine light fall, but on the relation of man to his Creator, and on the laws of his faith and life. God dictated to Moses the laws which regulate the duties of man towards God and towards his fellow-man; he left it to Newton to discover the laws which govern the universe. The inspiration of the Sacred Volume relates not only to religion and morality, but to religion and morality alone, and apart from any mere human science.

'I have read the Bible over and over again, with the greatest care, with no intention either of criticizing it or apologizing for it, but with the single aim of learning to understand its character and meaning aright.

The more I have advanced in this study, and have been able to live as it were in the Bible, the more clearly have I apprehended two contemporaneous facts, a divine fact and a human fact, which are at the same time entirely distinct and closely connected. In every part of the Bible I find God and man: God, a real and personal being, not affected by any external incident, and in whom there is no change, always the same and immoveable though the centre of universal movement, and Himself giving this unprecedented definition of Himself, "I am that I am;" and man, an incomplete, imperfect being, subject to change, full of flaws and contradictions, of lofty instincts and degrading tendencies, inquiring and yet ignorant, capable of good and evil, and able to attain perfection in spite of his imperfection. Throughout the whole Bible we see God and man, their union and their antagonism: God watching over man and guiding him; man sometimes accepting and sometimes rejecting the influence of God. If I might be allowed to use such an expression, I would say that the Divine person and the human person are brought face to face with each other; we see them acting on each other, and influencing events. We see the education of man after his creation, the education of a religious and moral being, neither more nor less. At the same time, whilst God elevates he does not transform mankind; he created man intelligent and free; he illuminates the laws of his spiritual and moral life with a Divine light; but he leaves him to struggle with great dangers and much peril, until he learns the right use of his intellect and will. And at every period, in all circumstances, even whilst he still continues to influence him, God takes man just as he finds him, with all his passions, vices, weakness, error, and ignorance, just what he has made himself, and is making himself every day, by the good or evil use of his intellect and his will. This, I say, is the Bible, and its history of the relations between God and man.

'What a striking contrast is brought out in this history, and yet what a close and strong bond between those whom I scarcely dare to call the two performers! In no tradition or poetical invention, in no religious mythology does God appear so exalted, so pure, so free from all the imperfection and disquietude of human nature, so immutable and serene, so truly God as in the Bible. On the other hand, among no people, in no historical narrative or document is man portrayed as more violent, more barbarous, more brutal, more cruel, more prone to ingratitude and rebellion against God, than among the Hebrews. Nowhere else, and in no other history does the distance seem so great between the divine sphere and the human region—between the sovereign and his subjects. And yet the Israelites never separate themselves from God. In spite of their vices and evil passions they always turn again to the Lord, and always acknowledge his law and his government, even at the very time that they violate the one and rebel against the other. God is, however, nowhere manifested as so solicitous with regard to man—at the same time so exacting and so sympathetic; he does not change a man at one stroke, and by a single act of his sovereign will; he watches all his short-comings, his weakness and his errors, but never forsakes him; he holds the torch of Divine light always before his eyes, and never loses his interest in the destiny of mankind. Religion and morality are the subjects which not only predominate, but which are exclusively presented in the sacred volume: nowhere else have the aspirations and labours of human science held so insignificant a position in human thought and society; God, and the relation between man and God,—this, and this only, occupies every page of the Bible.

'I do not hesitate to affirm that science, with its special and manifold subjects, astronomy, geology, geography, chronology, physical science, historical criticism, all are foreign to the plan and design of the Holy Scriptures. The study of science is the work of the human intellect, and of the human intellect alone: science is a fruit that ripens slowly, and is only brought to perfection by the intellectual labour of many generations. If then, in addition to those facts which are expressly declared to be miraculous, you find statements and assertions in the Bible which are in opposition to the established truths of science, do not be astonished or dismayed; it is not the word of God on these subjects; it is the language of the men of that age, and it accords with the measure of their knowledge, or rather of their ignorance; it is the language which they spoke, and in which it was necessary to speak to them if they were to understand what was said.

'The fact is so simple that I am astonished that it should be necessary to assert it: in all times and places, among all nations and in every age, there are spontaneous instincts, and common aspirations and ideas in matters of religion and morality, which not only clothe themselves, as it were, in the same language, but have the power of making their language intelligible to all those to whom it is addressed, in spite of the difference which there may be in their several degrees of education and civilization. But we meet with nothing similar in purely scientific matters; the majority of men see and speak, not in accordance with the facts of science, but according to appearances; and they understand, or do not understand, they listen, or do not listen, just in so far as they have any knowledge of science, or are ignorant of it. What would the Hebrews in the desert have said, or the Jews who gathered round the Apostles, or the savages of Polynesia addressed by the first Christian missionaries, if they had been told that it is the earth which revolves round the sun, and that the earth is a spheroid, inhabitable and inhabited at the opposite points of its circumference? What more natural and inevitable than the agreement of the language of Scripture with the imperfect knowledge which men possessed of scientific subjects, even although the light of Divine inspiration was, at the same time, shed upon the laws which govern the spiritual and moral nature of human beings?

'No one admires and honours science more than I do: the study of science is one of man's highest vocations, but it has nothing to do with the relation between man and God, and the influence of God upon man. God is not a lofty philosopher who reveals scientific truths to men in order that they may have the noble pleasure of contemplating and disseminating them; the search for these truths is a purely human labour. The divine work is grander and more complicated, and it is essentially practical. That which all men and every man needs and craves, the most ignorant as well as the most learned, that which humanity demands from God is the knowledge of those religious and moral truths which ought to influence the soul and life, and in accordance with which the life of the future will be regulated. God meets this requirement of the whole human race ; and the Bible is addressed to all that they may be saved by leading a new life, not that they may be well taught in matters of science.'[1]

If Calvin had lived in the nineteenth century I am inclined to believe that his clear and vigorous intellect would have preserved him from falling into this error of attributing universal infallibility to every word contained in the Bible, and that he would have recognised the aim and the true tendency of those Divine revelations of which the Bible is so noble a monument. Even a hundred years after his death the labours of the great critics of the seventeenth century, of Richard Simon, Bayle, and John Leclerc, would have helped him, by the clear light which they threw on this question, and would have shown him how to shield the Christian faith effectually both from improper attacks and from the legitimate discoveries of human science. The domain of science is not the same as that of Christian faith, nor are they equal ; the very aim of revelation has been to enunciate truths, and to shed a light into the soul which no amount of scientific labour would have sufficed to procure. This is the real and true character of the Bible ; it is from this that all its authority proceeds, and by this, at the same time, that the limits of its sphere are defined.

[1] *Méditations sur la Religion chrétienne*, vol. i. p. 151 ; vol. iii. p. 17.

CHAPTER VII.

CALVIN'S THEORY OF FREE-WILL AND PREDESTINATION.

CALVIN'S second grave error consists, as I think, in his theory of free-will and predestination. He denies free-will, and believes that the destiny of every man, his future salvation or damnation, is determined from all eternity by the irrevocable decrees of God; and at the same time that he affirms this two-fold doctrine, he exhausts himself in ineffectual attempts to assert and uphold the moral obligation and responsibility of man in this dual condition.

I have no wish at the present time to enter into a discussion which, in all times and in every country, has divided, and will continue to divide, all serious and earnest men, whether they are theologians or philosophers. I repeat that this discussion will continue to cause division, because it turns upon a problem which men cannot help discussing, and which they are not able to solve—that is, the reconciliation of human freedom with Divine prescience and omnipotence. Forty years ago, in my course of 'Lectures on the History of Civilization in France,' I gave a historical account of this difficult question, and of the discussion concerning it between Pelagius and St. Augustine in the fifth century. And now, in order to describe Calvin's thoughts on this subject with accuracy, and to show their influence on his life, I must recall some of the ideas which I developed forty years ago, as well as those which I have more recently expressed in my 'Meditations on the Christian Religion,' with regard to the intimate union of Christianity and morality.

In order to understand and appreciate that fact connected with man which we call his freedom, his free-will, we must disengage it from all foreign elements, and consider it apart from them. Owing to the want of this precaution, it has been very often misunderstood; men have not studied the fact of free-will, and that fact only: they have looked at it and described it in a confused manner, together with a number of other facts which are, so to speak, bound up with it in the moral life of mankind, and yet which differ from it very essentially. For example, free-will has been said to consist in the power of choosing between different motives of action; and the act of deliberation, together with the act of judgment which follows it, have been said to constitute the essential part of free-will. It is nothing of the kind; these are the acts of the intellect, and not of the will; different motives of action—interests, opinions, inclinations, and others—pass before the intellect, which deliberates, compares, assigns a value, weighs, and ultimately passes judgment. This is a preparatory labour which precedes the action of the will, but does not constitute that action. When the act of deliberation has taken place, when a man has investigated the motives presented to him and their worth, then comes in an entirely new fact,—the action of the will. The man forms a resolution, that is to say, we come to a new series of facts which have their origin in the man himself, of which he looks upon himself as the author; which exist because it is his will, and would not exist if it were not his will; which would be other than they are if he chose to make them other than they are. Keep apart from this act all recollection of the deliberation of the intellect, of motives recognised and appreciated, concentrate your thoughts on that single moment when the man 'forms his resolution,' when he says 'I will,' and ask yourself —ask the man himself to tell you in all sincerity whether he could not have willed differently. Undoubtedly you would answer, as he would answer, 'Yes.' And it is at this moment and in this manner that the freedom of the human will is revealed. It resides altogether in the resolution which a man forms as the result of deliberation; it is this power of forming a resolution which is the special action of the man, existing by his will and his will only; it is a distinct act, separate from all the facts which precede and surround it; it is the same under the most dissimilar circumstances, always alike whatever may be its motives or results.

This action of the will is recognised at the very moment of its exercise; we have the same knowledge of our freedom as of our existence; we feel and know that we are free. But at the same time that we know ourselves to be free, and recognise in ourselves the faculty of originating by our own will a certain series of actions, at that very time we discover that our will is placed under the control of a certain law which constrains but does not coerce us; and which takes different names,—is called the moral law, reason, justice, good sense,—according to the occasions on which it is applied. Man is free, but even according to his own notion this is not an arbitrary freedom; he may use it in an absurd, mad, unjust, or guilty manner; but every time that he does use it, there is a certain law which ought to govern him. The study of this law is his duty: it is the task imposed upon him by his freedom.

We soon perceive that we can never altogether perform this task, that we can never act in perfect accordance with reason or the moral law; that whilst we are always free, that is, morally capable of conforming to the law, we do not in fact accomplish all that we ought to do, or all that we can do. Whenever we question ourselves closely, and answer sincerely, we are compelled to acknowledge, 'I could have done it if I would;' our will has been weak and cowardly, and has not gone to the full extent of our duty or our power. Hence arises a feeling which is found in all men under different forms, the feeling of the need of external help, of some support for the human will, of a strength to be added to its strength which may sustain it in time of need. Man seeks this support, this help in time of need on all sides; he asks it from the encouragement of friends, from the counsel of the wise, from the example and approbation of his fellows, and from fear of punishment. There is no one who cannot find in his own daily conduct innumerable proofs of this impulse of the soul, this eagerness to find out of itself an aid to the liberty which it feels to be at the same time real but insufficient; and as the visible world and human society do not always respond to this desire, as they also are tainted with the same insufficiency, which is at length perceived, the soul seeks the support which it needs in something apart from the visible world, above these human relations; it addresses itself to God, and calls to him for help. Prayer is the most elevated, but not the only form under which this universal feeling of the weakness of the human will, and its resort to an external and yet kindred strength, is manifested.

In addition to these facts which occur in the human soul and are clearly manifested whenever we make use of our free-will, there is another fact more obscure, but which I consider equally capable of proof. Certain changes, certain moral phenomena take place and are manifest in us, the origin of which we cannot refer to any act of our own will, and of which we do not recognise ourselves as the author. I will take an example of this class of facts in the first place from the domain of intellect, where they occur more frequently and can be more easily investigated. I suppose there is no one who has not at some time or other made painful efforts at night to recall some idea, some event, and fallen asleep without succeeding in the attempt; waking on the morrow, he has immediately and without effort accomplished his aim. I draw one single deduction from this; that, independently of the voluntary and premeditated activity of the mind, there is a certain unconscious and involuntary action of the intellect which we do not control, which we cannot follow in its development, and which, nevertheless, is real and fruitful in result,—a kind of unconscious growth which is not the act of our will, but bears fruit spontaneously. Now that which takes place in the realm of intellect takes place also in the moral world; certain changes take place in the man which he cannot attribute to himself and which he cannot account for by the action of his own will. On a certain day or at a certain moment he finds himself in an altogether new moral condition, quite unlike that to which he is accustomed and which he knows. He cannot discover the sources of these changes; he has no recollection of having acquiesced in or originated them. In other words, the moral man, even in the exercise of his own free-will, is not altogether complete in himself; he learns from experience and feels that causes and powers, or to speak more correctly, a cause, a power external to himself, acts on him and changes him without reference to his own will: in his moral life as well as in the whole of his destiny he finds the incomprehensible and the unknown.

Thus in the unconscious and free development of the human soul, moral and religious facts are evolved, called forth and united naturally. Man recognises of himself the distinction between moral good and evil, recognises moral law, moral liberty, moral responsibility, moral excellence or unworthiness; and at the same time he recognises that the moral law is not a human invention imposed by human consent, neither is it one of those immutable laws by which the material world is governed. That is, he recognises a higher power from whom the moral law emanates, whom it reveals, and in whose presence he either keeps or violates this law. God a moral ruler, and man a free subject, are revealed to us side by side in the facts which constitute the moral nature of man.

And just as a moral law without a sovereign legislator who ordains it is an incomplete and inexplicable fact, a river without a source, so also man's moral responsibility without a supreme judge who applies the law, is incomplete and inexplicable,—a river without an outlet, which flows on until it loses itself we know not where. God is implied in the moral law as its first author, and God is included in the moral responsibility of man as his ultimate judge.

But if a man discovers and acknowledges the existence of God in himself and in the world around him, he cannot study and investigate, or explain, nor does he know God as he knows himself and the external world which we call nature. Man and the external world are mirrors in which God is reflected; but this reflection or revelation is limited by the measure and limitations of our own mind, and does not manifest the plenitude and immensity of the divine nature. Those special and direct revelations which are treasured up for us in the sacred volume only disclose an infinite perspective of divine action, they do not give a full and clear knowledge of that action. Even when we acknowledge and worship God, we find that there is that in him which is not only unknown, but unknowable by man; and that although he has manifested himself, he is still impenetrable and inexplicable. Why has God created man? Why has he created him free, that is, capable of deciding his actions by his own will alone, in spite of the many external motives which seek to influence him, and in a world governed by fixed and inflexible laws? What is the nature and what the extent of the moral responsibility which, according to his own account, man as a free being incurs? What part was assigned to him, and what influence did God give him over his own life and his own destiny when he created him free? Is it possible that he assigned him no part at all, no influence at all, that beforehand and irrevocably he decided the life and fate of man whom he created free, as he did that of the material world which is governed by inflexible laws? Do we not borrow the terms of merely human language when we use the word prescience as applied to God,—God an eternal being, everywhere eternally present, to whom we cannot apply our notions of space and time, and of that succession of events in the midst of which our fleeting life passes? These are questions of supreme importance which we naturally ask ourselves, and which bear witness to the nobility of human nature, but which we are not permitted to answer; for in order to answer them we should need to know and comprehend God, his nature and his designs, as God knows and comprehends himself and his own actions. There is no answer to these questions; even in the midst of Christian light man must resign himself to Christian ignorance; all his knowledge of his own being and of the world around him will never give him a knowledge of God, or of the design of God in the creation of the world and of mankind.

And this brings me to Calvin's great mistake. He was much more engrossed in speculations concerning God than in the observation of mankind. God is, so to say, the fixed centre and starting-point of all his thoughts. He meditates and imagines, and if I dared I would say that he presents God to us, and describes him as if he knew him thoroughly, and had exclusive possession of him. He then summons man into the presence of God, and denies or calmly rejects everything in him which does not accord with or cannot be adjusted to the God whom he has conceived and depicted. He denies the free-will of man and affirms his predestination, because he imagines that man's free-will is opposed to the idea which he has formed of the omnipotence and omniscience of God, and that his predestination is necessary to it. Calvin had a very imperfect knowledge and understanding of man because he professed to know and understand too much about God.

I find proof in the works of Dr. Chalmers, the most eminent Protestant theologian of our time, a faithful follower of Calvin, and a man profoundly versed in science, that the state of Calvin's mind must, in fact, have been that which I have described ; and that at first he was led to deny the free-will of man and affirm his predestination, in order to prove his assumed knowledge of the nature of God and of his design in creating the universe. I find the following passage in Chalmers' 'Institutes of Theology :'—

'It is clear, that were there no such necessity in the world of matter—did it not in every instance take a precise direction from the laws and the forces which the Deity hath established over it—were there any of its phenomena, whereof no other account could be given, than that they sprung from a random contingency, in virtue of which another set of phenomena might have as readily occurred as the actual ones ;— then, at this rate, the world of inanimate things would drift uncontrollably away from the authority of its

God; nor would it be any longer his will that overruled the condition and the history of the universe which he formed. Now, it is the very same with the world of mind. .... If this class of events, if the movements of intelligent and animated nature, can be referred to no moving forces directed by and dependent upon him, of whom we have been taught to believe, that he hath ordained the mechanism of the spiritual world, and presides over all the evolutions of it—if amid the diversity of the operations by which we are surrounded, those of the will and of the mind form an exception to the doctrine that it is God who worketh all in all—then, by far the most dignified and interesting of all his creations is wrested from the dominion of him who gave it birth; .... and in the most emphatic sense of the term might it be said, that there is a universe without a Lord—an empire without an Imperial Sovereign to overrule its destinies.

'Both the power and the prescience of God are involved in this question. It seems strange that the Creator of all should not be the governor of all; or that the universe which proceeded from his hands should have been so constituted in any of its departments as to have an independent history of its own, placed beyond the sovereignty and the control of him who gave it birth. But so it would be on the hypothesis of a self-determining power in any of the creatures. .... To avert this conclusion, all must be determinate, and all, both in the mental and material world, be under the absolute control of him who made all, and who upholds all.'[1]

[1] Chalmers, *Institutes of Theology*, vol. ii. pp. 351-355.

According, therefore, to Calvin and Chalmers, the moral world and the material universe are on the same footing, and are governed by laws of the same nature; they have deduced this opinion from their own conception of God, and the knowledge which they believe themselves to possess of his nature, his designs, and his relation to his creatures. God, they say, is an absolute monarch; and in no part of his realm, from no one of his subjects, will he allow of any intervention, any action, or any will opposed to his own law, and because of this inexorable and universal law they deny the free-will of man.

Strange denial, which has been condemned beforehand by God himself! God is infinitely more powerful and more incomprehensible than Calvin and Chalmers have imagined him to be. Among the infinitude of his creatures there is one being whom he has created and placed high above all others on this earth, and whom he has distinguished by his own mark placed upon him. God has thought fit to create man, and to make him *in his own image*, that is to say, a free being, capable of deliberate acts of intelligence and will.

It is the Bible which tells us this — the book which contains the record of Divine revelation; man's first act according to the Bible, the first historical fact recorded of him in his relation towards God, is an act of disobedience, that is, an act of free-will. I repeat my questions: Why has God desired this, and created man thus? What position and what share of action has God assigned to man in the circle of his designs and works? We do not know, and we shall never know. But, with all our ignorance, we do wrong to disown the sublime gift which we have received from God, and to deny our own free-will at the very time that we are using it.

Calvin was not a theologian and a moralist only, he did other things besides the writing of books; he took part in human affairs, and directed and controlled the social struggles and convulsions of his age. At all times, his actions were prompted and regulated by his opinions: he did not believe in man's free-will, and he treated it with severity and a kind of contempt; he had entire faith in the authority of God and the law of God, and he worked with the utmost zeal to secure the triumph of divine authority and law. In everything which had reference to human opinions and actions, to the thought and conduct of private individuals, to public or private life, Calvin laboured to introduce and to insure the ascendency of the doctrines and precepts, the discipline and morality, of which he found either the germs or the formal expression in the sacred volume; that is, in the Divine revelation to man. He had the strength arising from the sincerity of his convictions and the disinterestedness of his motives; he was exacting and rigorous towards himself, and therefore he was exacting and rigorous to others also; he believed and asserted that he had more right over other men's opinions and actions than he ought to have claimed, and he did not show sufficient respect to their rights. He was affectionate and faithful to his friends, but he often lacked sympathy for men in general, and justice to his enemies. Some of his faults were, no doubt, owing to his natural character and disposition; but the convictions which he held so firmly and had systematized with such care, had a still greater share in the occasional severity and injustice of his conduct towards others. Perhaps no man was ever more devoted to that which he believed to be the truth than Calvin ; no man has shown more fearless courage in running every risk, making every sacrifice, in order to serve the cause to which he had given his faith. This is his noblest and most beautiful characteristic, one that is manifested at every step during the whole course of his life, even in his very errors and those results of them which are most to be regretted.

And here, with great regret, I must close this inquiry into Calvin's fundamental principles as they are disclosed in his 'Institutes of the Christian Religion:' an exhaustive discussion of their merits and defects would necessitate a much more complete development than I am able at this time to give them. I therefore return to my picture of the character and genius of Calvin as they are shown in the labours and struggles in which he so rapidly wore out his life.

CHAPTER VIII.

CALVIN PREACHES RELIGIOUS REFORM IN ITALY. THE DUCHESS OF
FERRARA. CALVIN'S FLIGHT FROM AOSTA.

TOWARDS the close of 1535, when the first edition, or, to speak more accurately, the first sketch of his 'Christian Institutes' had been prepared, or possibly published at Basle, Calvin had not as yet come to any definite conclusion with regard to his ultimate abode and life-work; he was engrossed in the propagation of his faith, and wandered about, as one may say, in search of places which might seem to promise the best means and chances of success for his labours. He resolved to visit Italy and, like others, to preach reform in the very stronghold of the ancient Church. I say 'like others,' for the Reformation already possessed more or less open adherents in Italy—reformers who were sincere and active even when they were timid. Their chief protector was Renée of France, duchess of Ferrara and daughter of Louis XII.: they gathered round her, secure of her favour, and at times tolerated by her husband Hercules d'Este, Duke of Ferrara; but their religious labours were always to some extent disguised by their love of learning and literature. Either from prudence or in the interest of his cause, Calvin did not travel in Italy under his own name, nor did he pass by it at Ferrara ; he was known as Charles d'Espeville, a name which he often assumed to the end of his life whenever he wished to write without compromising his friends. At the court of Ferrara he soon found, or rather gained, admirers and disciples, some of them ardent and enthusiastic like M. and Madame de Soubise, others brilliant and vacillating like the poet Clement Marot. But Calvin's most important and valuable conquest at Ferrara was the Duchess Renée herself. She was a princess of insignificant appearance, little and deformed, but she possessed rare intelligence and a very noble nature ; she was deeply interested in the study of religion as well as that of literature, and was capable of making great efforts and sacrifices for the Christian faith, although she never forgot the requirements of her position and royal birth. She had married her eldest daughter to Francis, Duke de Guise, and in 1557, at the close of the disasters of the army commanded by the duke in Italy, 'she saved,' says Brantôme, ' more than ten thousand souls, poor Frenchmen, soldiers and others, who would have died of hunger and want if it had not been for her; they passed through Ferrara and she succoured them all, as many as ever there were, supplying their wants and giving them money : so much so, that I have heard from one of her *maîtres d'hôtel* that their passage through the place cost her more than ten thousand crowns; and when the *intendants* of her palace remonstrated at the excessive expense, she said nothing more to them than—"What would you have me do ? They are poor Frenchmen of my nation, and if God had given me a beard on my chin, and I had been a man, they would have been my subjects; and indeed they would be my subjects now if that cursed Salic law did not press so hardly upon me."'

Some years later, after 1559, the duchess became a widow, and she then returned to France, and lived in her own castle of Montargis; in 1562, in the midst of the civil war, she sheltered in it a considerable number of Calvinists, some of them men of rank; her grandson Henry, Duke de Guise, besieged the castle, and summoned her to deliver up her guests. 'Take good care of what you are doing,' was Renée's answer to the duke's envoy; 'know that, except the king himself, no one has any right to dictate to me, and if you execute your threats, I will be the first to enter the breach, and I will try if you are bold enough to kill a king's daughter, whose death both heaven and earth will be compelled to avenge on you and your descendants, down to the children in their cradles.'

Such a victory for the Reformation, and such a protector for the reformers, were well worthy of the affectionate esteem and great consideration which Calvin constantly showed the Duchess of Ferrara from 1536 to 1564. During his short sojourn in Italy he had evidently acquired that ascendency over her which a powerful nature always obtains over a generous one, and a religious leader exercises over his sincere adherents. There is no indication of his having ever seen her again; but he was in constant correspondence with her, and he became truly, in the language of the seventeenth century, the director of her conscience. In this difficult task he displayed an admirable admixture of religious severity and wise moderation;

he was prompt in his warnings when he found the duchess weak, but very careful not to wound her by unnecessary severity, or to require anything at her hands which was inconsistent with her position; he took pains to put her on her guard against the irregularities of her servants, but did this without any meddlesome interference in her affairs or the affection she felt for her family. In 1554 she asked him to send her a chaplain for herself, and two widow ladies 'to take charge of and have rule over the daughters of her house.' Calvin sent her a reformed minister, Francis Morel, who was known as Monsieur de Colonges. 'I think,' wrote Calvin, 'you will find him so satisfactory that you will have good reason to thank God. As he is a gentleman of good birth, he will be so much the better received by those who will never listen to good men if they are contemptible in the world's eyes. The truth is that we must strive after that which is highest, and even noble birth is not always to be desired if a man prizes it too highly and is hindered, because of it, from serving God.'[1] In 1555 the duchess was compelled to witness the cruelty of her husband Hercules, Duke of Ferrara, towards the reformers, and even to submit to his wishes with regard to Catholic ceremonies: 'I am sure,' wrote Calvin, 'that you have been compelled to swerve from the right path, or you could not have satisfied those who are of this world; for it is an evil sign that they who offered such fierce opposition, in order to turn you from the service of God, now leave you in peace. But, Madam, since our good God is always ready to have mercy upon us, and stretches out his hand when

[1] August 6th, 1554. *Lettres Françaises de Calvin*, vol. i. p. 428.

we stumble so that we may not fall utterly, I pray you to take courage; and if the enemy for once, by reason of your weakness, has had the advantage over you, yet do not let him think that he has gained any real victory; let him rather feel that those whom God has raised have twofold strength to sustain them against all assaults.'[1] When the duchess sheltered the reformers in her chateau of Montargis, in 1562, and gave such a haughty refusal to the summons of the Duke de Guise that she should deliver them up, Calvin congratulated her in a sternly eloquent epistle: 'I have often thought, Madam, that God had reserved some trials for your old age in order to indemnify himself for all the arrears that you owe him on account of your timidity in the past. I speak according to the manner of men, for if you had done a hundred, a thousand times more, it would not have been enough to pay what you owe him from day to day for the infinite benefits which he continues to grant you. But I understand that he has shown you singular honour, and has employed you in no less a service than that of bearing his banner, so that you may be a refuge for the members of Christ.'[2]

In 1564 Calvin was informed that the duchess was deeply grieved at the violent hatred which the reformers continued to feel for the memory of her son-in-law, Francis, Duke de Guise, who had been assassinated the previous year by Poltrot, and by their assertion that he would be condemned to everlasting punishment; he was touched by her sorrow, and wrote to her four months before his own death: 'Although

[1] February 2d, 1553. *Lettres Françaises*, vol. ii. p. 5.
[2] May 10th, 1563. *Ibid.* vol. ii. p. 514.

we may all have said, "Woe to him by whom the offence cometh,' yet there has been reason why we should lament and weep, in that a good cause has been very badly conducted. And how could the Duke de Guise, who had kindled the fire, be spared, if the evil which he committed vexed the souls of all good men. I myself, even though I always prayed God to have mercy upon him, yet verily I often implored the Lord to lay his hand upon him and deliver the Church from him, if it was not his will to turn his heart. And, I can assure you, that very often during the war, if it had not been for me, impetuous and resolute men would have attempted to rid the world of him; and they were kept back by my exhortations only. Nevertheless, to say that he will be damned is to go too far, unless we have sure and certain signs of his condemnation. In which matter, we must guard against rash presumption, for there is one judge only, before whose throne we must all render up an account.'[1]

Surely, very few men in the sixteenth century—I do not speak of any other—were liberal and largehearted enough to use such language concerning the death and the future state of their most formidable enemy.

I do not hesitate to affirm, that the great Catholic bishops, who in the seventeenth century directed the consciences of the mightiest men in France, did not fulfil this difficult task with more Christian firmness, intelligent justice, and knowledge of the world, than Calvin displayed in his intercourse with the Duchess of Ferrara. And the duchess was not the only

[1] January 24, 1564. *Lettres Françaises de Calvin*, vol. ii. p. 533.

person towards whom he fulfilled this duty of a Christian pastor. His correspondence shows that he exercised a similar influence, in a spirit equally lofty and judicious, over the consciences of many Protestants.

The severity of Hercules d'Este towards the Protestants obliged Calvin to leave Ferrara. He knew no more than when he had arrived there some months previously, where he should ultimately take up his abode, nor how he should carry on the work to which he had devoted his life. He wandered from place to place in northern Italy, tarrying where he found friends, and teaching and preaching religious reform wherever he went. Sometimes he was received well, at others he was pursued by enemies who were embittered against his doctrines and himself, for he had already become famous. In 1536 he arrived in Piedmont and stayed there some weeks, not in the city of Aosta itself, but in the neighbourhood, at the house of a family of high rank, where several of his adherents were assembled to meet him. But the alarm was given to the civil and ecclesiastical authorities of Piedmont: a council was held at Aosta, which was reinforced by a strong manifestation of popular-feeling. 'All the corporations in the country renewed to the bishop the oath of fidelity which they had taken to his royal highness, binding themselves to live and die in obedience to him, and in the Apostolic and Roman faith.' Orders were given to arrest Calvin 'and all others of his party.' He escaped, but not without difficulty; he had to traverse perilous Alpine passes, and, according to an ancient tradition, was followed by 'the Marshal d'Aosta, Count of

Chalans, who pursued him to the very foot of the mountains with a drawn sword in his hand.' In 1541, five years later, a fountain surmounted by a cross was erected, in the principal street of Aosta, in the market-place, and the following inscription may now be seen on the pedestal :—

Hanc
CALVINI FUGA,
Erexit Anno MDXLI.
Religionis constantia reparavit
Anno MDCCXLI.
Civium pietas
Renovavit et adornavit
Anno MDCCCXLI.

'This cross, erected in 1541, in memory of Calvin's flight, restored in 1741 by faithful believers, was renewed and ornamented in 1841 by the piety of the citizens.'

The cross of Aosta and its inscription are not the only monuments of Calvin's visit to Piedmont; local tradition has preserved many other memorials: Calvin's *farm* and Calvin's *bridge* are still shown in the valley of Aosta; and the pass of Duranda, one of the lofty passes on the borders of Valais which he ascended when he fled from Piedmont, is still known as Calvin's *window*.

Driven out of Italy, he returned to France; not, however, that he desired to remain there, or would have been able to do so, for there was no more safety for him in France than in Italy; his intention was to establish himself at Basle or Strasburg; but either attracted by recollections of home, or influenced by other motives of which we are ignorant, he desired once again to see the place of his birth, and those members of his family who were still living. He reached Noyon, and spent some time there, apparently meeting with no opposition; at Noyon also he preached the Reformation and made proselytes. Among others he induced one of his sisters, Mary, and his only remaining brother, Anthony, to share his belief and follow him to a new country; accompanied by them, he set out for Basle; but as hostilities had again broken out between Francis I. and Charles V. he did not go by way of Lorraine, where the war was being carried on, but by Geneva. He arrived there towards the end of August 1536, not intending, so he says, to stay more than a single night. It was at Geneva, however, after many severe trials, that he was to be established and to find the great work of his life.

Great ideas, great men, and great events cannot be measured by the magnitude of their cradles. Geneva at that time seems not to have had more than from 12,000 to 15,000 inhabitants, and it was not then a place of renown; but within its narrow limits it was the scene of every crisis and every problem, great or small, which can agitate human society. It had only just obtained the national independence which it was still struggling to defend, and which it had wrested from its former masters, the dukes of Savoy, and from the hands of its own bishops. Its form of government as an independent state was still imperfect and unsettled, and was undergoing many experiments. Religious reform had been inaugurated at the same time as political freedom, but as yet it had not been condensed and embodied either in doctrine or in ecclesiastical organization and discipline. There was an urgent need of moral reform, for the ancient creeds and authorities had strangely tolerated the decay of public morality; and their downfall had been followed by an increase of licence and profligacy. Religious reform made moral reform all the more necessary, but did not succeed in accomplishing it. In fact, Geneva presented the spectacle of a tottering republic, a wavering faith, a nascent church; State and Church were sometimes confused together, at others entirely separated, and there were no definite rules recognised by both Church and State in their mutual relation; whilst to all these public difficulties must be added the frightful immorality of private individuals. What was the meaning of these numerous indications? What would be the result of a complication in which everything as yet seemed dark and uncertain? Was it life-giving power that was at work, or unfruitful anarchy? Such were the questions suggested in the sixteenth century, in Geneva as well as in several of the great European States; but in Geneva they were put forward more distinctly, emphatically, and urgently than elsewhere.

Geneva became a celebrated city, because she was able to answer these questions in a manner that for three centuries has been satisfactory, whilst it is to Calvin that the answers are due.

CHAPTER IX.

WILLIAM FAREL. CALVIN IN GENEVA.

WHEN Calvin reached Geneva towards the end of August 1536, with the intention of resuming his journey on the following day, another reformer, a man who was earnest, eloquent, and fearless, was living there. This was William Farel, also a Frenchman, and one who, like Calvin, after having tried to propagate reform in France, had left it, as he had done, and travelled in Switzerland, to Basle, Berne, and Neufchatel, teaching and preaching with great fervour. Farel had now lived for some time at Geneva, where he was working with his whole soul to ensure the triumph of reform over all its adversaries, whether Genevese or strangers, whilst they opposed him with equal zeal. After more than two years of alternate success and reverses, of public discussion and civil war, Farel succeeded in getting the whole question stated in the following terms to the inhabitants of Geneva, who were assembled in the church of St. Peter :—' By a decree of the Council of Two Hundred you are assembled here, that it may be known if there are any among you who have anything to say against the Word of God, and the doctrine which is preached to us in this city. . . . . If so, let them speak, so that we may know if there are any who are not willing to live according to the Gospel which has been proclaimed to us since the abolition of the mass and of the papal sacrifice.' 'Upon which,' says the Register, 'without one single opposing voice, it was unanimously agreed to, and carried by the holding up of hands; and a promise, and an oath taken to God that all the people would live according to this holy evangelical law and the Word of God which has been made known to them, forsaking all masses and other papal ceremonies and frauds, images and idols, and living together in unity and in obedience to the law.'

The latest and most accurate historian of the Church of Geneva, says: 'That day, the 21st of May, 1536, is the true date of the Reformation at Geneva. From that time the citizens, pressing to their hearts a faith which was sanctified by misfortune, prepared themselves for the sacrifices and glory of the future, and, like the Hebrews on the frontiers of Canaan, they repeated Joshua's oath, "As for me and my house we will serve the Lord."'[1]

Farel had conquered, but his victory gave him great uneasiness and apprehension. He was as conscientious as he was courageous, and did not deceive himself as to the defects of his work; the reformed faith was triumphant at Geneva, but the foundations of the reformed Church were not laid, nor did Farel feel that he was capable of establishing a church: he lacked the knowledge and authority, the intellect and judicious tact which are necessary for such a task;

[1] Gaberel, ancien Pasteur. *Histoire de l'Église de Genève*, vol. i. p. 261.

his vocation was religious warfare, not the organization of a new religious society. In the midst of his perplexity, a French refugee at Geneva, the canon Louis du Tillet,—who was, as we have seen, a lukewarm reformer, and had formerly received Calvin at Angoulême, leaving France with him afterwards,—hurried to Farel's house and told him that Calvin, the author of the 'Institutes of the Christian Religion,' had just arrived; that he had been driven out of Italy, where he had gained great renown teaching and preaching the reformed religion; but that he was only passing through Geneva, and was on his way to Basle or Strasburg. Farel immediately hurried to Calvin, implored him to stay at Geneva, to establish himself there, and work with him to secure the complete triumph of the reformed religion. Calvin refused, pleading the studies he had commenced, his desire of pursuing them, and his dislike to a public and stormy life. Farel pressed him eagerly; Calvin persisted in his refusal. 'When he saw,' says Calvin, 'that he could gain nothing by prayer, he tried imprecation, demanding that it might please God to curse my retirement and the tranquillity which I was seeking for my studies, if I held back and refused to give succour and aid at a time of such urgent need. And these words terrified and shook me as if God from on high had stretched out his hand upon me to stop me, so that I renounced the journey which I had undertaken; but conscious of my diffidence and timidity, I refused to bind myself to undertake any definite office.'[1] At first he only engaged to give instruction, in St. Peter's church, in the Holy Scriptures; he began to do so

[1] Calvin's Preface to the *Commentaries on the Psalms*.

on the 1st of September, and with such success that, on the 5th of the month, Farel said at a meeting of the Council of State, that 'the lectures which had been commenced in the cathedral by *the Frenchman* were absolutely necessary, and he entreated the Council to retain that minister and provide for his maintenance.' The Council consented, but they did not assign Calvin any official function, and merely spoke of him as *the Frenchman*.[1]

Calvin's powers were almost immediately manifested on a very solemn occasion. A conference had been arranged at which Catholics and Reformers should meet and freely discuss their differences of faith and ecclesiastical discipline, and it was held at Lausanne, towards the close of September 1536. Both Farel and Calvin were present, Farel as the chief representative of Geneva, Calvin as his ally and auxiliary. The conference lasted seven days, and until the 5th Farel took the lead in the debate; Calvin was silent. At length he took up the question of the real presence of Christ at the sacrament of the Lord's Supper, and after expressing his ideas as to the nature of the debate itself, he protested strongly against the reproach of the Catholics against the Reformers—that they despised the Fathers of the Church, their belief and traditions : ' We read them, and learn more from them than you do,' said Calvin ; 'but we cannot submit unreservedly to their judgment, because the Word of God forbids us to do so. How can you dare to assert that whoever does not acknowledge the absolute authority of the Fathers thereby rejects all authority whatsoever, even that of the law and the

[1] 'Iste Gallus.'

rulers of his country?' And here he referred to all the principal Fathers of the Church, especially Tertullian, St. Augustine, and Chrysostom; he traced back all their thoughts to the New Testament itself, to the Epistles of St. Paul, and that with so much learning and eloquence that Joseph Jandy, a monk who was present at the conference, suddenly started up and called out 'that at length he had found the truth and could understand the teaching of the Gospel ; that if he did not receive it he should commit the sin against the Holy Ghost ; that he now confessed his errors, and prayed God to grant the same grace to his brethren that they might also confess theirs.'

Calvin's arguments and eloquence produced so deep an impression, both in the conference and elsewhere, that the reformed religion was formally adopted and proclaimed at Lausanne and throughout the Pays de Vaud, as it had formerly been at Geneva, and Calvin returned to the latter city towards the middle of October with greatly augmented fame and influence.

He had need of it ; for the task which awaited him and which he imposed upon himself was indescribably complicated and arduous. He desired to establish and promote Christian faith in accordance with his own views ;—to secure to the religious society which had been founded in virtue of that faith, on the one hand religious independence from state control, and on the other due authority and power in matters of religion over its members and faithful adherents ;— to reform public and private morality both in civil and religious society, in the name of the allied powers of Church and State, and by their mutual help. Such was the threefold design which Calvin hoped to accomplish. No doubt he had not set it very distinctly before him, nor had he fully realized all that it involved and all its difficulties, but he commenced the struggle with a stout heart and resolute mind.

He returned to Geneva with Farel in October 1536, was elected pastor and, under this title, solemnly installed in the church of St. Peter. The first time that he preached there the crowd thronged around him with loud expressions of satisfaction, and he was obliged to promise those who had been unable to hear him that he would preach again on the following day. He and Farel together drew up a confession of faith : 'a brief formula of belief and doctrine,' says Beza, 'to give some shape to the newly established Church. Calvin also wrote a catechism, not that which we have at the present time, arranged in questions and answers, but one which consisted of brief summaries of all the principal tenets of our religion.' On the 10th of November in the same year, Farel submitted the confession to the Council of Two Hundred, who ordained 'that the articles should be regularly observed by the citizens,' but did not definitely adopt them, and adjourned the discussion of them to another day.

This first confession of faith by the reformed Church in France was simple in form, moderate in tone, and free from many of the theological controversies which afterwards arose among the reformers ; its principal object was to separate the reformed faith clearly and entirely from the Church of Rome, its traditions, its priestcraft, and its worship ; at the same time it was entirely in harmony with the facts, dogmas, and precepts contained in the Scriptures, the authority of which it asserted as the fixed basis and law of Christian faith. The confession is divided into twenty-one articles. The starting-point of the three first is the word and law of God 'as they are contained in the Holy Scriptures,' and at their close all the Ten Commandments are inserted according to the version given in the Book of Exodus. The ten subsequent articles enumerate and announce the fundamental doctrines of evangelical orthodoxy; namely, the natural depravity of man, the redemption by our Lord Jesus Christ, the necessity of faith in Christ for regeneration and salvation, and they end with the insertion of the whole of the Apostles' Creed and the Lord's Prayer, together with this previous declaration: 'All that Jesus Christ did and suffered for our redemption, we believe truly and without doubt as it is stated in the creed which is recited in the Church.' The eight remaining articles treat of the sacraments of the Church, which they reduce to two, baptism and the Lord's Supper; they very briefly indicate the essential principles of ecclesiastical organization, the duties of the pastor to his flock, and of believers to the civil powers : 'By which we mean that every Christian is bound to pray to God for the prosperity of the rulers and governors of the country in which he lives, to obey the statutes and decrees which are not in opposition to the commandments of God, to strive to promote the public welfare, peace, and profit, and to take no part in schemes which may provoke danger and dissension.' At the same time in the hands of the Church, and to be exercised by its authority, these articles formally establish 'the punishment of excommunication which we hold to be a sacred and salutary weapon in the hands of believers, so that the wicked by their evil conversation may not corrupt the good and dishonour Christ. We hold that it is expedient and according to the ordinance of God, that all open idolaters, blasphemers, murderers, thieves, adulterers and false witnesses, all seditious and quarrelsome persons, slanderers, pugilists, drunkards, and spendthrifts, if they do not amend their lives after they have been duly admonished, shall be cut off from communion with believers until they have given satisfactory proof of repentance.'[1]

Objections and complaints broke out, before long, against a rule of such religious and moral austerity: the bold innovators, who in their struggles with dukes and bishops had recently established the political independence of their country, were as much accustomed to licence in their manner of life as to freedom of thought. They accused Calvin of exceeding the duties of his office: 'It was his place,' they said, 'to explain the Scriptures; what right had he to meddle with other things, to talk about morals and find fault? He was to show that they were right in not having anything more to do with mass, and the Pope, and confession, and all the rest of it; was he going to revive an office which they had abolished, and make himself confessor to, and inflict penance on the whole city?' Calvin did not deceive himself as to the danger of these attacks: 'We are exposed to the most serious difficulties,' he wrote to his friend Bullinger, 'for the people in breaking off the yoke

[1] Gaberel, vol. i. *Pièces Justificatives*, p. 120.

of the priests think that they have shaken off all authority in this world. Many of the citizens say, " The knowledge of the Gospel is enough for us; we know how to read it, and our actions are nothing to you." The greater number are inclined to look upon us as preachers rather than pastors. Oh, what a difficult thing the rebuilding of the Church will be! We shall have to struggle against all the worst passions of flesh and blood!'

But Calvin and Farel were of the number of those who gain strength and courage in the face of danger; they addressed a long memorial to the Council, in which they demanded that the provisional vote of the previous 10th of November on the organization of the Church, should be replaced by a decisive vote; and they pointed out the measures which they looked upon as essential in a Christian government,—monthly celebration of the Lord's Supper, excommunication to be put in force, the introduction of psalm-singing in public worship, instruction of children in Christian doctrine, and the regulation of marriages. The Council adjourned the consideration of, or discarded some of these measures, and accepted others; although they were partisans of Calvin and Farel, the magistrates were disposed to try conciliation and patience. The two reformers, on their side, showed their moderation by consenting to the modifications which the magistrates desired, and on the 16th of January, 1537, the Council definitely accepted the confession of faith, and all the most important resolutions in the scheme of moral and religious discipline which Calvin and Farel had drawn up.

Their scheme was put into execution at once; and

although it was not carried out in what the two reformers considered a complete and satisfactory manner, still the attempt was bold and dangerous enough in the state of men's minds at that time. One of the magistrates entrusted with executive power, the syndic Ami Portal, was a fearless and devoted friend of Calvin's; he unhesitatingly applied the measures for the promotion of moral and religious discipline; gaming-houses were closed; gamblers were seized with loaded dice,—one of them was condemned to sit for an hour at St. Gervais, with his cards suspended round his neck; a convicted adulterer was led through the streets with his accomplice and then expelled from the town; and all masquerades and immodest dances were prohibited. 'I do not condemn amusements as such,' said Calvin; 'dances and cards are not in themselves evil, but how easily these pleasures succeed in making slaves of those who are addicted to them! Wherever wrong-doing has become an old-established custom we must avoid every risk of falling back into it.'

This moral police force was at first well received; rich and poor, great and small, were alike subject to it, and neither family influence nor political merit could ensure exemption. A man of some distinction, who was found guilty of offence, urged in extenuation of it the services which he had rendered to Geneva in the hour of peril when her national independence was at stake. Calvin, to whom he had appealed, answered: 'It is the act of a disloyal citizen to claim the right of doing evil and setting a bad example, as a recompense for the blood which he has shed for his country.' Moral instinct as well as secret jealousy causes men to take pleasure in the contemplation of virtuous and impartial severity, but they are none the less influenced by the clamour of discontented men, and assertions of the right of liberty.

There was a violent outbreak at Geneva. Two Anabaptists arrived there, and were favourably received by the adversaries of the two reformers; they were members of a sect which was at that time in great disrepute, both on account of the profligacy which it was supposed to sanction, and of the mystical doctrines, immoral or anarchical, held by its members, or attributed to them. Calvin and Farel were uneasy at this introduction of a new element of disorder, and were always ready to take part in the intellectual contest which was kept up on both sides. They demanded a public conference, at which the two Anabaptists could be openly heard and refuted. At first the magistrates refused their request: 'It would be dangerous,' they said, 'on account of the *tenderness* of the public mind; it would be better to hear these men in the council.' Farel persisted; the magistrates gave way: 'The usual conditions of these theological tournaments were proposed to the strangers,' says the historian of Geneva,[1] and they consented to submit to banishment or death in case of defeat. The discussion lasted for three days. The subjects of the most important debates were, the sacrament of baptism and the nature of the soul. Philosophy can show no more luminous demonstration of the immortality of the soul than that uttered by Calvin. The reasoning of his opponents does not seem to have been very conclusive. There were many,

[1] Gaberel, vol. i. p. 281.

however, who took their part; for those who were secretly vicious were delighted to find that the words of the Anabaptists made excuses for them; therefore they held their reasons to be good and valid, and refused to examine those of the ministers. At the end of three days the Council seeing that the breach was widening daily, and that the faith of many began to totter, commanded that the discussion should cease, and summoned the Anabaptists before them : 'You see,' said the first syndic, 'that we listen to each one, and that when we have heard your arguments you cannot prove them to be valid by the Scriptures. Since therefore you will not retract your errors and turn to God, we banish you for ever from our land.' The two Anabaptists left Geneva.

Calvin and Farel were victorious, but they were keenly alive to the incompleteness of their victory, and the necessity of making some powerful impression upon the minds of the people. They had recourse to the two most legitimate and efficacious plans which they could have adopted: they increased their intimacy with the citizens, multiplied their visits and the religious instruction given in private houses, and, acting with the magistrates, they caused the confession to be printed and distributed among the people. They thus placed their doctrines and precepts within the reach of all, and they took great pains to find out the opinions of the citizens, to strengthen and encourage believers, and to enlighten and confirm those who hesitated. There was another French refugee at Geneva, Courault, formerly a monk, then a preacher of reform, received with favour by the Queen of Navarre, now old and blind, but eloquent, impetuous, and indefatigable ; he became their colleague in the ministry, and their most popular agent. The assiduous labours of the reformers had the effect which is invariably produced in the early and violent stages of moral and social disturbances. Men's passions on both sides became equally excited; the two parties were sharply divided and hopelessly separated : the Libertines, as they were already called, became more turbulent and aggressive ; the orthodox believers more harsh and exclusive. Calvin and Farel demanded that one of the syndics, accompanied by certain officers, should enter every house, in order to obtain the adhesion of the inmates to the confession. The Council consented to take this step, but to the demand for religious observance of the confession they added the following restriction, 'as far as may be.' The result of these domiciliary visits was to show the complete separation and mutual opposition of the two parties ; many of the citizens, some of them men of good position, others humble and obscure, refused their adhesion to the confession ; one of the first of these sent word to the Council that 'as to him and his servant there were certain articles of the confession of faith which they were quite ready to agree to, but that they could not take any oath about the ten commandments of God, because they were exceedingly difficult to keep.' Similar declarations, and the immorality of those who made them, filled the pastors and their allies with alarm and anger; in September 1537, when they were about to celebrate the Lord's Supper, Calvin and Farel demanded that the abettors of the Anabaptists should be censured before they were allowed to partake of it;

once again the magistrates consented, but they implored the pastors to be careful and 'to exhort the people without casting them out of the right path.' Both pastors and magistrates felt that they were on the verge of a crisis; the magistrates, although they did not in theory acknowledge liberty of conscience, yet in point of fact respected it, fearing that, unless they did so, public order would be seriously disturbed, and the city depopulated; the pastors were afraid that the civil powers would attack the independence and rights of the Church, and were more and more anxious to assert and use them so that they might be secured. The commencement of the year 1538 was at hand, the time when the magistrates were to be re-elected by the citizens; the pastors insisted on the acknowledgment of their right of excommunication before they would consent to celebrate the Lord's Supper; the Council considered this threat too dangerous, and declared that communion must be refused to no one. The pastors gave way for the moment, for they were themselves anxious as to the sentiments of the people and the result of the approaching elections, and as we have seen already, Calvin was not incapable either of prudence or patience. The elections were unfavourable to him; three at least of the four new syndics were taken from the ranks of his enemies. The pastors restrained themselves for some weeks longer, and were content to do no more than call the attention of the Council to 'certain immoralities in the city both by night and day, as well as indecent songs and language.' The new magistrates, on their side, received these complaints

The irritation which this step produced was extreme, and was felt, not only by the pastors, but also by their pious and austere partisans; they resolved to lay their complaint solemnly before the Council. Calvin and Farel appeared before them, accompanied by fourteen pious burgesses of note.[1] Farel began abruptly, 'You have acted badly, wickedly, iniquitously,' said he, 'in putting Courault in prison. I demand that the matter be brought before the Council of Two Hundred. Ah, sirs, you should remember that without me you would not be here now.'

A Burgess. 'Yes, sirs, the pastors shall preach in spite of you.'

The Syndics. 'Courault has been imprisoned for abusive language to the magistrates; he will stay in prison until justice is done. And you, sirs, the preachers, will you obey the decree of Berne touching the Lord's Supper?'

The Pastors. 'We will only do what God commands us.'

The Burgesses. 'Set Courault at liberty. We will give bail for him.'

The Syndics. 'It is not the custom, seeing that he is imprisoned for contempt of justice.'

A Burgess. 'You have imprisoned him on the testimony of false witnesses; there are traitors here, and I know very well which they are.'

They separated, the magistrates surprised and provoked, the pastors and their friends more than ever resolved upon resistance. That same evening the magistrates sent a messenger to ask Calvin and Farel:—'Will you preach to-morrow, Easter Sunday,

[1] April 20, 1538.

and administer the Communion according to the tenor of the letters from Berne?' Calvin was alone, and he refused to give any answer: 'Then,' said the messenger, 'on the part of the magistrates I forbid you to preach to-morrow; they will find some one else.'

After having taken counsel together during the evening, Calvin and Farel resolved to preach on the morrow, not in order that they might administer the Lord's Supper, but in order to reproach their enemies, magistrates and citizens, with their conduct towards the defenders of the Reformation. The report spread rapidly that the pastors intended to preach in spite of the prohibition of the Council. Early on the morrow a dense crowd, friends and enemies, filled the churches of St. Peter and St. Gervais. Farel entered the pulpit at St. Gervais: 'I shall not administer the Sacrament,' said he, 'but I tell you that it is not from dislike to the Bernese rite, it is because your own dispositions render all communion with Jesus Christ impossible. There must be faith in order to hold communion with him, but you revile the Gospel! There must be charity, but you are here with swords and with sticks! There must be repentance; how have you spent the night that is past?' and he launched into a description of excesses which were familiar enough to the Libertines. Angry exclamations were heard on all sides; swords were drawn at no great distance from Farel; his friends surrounded him; he descended from the pulpit, and left the church walking slowly, his head thrown back, fiercely threatened but not attacked. Similar scenes took place around Calvin in St. Peter's church. On the following day[1] the Council resolved to adopt the Bernese rite definitely, and to depose the preachers who showed such contempt for the law, 'allowing them to remain in Geneva until others had been found to take their places.' The next day these two resolutions were confirmed by the general assembly, convened for that purpose, and an order to Farel and Calvin was added to 'leave the town in three days.'

The Genevese populace was undoubtedly hostile to the two reformers, to the supremacy of their faith, and the severity of their discipline and morality; their hostility was not without a confused sense of the right to liberty in matters of belief, although it also arose from vulgar antipathy to the moral results of the Christian faith and law.

Bonnivard, an old and valued friend of Geneva, often imprisoned and persecuted for the Genevese cause, and at that time living at Berne, had predicted this revolutionary violence: 'You hated the priests,' he said to the Genevese, 'for being a great deal too much like yourselves; you will hate the preachers for being a great deal too unlike yourselves; you will not have had them two years before you will wish them with the priests, and you will send them off with no other wages for their work than good blows with a cudgel. The same thing will happen in Geneva which happens among any people who have groaned for a long time beneath a hard and tyrannical power; delighted to feel themselves free, their love of liberty is changed to a love of licence; every man will be his own master and will live as he pleases.'

When Calvin received the order to leave Geneva

[1] April 22, 1538.

within three days: 'Well,' said he, 'so be it; if we had served man this would be a bad return, but we serve a great master who will reward us.' Calvin was not presumptuous, but he was proud, and he distrusted men almost as much as he trusted God; he left Geneva dejected and sad, and yet with a feeling of relief: 'Whenever I think how wretched I was in Geneva,' he wrote a little later, 'I tremble throughout my whole being; when I had to administer the sacrament, I was tortured by anxiety for the state of the souls of those for whom I should one day have to render an account before God; there were many whose faith seemed to me uncertain, nay doubtful, and yet they all thronged to the table of the Lord without distinction. I cannot tell you with what torments my conscience was beset, day and night.'[1]

Calvin did not know that he had sown seeds in Geneva which would soon spring up and bear fruit.

[1] Stähelin, 1860, vol. i. p. 157.

day[1] the Council resolved to adopt the Bernese rite definitely, and to depose the preachers who showed such contempt for the law, 'allowing them to remain in Geneva until others had been found to take their places.' The next day these two resolutions were confirmed by the general assembly, convened for that purpose, and an order to Farel and Calvin was added to 'leave the town in three days.'

The Genevese populace was undoubtedly hostile to the two reformers, to the supremacy of their faith, and the severity of their discipline and morality; their hostility was not without a confused sense of the right to liberty in matters of belief, although it also arose from vulgar antipathy to the moral results of the Christian faith and law.

Bonnivard, an old and valued friend of Geneva, often imprisoned and persecuted for the Genevese cause, and at that time living at Berne, had predicted this revolutionary violence: 'You hated the priests,' he said to the Genevese, 'for being a great deal too much like yourselves; you will hate the preachers for being a great deal too unlike yourselves; you will not have had them two years before you will wish them with the priests, and you will send them off with no other wages for their work than good blows with a cudgel. The same thing will happen in Geneva which happens among any people who have groaned for a long time beneath a hard and tyrannical power; delighted to feel themselves free, their love of liberty is changed to a love of licence; every man will be his own master and will live as he pleases.'

When Calvin received the order to leave Geneva

[1] April 22, 1538.

within three days: 'Well,' said he, 'so be it; if we had served man this would be a bad return, but we serve a great master who will reward us.' Calvin was not presumptuous, but he was proud, and he distrusted men almost as much as he trusted God; he left Geneva dejected and sad, and yet with a feeling of relief: 'Whenever I think how wretched I was in Geneva,' he wrote a little later, 'I tremble throughout my whole being; when I had to administer the sacrament, I was tortured by anxiety for the state of the souls of those for whom I should one day have to render an account before God; there were many whose faith seemed to me uncertain, nay doubtful, and yet they all thronged to the table of the Lord without distinction. I cannot tell you with what torments my conscience was beset, day and night.'[1]

Calvin did not know that he had sown seeds in Geneva which would soon spring up and bear fruit.

[1] Stähelin, 1860, vol. i. p. 157.

CHAPTER X.

CALVIN'S POLEMICS.

FOR four months Calvin wandered in Switzerland, visiting the different centres of the Reformation, Berne, Zurich, Lausanne, and Basle; sometimes doing his best to prove the lawfulness of his actions at Geneva and of their motives, at others acquiescing, although without hope of success, in the attempts of some of his friends to bring about a reconciliation with the Genevese. It was at Strasburg that he finally resolved to establish himself: about fifteen hundred Frenchmen, who had adopted the reformed faith and were fugitives like himself, had found an asylum there; two celebrated reformers, who were already his friends, Bucer and Capito, lived there and possessed great influence; they pressed him to join them: 'It was,' says Calvin, 'a similar appeal to that of Farel, which had formerly touched me so deeply: I yielded, like Jonah,[1] to the warning which called me to another work.'

He arrived at Strasburg in the early part of September 1538, and preached with his accustomed success before the assembled French refugees. The magistrates immediately authorized him to organize a religious congregation of his countrymen, he received the right of citizenship, was appointed professor of theology, and commenced a life of study

[1] Jonah, chap. i.

and religious instruction, the only life that was in harmony, so he said, 'with my timid, weak, and even pusillanimous nature.' Wearied and disgusted with his first combat, he was far from foreseeing the destiny for which he was reserved, as the heroic champion of the reformed faith.

No sooner was he settled at Strasburg than he was unexpectedly called upon to take up arms in defence of Geneva, the city which had just banished him. In April 1539, Cardinal Sadolet, Bishop of Carpentras, one of the most learned, most highly esteemed, and moderate of the prelates at the court of Rome, wrote a long letter to the Genevese, with the object of inducing them to return to the bosom of the Church of Rome. The banishment of Calvin had probably inspired him with some hope of the possibility of such an event. The letter was singularly prudent and temperate, free from all personal attack and special controversy: its sole aim was to urge the following argument, that eternal salvation being the first and chief interest of the human soul, there was more certainty of obtaining it by faith and humble submission to the Catholic church, than by accepting the audacious and vagrant doctrines of the innovators. The cardinal made numerous appeals to the authority of St. Paul, the favourite apostle of the reformers; and he ended his letter with an eloquent description of the different positions in which two Christians would find themselves at the Day of Judgment, in presence of the Supreme Judge, one of whom had humbly obeyed the teaching and authority of the Church, whilst the other had set up his own intellect and his own will as the law of his faith and life. Without a single reproach or threat, and in a tone of confident though sorrowful affection, the cardinal recalled the children who had gone astray, warned them of their great danger, and entreated them to return to the home of their fathers.

He had not named Calvin, or any other of the now celebrated reformers; but Calvin was not a man to take advantage of this discreet forbearance, or to screen himself behind the cardinal's silence concerning him. As soon as the letter to the Genevese was promulgated, the man who had been banished from Geneva, considering that he was attacked without being named, published a grand answer to it, in which he addressed the cardinal as his own opponent. He began by acknowledging, in very courteous terms, the high character, intellect, learning, and moderate language of the prelate, and disavowing any personal animosity or annoyance on his own part. Acknowledging the dignity and importance of their mutual position, he then, in his own name, in the names of his friends the reformers, and his disciples the Genevese, undertook the defence of their common cause, the Reformation—its principles and its aims. His defence was in reality an open and powerful attack upon the Church of Rome, its deviations from the Gospel teaching, its usurpations, immorality, and vice. 'I cannot consent to allow you,' said he, 'to stir up against us the hatred of ill-informed persons, by giving the name of Church to such a profligate institution, as if we intended to make war against the Church. We are armed not only with the Word of God, but also with the writings of the Fathers of the Church, by which means we can fight against, overthrow, and destroy your empire; you hold up in opposition to us the authority of the Church as if it were the shield of Ajax, but I will take it from you, and show you by means of a few striking examples how very far you are removed from that sacred antiquity. . . . Recall to your minds the ancient form of the Church, such as it was among the Greeks in the time of Basil and Chrysostom, among the Latins in the time of Cyprian, Ambrose, and Augustine, of which the records remain in their own writings, and then look at the ruins of it that exist in your midst. . . . We ask for Christian liberty, which has been oppressed and stifled under human traditions. . . . Have we not restored the rights of criminal and civil jurisdiction to the magistrates, from whom they had been fraudulently abstracted by the pretexts of episcopacy and priestcraft? . . . Do not take to yourselves the credit of a peaceful reign; there has been peace only because Christ has been silent. I grant that this new expansion of the Gospel has given rise to great strife which no one foresaw; but do not impute this to our followers; they are ready to give a reason for the faith that is in them at all times and to all men. . . . God grant, O Cardinal! that thou and all thy followers may one day recognise that it is Christ our Saviour, he who reconciles us to God the Father, who can alone unite his scattered Church, and re-establish it in the bond of true unity.'

It is an easy and vulgar manner of writing history to depict exclusively the most salient features of men and parties, and to describe only those views and violent passions which separate them most strongly. I have no taste for this superficial and crude method: truth demands that we should penetrate beyond the mere surface of minds and characters, that we should also show their inmost nature, and point out the larger views and juster feelings which have sometimes led opponents to seek to understand and approach each other. This is what I have just done with regard to Sadolet and Calvin; for a time I have left out of sight their striking points of difference and the subjects on which they profoundly offended each other, and have shown them as they appeared in 1539, in their polite and reserved polemics. The differences of principle and action which separated them were not rendered less deep and obvious by their mutual forbearance, and the contest between the two causes to which they were devoted, the Church of Rome and the Reformation, was carried on by them all the same. Both show themselves, in fact, just what they are, they and their followers: the cardinal is old, and Calvin is young;—one is timid, the other bold;—one tries to arrest a great movement in the human soul and human society which alarms and exhausts him;—the other throws himself into the movement with all confidence, and strives to help on the human soul and human society in the path which they have just entered.

The two letters made a great noise throughout Europe: 'Here is a work which has hands and feet,' said Luther when he read that of Calvin; 'I thank God for raising up such men.' The letters were forgotten, the cardinal's attempt was futile, but the impulse given by Calvin spread and increased.

I have tried to find in the history of the time some other traces of the intercourse thus commenced between two men, both of whom, although so unequal, were very remarkable, and both of whom were earnest. I was struck by a few lines in a remarkable work published by M. Felix Bungener, pastor at Geneva, and entitled 'Calvin, his Life, his Work, and his Books;'[1] in which he refers to a visit said to have been paid to Calvin at Geneva by Sadolet, at some unknown period after their epistolary controversy. The fact seems to me not impossible, but very difficult to reconcile with the facts and dates in the lives of the two men from 1539 to 1547, the date of the cardinal's death. I asked M. Bungener himself from what contemporaneous documents he had extracted this anecdote, or by what testimony it was supported. He acknowledged, with great candour, the difficulty of procuring any such corroboration in its favour, and added (I make it a point of duty to reproduce his exact words) : 'I never placed entire confidence in the story which struck you in my " Calvin." I inserted it at first on the authority of local tradition; every one at Geneva believes it, and I believed it, like every one else. But I had also further authority than tradition; I found it in Drelincourt's "Défense de Calvin," published at Geneva in 1667, in the following passage:

'" It is said, and illustrious members of the Church of Rome have also heard it said, that Cardinal Sadolet, passing through Geneva *incognito*, as they call it, wished to see Calvin, who had written against him, and so he went to call upon him. He expected to find a palace, or at least a magnificently furnished mansion, well filled with servants. Instead of that he was greatly surprised when he was directed to a small house, and when, having knocked at the door, Calvin himself, very simply dressed, came to open it. The cardinal was astounded to find that

[1] Bungener, p. 503. 1862.

this was the celebrated and renowned Calvin, for whose writings he entertained so much admiration; and he could not help expressing his astonishment and surprise. But Calvin told him to remember that in what he had done he had not taken counsel with flesh and blood; and that his aim had not been to make himself rich and powerful in this world, but to glorify God and defend the truth. Report adds that the illustrious cardinal conversed for some time with Calvin, and was greatly edified." [1]

Even if we admit the visit, I doubt—and M. Bungener doubts also—whether it made the impression upon the two men which is attributed to it in the chronicle. The cardinal was probably not so much astonished at Calvin's humble dwelling; and Calvin did not take so much pains to explain why he did not live more sumptuously, and by what more lofty motives than the desire of making himself rich and powerful in this world his life was governed. They were both certainly capable of understanding each other very much better than this. Calvin's entire disinterestedness, and the extreme simplicity of his habits, had been abundantly shown and were well known at that time. Wherever he lived, and as long as he lived, at Basle, Strasburg, and Geneva, he had scarcely the bare necessaries for the most simple and humble existence: he received a stipend sometimes from the small and parsimonious municipal governments of the places in which he resided, at others from private friends who were intimate with him and knew his needs. He arranged all domestic matters with the most scrupulous exactness; he wanted no more than would suffice regularly

---

[1] Drelincourt, *La Défense de Calvin*, p. 187. Geneva, 1667.

to supply the needs of every day, and would leave him free from anxiety on the subject. All his thoughts were entirely engrossed by his Christian work in the world and his intellectual life.

He lived thus for three years at Strasburg, preaching, teaching, and writing; passing from his labours in translating and explaining the Scriptures to the partly ecclesiastical, partly political missions which were entrusted to him, and which took him to those meetings at which the general work of the Reformation had to be discussed and decided. It was at this period that he published his treatise 'On the Lord's Supper,' his 'Commentary on the Epistle of St. Paul to the Romans,' and his revision of the 'Translation of the Bible,' by his fellow-countryman Robert Olivétan. From 1539 to 1541 he was sent by the magistrates of Strasburg and the dukes of Brunswick-Lunebourg, as one of their delegates, to the diets or conferences of Frankfort, Hagenau, Worms, and Ratisbon ; the object of these meetings was sometimes to attempt to establish agreement and unity between the different reformed churches, at others to seek some solution for the difficulties which arose between the civil and religious authorities,—the Empire and the new churches. On all these occasions, and especially at the time of the controversy between Luther and Zwingli on the nature of the eucharist, Calvin's conduct was that of a conciliatory and politic theologian, skilful in distinguishing essential points from those which are of secondary importance, and inclined to seek for some compromise on the secondary, which might assist but not prejudge or endanger, any decision ultimately formed on the essential points. He had no desire to undertake these difficult missions: 'Although I continued,' he says, 'to be always like myself, that is, unwilling to take part in great meetings, I do not know how it was that I was always driven, as if by force, to the diets, where, whether I liked it or no, I always found myself in the company of many people.' In a recent and very intelligent history of Calvin by a German author, I find the following passage: 'The young Frenchman, with his reserved and rather shy manners, must have been a singular apparition among the princes and most eminent men of learning in the German empire amongst whom he was suddenly thrown. As they often spoke in German he did not always understand what was being discussed, and his position was rather that of a learned and reliable man whom his friends had summoned to give them valuable advice, than that of one who took an active part in official debates.'[1]

Calvin had not attended these meetings long before he acquired a very strong feeling of their inefficiency, and of his want of power to give predominance to his own views: 'Certainly,' he wrote, after the first meeting of the Diet of Ratisbon, 'if this results in anything satisfactory it will be greatly opposed to my expectations.' In fact, he did not succeed in harmonizing the doctrines of the reformed German, Swiss, and French churches, nor could he reconcile the Lutherans and Zwinglians on the question of the Eucharist. Neither side had yet learnt, either by experience or common danger, to unite in their great common ground of Christian belief, and to concede mutual liberty in the points on which they differed in knowledge as a nation, or as a sect.

[1] Stähelin, vol. i. p. 233.

CHAPTER XI.

CALVIN, LUTHER, AND MELANCTHON. CALVIN IN SEARCH
OF A WIFE.

CALVIN'S presence at these religious congresses was not devoid of pleasure and valuable result to himself. He was brought into personal relation with almost all of the most eminent men in the different reformed churches; and he soon obtained such a high place in their esteem that with one consent they called him *The Theologian*, being struck not only by the extent of his knowledge, but by the clear insight and courage which he displayed, in dealing with the difficult questions which they had to discuss. There was one important meeting—perhaps the most important of any for the Reformation—which did not, however, take place at these conferences—Calvin did not meet Luther; the two great reformers never once saw each other and talked together. Calvin, no doubt, regretted it keenly, for he ardently desired the unity of the reformed churches. He wrote to the learned Bullinger of Zurich: 'Nothing is more important, not only for us but for the whole Christian Church, than the maintenance of true harmony between those men to whom the Lord has confided great powers. This is the point on which Satan has fixed his eyes; he desires nothing so much as to excite quarrels among us, and to isolate us from each other.' Calvin was especially troubled at the controversy between Luther and Zwingli on the subject of the eucharist: 'Although I have the highest opinion of Luther's piety,' he wrote to his friend Bucer, 'I do not really know what I ought to think of him; even his friends acknowledge that there is a good dose of self-esteem in his firmness, and it does not seem to me at all improbable. The Swiss may therefore be excused if they distrust the attempts at re-union; Luther's offensive pride compels them to do so.'

A message, and a few words uttered by Luther, modified these impressions. Calvin wrote to Farel: 'Craton, one of our engravers, has just come from Wittenberg; he has brought a letter from Luther to Bucer, in which Luther says, " Greet Calvin—whose little works I have read with remarkable pleasure —affectionately." Philip (Melancthon) also writes: " Calvin is in high favour here." He also desired the messenger to say that certain persons, wishing to irritate Martin (Luther), had pointed out several passages in my works in which I alluded to him and his followers in very bitter terms. Luther examined the passages, and saw that he was undoubtedly the person referred to; he ended by saying, " I hope Calvin will think better of me one day; we ought to bear with something from so excellent a man." If we are not melted by so much gentleness,' adds Calvin, 'we must be stones; as for me, I am melted.'

The controversy concerning the eucharist still raged as fiercely as ever between the two schools, but Calvin's feelings had evidently undergone a change. ' I implore you,' he wrote to Bullinger, who was a Zwinglian, ' never to forget how great a man Luther is. Think with what courage, what constancy, what power he has devoted himself to spreading the doctrine of salvation far and near. As for me, I have often said, and I say it again, though he should call me *devil*, I would still give him due honour, and recognise him as a mighty servant of the Lord.' A little later Calvin went beyond even this. He wrote to Luther: ' If I could only fly to you and enjoy your society, even for a few hours! But since this happiness is not granted to me here, below, I hope that it may soon be granted me in the kingdom of God. Farewell, then, most illustrious man, eminent minister of Christ, father for ever venerable to me! May the Lord continue to direct you by his Holy Spirit for the common good of his Church!'

Melancthon was charged to give this letter to Luther, but finding no doubt that his master was not in the right humour to receive it, the timid disciple kept the letter, and Luther never knew of it. I do not know if it would have had the effect of calming his irritation, but it remains as a noble expression of the sentiments which Calvin entertained for him, and which he continued to express even after Luther's death.

During the Diets of 1539 and 1542, Calvin frequently met Melancthon, and they became close friends. When men are earnest and sincere, they are drawn together, and united by their points of difference almost as powerfully as by their common sympathies. Melancthon attracted Calvin by the cultivation and fertility of his intellect, by its comprehensiveness as well as its subtlety and elegance ; he was at the same time philosophical and literary, as well versed in the ancient Greek and Latin literature as in Christian history and theology. He belonged quite as much to the Restoration of literature in the sixteenth century as to the Reformation. All these things influenced Calvin, who was keenly alive to the charm of great learning and fine language. Moreover Melancthon shared the greater number of his own views on the principal religious questions which were at that time in dispute, especially his views on free-will and pre-destination. He was older than Calvin, and a man of much greater renown, and yet he showed him marked esteem and affection. During their early intercourse Calvin was the disciple, welcomed and treated with great favour by the celebrated man whose amiable nature was as great an attraction as his rare intellect and acquirements, so that he was no less honoured than delighted. He was not slow to perceive that these fine qualities were allied in Melancthon to defects which his own character and personal instincts caused him to feel keenly. Calvin was a man of great intellectual precision and courage, energetic, and of passionate intensity of character ; Melancthon was gentle, open to many influences, easily moved and intimidated either by friends or enemies, and inclined to make concessions in order to avoid a contest. Although Calvin was impressed by these characteristics, which were unfavourable to the common cause, yet he was no less alive to Melancthon's rare and attractive merits ; he remained faithful to his master, but the pupil soon became an independent and candid critic, and during the whole of their friendship he made it a duty to warn Melancthon, and put him on his guard against his weakness: 'You complain,' he wrote, 'of Luther's violence and blind intolerance; but must not this defect increase and grow from day to day, if every one trembles before him and gives way to him in everything? I gladly acknowledge that by your gentle and conciliatory manner you have kept many from quarrelling, or made peace between them. I approve of this moderation and prudence; but is it a reason for shrinking in terror from every contested question as from an abyss, for fear of opposing and offending some one? Do you not thus leave in uncertainty and perplexity a large number of friends who look to you and rely upon you as the man in whom they put their trust? Truly, as I have already told you more than once, it is not to our honour that we refuse to sign with our ink the doctrines which so many saints are sealing with their blood. You know why I address you with such earnestness: I would rather die with you a hundred times over than see you outlive your divine and native nobility. I am not afraid of that, but I am afraid that you will give our enemies a pretext that they have long desired for injuring you in one manner or another. Forgive these bitter complaints, which can do no good. May God guard thee, excellent man, whom I carry always in my heart! May the Lord still guide thee by his Holy Spirit, and sustain thee by his strength!'

It is possible that Calvin sometimes felt a secret pleasure in thus assuming towards Melancthon the attitude and language of an independent and severe judge; the noblest of human beings do not entirely escape from the small and ignoble defects of human nature, but, in spite of this, their nobility and rectitude are, on the whole, the true motives of their conduct. It was love of truth, sincere friendship for Melancthon, and zeal for their common cause, much more than a secret pleasure in the gratification of his own self-esteem, which led Calvin during the whole of their intercourse to address Melancthon in frank and dignified language. This was the tone of the last words—words imbued with the deepest tenderness—which he wrote concerning his friend when in 1560, having himself only a few more years to live, he heard of his death.

'O Philip Melancthon! for it is upon thee that I call, upon thee who now livest with Christ in God, and art waiting for us, until we shall also be gathered to that blessed rest! A hundred times, worn out with fatigue, and overwhelmed with care, thou hast laid thy head upon my breast and said, "Would to God that I might die here, on thy breast!" And I, a thousand times since then, have I earnestly desired that it had been granted us to be together. Certainly thou wouldst have been more valiant to face danger, and stronger to despise hatred, and bolder to disregard false accusations. Thus the wickedness of many would have been restrained, whose audacity was increased by what they called thy weakness.'

It would be difficult to reconcile truth, piety, and friendship more tenderly.

Calvin had now lived at Strasburg for more than two years—years of incessant work and arduous struggle. He had no other domestic enjoyment than his books, and occasionally the society of one or two young students who were invited to his humble home, no other relaxation than conversation from time to time with his friends, and journeys upon the different missions with which he was entrusted. He was scarcely thirty, and yet his health was already delicate and uncertain. He occasionally contemplated marriage, but entertained neither romantic nor worldly notions on the subject. On the 19th of May, 1539, he wrote to his most intimate friend Farel, and no doubt alluded to some suggestion which had been made to him: 'I will now speak more openly on the subject of marriage. I do not know if, before the departure of Michael, any one mentioned the person about whom I have written to you. Remember, I pray you, what I look for in a wife. I am not one of those idiotic lovers who can even adore defects when once they are captivated by beauty. The only beauty I care for in a woman is that she shall be modest, gentle, unobtrusive, economical, patient, and that I may expect her to look after my health. If you think that I do well to marry, pray see about it at once, lest some one else should be beforehand with you. If you do not think so, then let us give it up.' Some months later, on the 6th of February, 1540, he wrote again to Farel: 'In the midst of all these labours I have leisure enough to think of taking a wife. A young girl of noble birth and good fortune—far beyond my position—has been proposed to me. But there were two reasons against the marriage. She did not understand our language, and I was afraid that she might think too much of her birth and education. Her brother, a very pious man, urged the marriage strongly, from no other motive than his affection for me, which blinded him so that he forgot himself; his wife entreated as earnestly as he did, and I should have been compelled to give my hand, if the Lord had not delivered me. I answered that I would do nothing unless the young lady promised at once to devote herself to the study of French. She asked for time to consider. I immediately sent my brother, and a worthy man whom I know, in search of another person; and if she is as good as her reputation, she will bring me an ample marriage portion without any money, for all who know her speak of her with admiration. If the thing succeeds according to our hopes, the marriage will take place not later than March 10th. God grant that you may be present to bless our union! I shall feel rather foolish if my expectations come to nothing, but I fully believe that the Lord will help me, and so I act as if the thing were certain.' Three weeks later, on the 26th of February, 1540, Calvin wrote once more to Farel: 'I am afraid that if you wait for my wedding it will be a long time before you come. My wife is not yet found, and I am afraid that I must look again for her. Three days after my brother's return, I received certain information about the young lady in question which compelled me to send him back at once, in order to break off the engagement.'

His friend Bucer now came to his aid, spared him the trouble of a fresh search and saved him from further uncertainty. John Störder, an Anabaptist from Liège, had been converted to the orthodox faith by Calvin, and had since died of the plague; his widow now lived at Strasburg. Her name was Idelette, and she was born at Buren, a little town in Gueldres; she had been left with three children, and in her humble position had gained the esteem and affection of all who knew her. Beza says: 'She was a grave and virtuous woman.' On Bucer's recommendation Calvin saw her and conversed with her, and was convinced, as he afterwards wrote to his friend Viret, 'that whatever sharp trial might be sent him, she would willingly be his companion in exile, poverty, and even unto death.' Their wedding was celebrated in September 1540, with considerable solemnity. Many of his friends, and deputies sent by different consistories in French Switzerland, were present at the marriage of an already celebrated reformer; a man from whom the members of the reformed faith in western Europe, in the midst of their struggles, expected much greater things than any that he had yet done.

CHAPTER XII.

CALVIN RETURNS TO GENEVA.

AFTER the banishment of Calvin and Farel, Geneva became a prey to moral and religious disturbances, and political perils which increased in significance from day to day. The Libertines were now in power, and, in a somewhat cynical manner, they put forward their ideas, their immoral doctrines, and their aims. Of the four syndics who called themselves members of the Reformed Church, one refused to be present at the reformed worship, another said that mass was not to be despised, and a third allowed it to be seen that he thought the supremacy of Berne might be advantageous to Geneva. The confession of faith which had been carried four years previously was attacked at a meeting of the Council. Education was not better treated than religion. A college had been established at the request of Calvin, and possessed a principal and professors who were pious and able men, acknowledged as such in Switzerland, and even in France; they were requested to preside at the sacramental tables, and to conform to the Bernese rites which Calvin and Farel had rejected. They also refused to do this, saying moreover that they had been engaged to teach pupils at the college and not to take part in religious services. They received orders to leave the city in three days, they and their families, and had great difficulty in obtaining permission to delay their departure for a fortnight. There were most outrageous displays of licentiousness and violence in the streets of the city, both by night and day. The pious and orderly citizens were alarmed and excited; they protested in vain against the immorality, and demanded that the banished pastors should be allowed to return and explain the motives of their conduct. The Government of Berne was also uneasy as to the state of Geneva, and sent envoys who supported this request. The syndics presented it to the General Council of the citizens, saying: 'Let those who wish the banished ministers to return to the city, that they may explain their conduct and resume their functions, hold up their hands!' Only four persons had the courage to do so, and the crowd immediately rushed upon these friends of the banished men, crying out: 'To the Rhone with the Williamists!'[1]

In the presence of such facts as these, the hopes of the ancient Catholic rulers of Geneva began to revive, and its last bishop, Pierre de la Baume (who had been made cardinal), the Duke of Savoy, and the Pope (Paul III.) prepared themselves for fresh efforts. A conference was established at Lyons, consisting of three cardinals and six archbishops or bishops, the object of which was to seek and put into operation means whereby the ancient Catholic religion might be re-established in Geneva. There was no lack of partisans or agents in Geneva itself. In addition to

[1] William was the Christian name of Farel.

the danger from the hopes of the Catholics, the city was threatened by the ambition of foreign states, especially by that of Berne, which had many adherents in Geneva. Conspiracy, sedition, trials, and political executions were added to religious dissensions: national independence was in as great danger as the Reformed Church.

Calvin's friends kept him well informed as to the position of affairs, and when he left Geneva he bore in his heart a very deep affection for the city in which he had first planted the banner of his cause. But neither the illusions of affection, nor the sorrows of exile, could blind his judgment with regard to what the conduct of his friends ought to be during their trials; and he unfailingly counselled moderation, patience, prudence, perseverance in their work, and that they should abide in the city where they had so much difficulty in performing it. There was to be no open schism, no voluntary separation, no abandonment of their native and national church, however gloomy the situation of that church might be, and however inefficient the pastors who ministered in the name of Christ. 'We must not,' he said, 'take offence at certain defects of doctrine, for where is the church which is altogether pure and perfect in this respect? It is enough that the grand and essential truths, on which God has founded his church, keep their place and are generally received.'

At the same time that he gave such wise advice, he endeavoured to keep up the courage of the believers, and to raise their hopes: 'Always turn, my beloved brethren, to this consolation; although the wicked strive to destroy your church, although your sins have merited more punishment than you can endure, yet the Lord will put an end to the chastisements which he has inflicted for your good. Consider your enemies; you will see that all their ways lead to confusion, although they may have achieved their desire.'[1]

In proportion as the immorality increased and the dangers became more apparent, a powerful reaction took place among the citizens of Geneva; the Libertines lost credit, and orderly and pious men resumed the position they had formerly held. The idea gained ground rapidly that the best remedy for all evils would be to recall Calvin and Farel, and openly to submit to their authority. A bookseller, one of Calvin's friends, was the first to inform him of the existence of this feeling. Calvin wrote immediately to Farel: 'Do what you can to prevent the thing from making progress, for I will not return. I would a thousand times rather die than allow myself to be nailed again to that cross, where my blood would flow daily from a thousand wounds. Certainly I rejoice at the tidings, but who knows if these men are truly converted and united together in the Lord? Unless it is so, this peace will be very soon broken again.' The idea of recalling Calvin made rapid progress at Geneva. On the 21st of September, 1540, the Council of State requested Ami Perrin, one of his faithful adherents, to find the means of inducing him to return. On the 20th of October the General Assembly voted that 'in order to promote the increase and advancement of the Word of God it was decreed to seek and send for Master John Calvin, who is a very learned man, to be the evangelical minister in

[1] Stähelin, ii. 286-290. Gaberel, ii. 304.

this city.' On the 22d a pressing official letter was addressed to him: 'Seeing that our people wish for you, we will deal with you in such a manner that you shall have good reason to be contented.' An appeal was also made to the magistrates of Strasburg to induce them to release Calvin from his engagements. At first they hesitated, for Calvin was not only an ornament to their city, but an honoured and useful representative in their transactions with the German Diets and Conferences. At that period Calvin had just set out for the Diet of Worms, and it was at Worms that the letter from Geneva was delivered to him. He wrote at once in answer to it, in very affectionate terms: 'If only in return for the kindness and courtesy which in every way you show me, I should not do my duty unless I made every effort in my power to comply with your request. But I cannot leave my vocation in Strasburg without the advice and consent of those whom our Lord has put in authority there.'

From October 1540 to April 1541, four successive messengers carried the entreaties of the Genevese to Strasburg, or wherever else Calvin was to be found. The people of Strasburg seemed inclined, although with regret, to consent to his leaving them. They had just sent him again to the Diet of Ratisbon, but they were struck by the importance of Geneva as the home and centre of the Reformation in France and Italy, and were willing to give up their own advantage to the general interest of the common cause. But Calvin himself was greatly perplexed: 'I knew well,' he wrote to Farel, 'that you would urge me to comply with the request; but if you had seen my anguish when this message reached me, you would have had pity on me. I was scarcely in possession of my senses. When I recall the life that I led in that place, I tremble to the very depths of my soul at the thought of returning. At that time I had often the greatest difficulty in stifling the desire of flight which would rise within me; but I felt that my hands and feet were bound to that city by the will of God. And now that his grace has set me free, shall I of my own will return thither and plunge again into an abyss of which I know the horror and the danger so well? .... Nevertheless the more I am inclined to recoil with terror from this task, the more I distrust myself. I therefore leave the thing to take its own way, and entreat my friends not to urge me in either direction. In any case I will never forsake the church of Geneva, which is dearer to me than my life. I am not seeking my own advantage, nor do I wish to make vain excuses; but I must see the will of God clearly in this matter, in order that I may walk in safety, and with his blessing.' This is a remarkable instance of the manner in which a noble nature may be attracted and yet alarmed by a great and difficult undertaking, and of the mingled eagerness and apprehension with which it may be approached.

But Calvin's hesitation was overcome by the urgent entreaties of the Genevese, and the advice of his most intimate friends. M. Bernard, one of the pastors who had remained in Geneva after his departure, wrote to tell him that on a day in February 1541, when he was in the pulpit, he saw that his hearers were deeply grieved at the destitution of the Church, and that he exhorted them to pray to the pastor of pastors, Jesus Christ, and implore him to put an end to this state of things; and, when he had spoken thus, every one thought of Calvin, and his name was on every tongue: 'As for me,' he continued, 'I blessed God that the stone which the builders had rejected had become the chief stone of the corner. Come to us, then, revered brother in Christ; you belong to us, for the Lord has given you to us. Come! for the Lord would require our blood at your hands, because it is you whom he has established as a shepherd over the house of Israel, which is among us.' On the 1st of May, 1541, the General Council formally revoked the decree of exile which had been pronounced in 1538, stated that 'Calvin and Farel were good men and men of God, and approved of all that the Council had done or might do to induce Calvin to return.' They had ceased to urge Farel's return, because Neufchâtel had explicitly refused to part with him. Calvin yielded: 'I thought the matter over conscientiously and with reverence, and when I saw that it was my duty I gave way, and consented to return to the flock from which I had been, as it were, torn away. But, as the Lord is my witness, I submitted with sorrow, tears, great solicitude, and anxiety. Not my will, O God, but thy will be done! I offer my heart as a sacrifice to the Lord.'

Calvin arrived at Geneva on the 12th of September, 1541,[1] after having spent a few days with Farel at Neufchâtel. A house, with a garden, had been pro-

---

[1] The 10th of September, according to a careful memoir by M. Amédée Roget, entitled *L'Église et l'État à Genève du Vivant de Calvin*. (Geneva, 1867.)

vided for him; and in the Registers of the Council for the month after his arrival, we find the following details :—

'Resolved to send for Maître Calvin's wife and household, and to provide him with all that is necessary for this purpose in men and money.'

'Resolved to buy Maître Calvin some broadcloth to make him a coat.'

'Cheque for eight crowns for Maître Calvin's coat.'

'Resolved that as Maître Calvin is a man of great learning, and well fitted to build up the Christian Church, and as he is put to great expense in entertaining strangers who pass through the city, that he shall receive a salary of 500 florins,[1] twelve measures of wheat, and two tubs of wine, and shall take the oaths here.'[2]

Beza says: 'He was received with singular affection by this unhappy people, who now acknowledged their faults, and were hungering and thirsting for the words of their faithful pastor, so that they did not cease to importune until he had been induced to return. And at length the rulers of Strasburg consented that he should leave them, though they stipulated that he should always remain a burgess of their city. They also requested him to retain the revenues of a prebend, which had been assigned as the salary of his professorship in theology. But he was a man who had no love whatsoever for the things of this world, and they could not succeed in persuading him to retain so much as a single farthing.'[3]

[1] Worth about 3,600 francs, or 150*l*. at the present time.
[2] Gaberel, vol. i. Appendix, p. 116.   [3] Beza, p. 31.

CHAPTER XIII.

CALVIN'S ECCLESIASTICAL POLITY.

CALVIN dreaded responsibility and warfare from afar and beforehand, but as soon as he had entered the arena all irresolution disappeared; he felt his own strength and did not scruple to use it. Two days after his arrival in Geneva, as soon as he had paid an official visit to the magistrates, he requested them, without any further delay, to nominate a commission which should have power to prepare the necessary reforms in the constitution and government of the Church. Six members were at once appointed, and a fortnight later, with the help of Calvin and his colleagues, they had drawn up a hundred and sixty-eight articles, which contained a complete scheme of ecclesiastical polity. This scheme was presented to the Council on the 26th of September, 1541. It was discussed during a whole month, and modified on many points in which the civil magistrates thought it too severe. It was adopted on the 9th of November by the Two Hundred, and was received on the 20th by the General Assembly. Several slight modifications were, however, made at the request of some of the citizens, and it was not until the 2d of January, 1542, that the Ecclesiastical Ordinances were definitely accepted by the General Assembly, consisting of 2,000 citizens. On the 14th of March, 1542, Calvin wrote: 'We have now a kind of ecclesiastical tribunal, and such a form of religious discipline as these troublous times will allow of. But do not think that we have obtained it without great effort.[1]

I will not attempt to give a detailed account of the internal organization of the Church of Geneva, nor of the peculiar nature of its relation to the State, which was the result of that organization. But I am anxious to define its first principles and to state its essential results with accuracy; not only because of the importance of the problems then solved, but also because the solution accepted at Geneva was so widely received. The religious system established by Calvin in the Church of Geneva was adopted by the reformed churches, and by Protestantism, properly so called, in France, Holland, Switzerland, and several of the United States of America. A local work does not spread in this manner unless it responds to some great instinct of humanity, to the general condition of men's minds, and to the wants of the time. Calvin's ideas were larger than he himself knew, and whilst he was laboriously discussing the Ecclesiastical Ordinances with the syndics of Geneva, he was in reality working for much greater states, although the foundations of some of them were not so much as laid at that time.

There were two principles to which Calvin attached the highest importance; I might almost call them his two supreme passions, for they were as pre-eminent in his religious system as they were in his life.

I. The distinction between religious and civil society; that is, between Church and State. I say distinction, not separation; it was an alliance between two societies, two powers, each independent of the other in its own domain, but combining in action, and giving each other mutual support.

II. The amendment and religious discipline of the life and morals of all members of the Church, who were to be placed under the inspection of the ecclesiastical powers, and subjected to their authority, with recourse, in extreme cases, to the civil power.

In speaking of Church and State, I use the language of the nineteenth century and not that of the sixteenth, and I do not explain Calvin's aims. He spoke only of the Christian Church and the Christian State. His Ordinances of 1542 were devised and framed for the Christian church of the little Christian republic of Geneva. They were, in fact, quite practicable in Geneva, which was a free and independent city, and had just solemnly embraced the reformed religion. Its two thousand citizens had been called together and consulted, and they had bound themselves to the Reformation by oath. Those who opposed this step had been bidden to seek a home in some other country. Thus both Church and State in Geneva had openly proclaimed themselves Christian. It only remained, therefore, to organize the Christian Church in accordance with the instructions given in Holy Scripture, and to connect the religious with the civil administration of this Christian State.

The constitution which was framed for the Christian Church of Geneva was, to a certain extent, both liberal and cautious; and, like the civil constitution of the Christian Genevese State, it was republican. Two supreme courts were instituted, both having somewhat of an elective character :—1. The Venerable Company of Pastors, whose power was spiritual and ecclesiastical; the members were to preach and teach the Christian faith, to administer the sacraments—more especially the Lord's Supper—and to act as members of the Consistory. 2. The pastors and certain laymen, called *elders*, formed the Consistory, a moral tribunal, and the guardian of ecclesiastical ordinances. The Consistory watched over the maintenance of Christian discipline; repressed moral disorders of every kind, in persons of all ranks; and thus introduced moral reform — of which Genevese society stood in great need—side by side with the religious reform already adopted. Church and State, civil and ecclesiastical rulers, and the veto of the citizens, all helped to form and keep up these two courts. 'In order that everything in the Church may be done in due order, all aspirants for the ministry are to be examined by the pastors; the object of the examination being to ascertain, first, the doctrine of the candidate—that is, if he possesses a thorough and sound knowledge of the Scriptures; secondly, if he is a fit and meet person to impart religious instruction to the people ; and thirdly, if he is a man of good character, and has always led a blameless life. A satisfactory examination is followed by the laying on of hands, in accordance with the apostolical custom, and the candidate is then eligible to be elected pastor. The election rests with the Venerable Company of Pastors, but the Council is at once communicated with, and sends some of its members to hear the candidate preach before the assembled ministers. On the following Sunday the name of the new minister is published in all the churches, together with an announcement that he has been elected and approved in the usual manner, but that if any one knows of anything to the prejudice of his character, it is to be communicated to one of the syndics before the next Sunday. On that day, if no valid objection has been raised, the new pastor takes the oaths before the Council and is publicly installed.' The twelve lay elders who, with six pastors, compose the Consistory, 'are chosen by the Council, in accordance with the indication of the pastors, and their election is confirmed by the Two Hundred. Their names are published on a Sunday, and, before the following Thursday, any objections which may be raised have to be laid before one of the syndics.' The power of excommunication belongs exclusively to this court, consisting of laymen and ecclesiastics.[1]

Calvin thus introduced two new and daring measures into the great European Reformation, in advance of anything attempted by its first authors. When Henry VIII. rescued the Church of England from the domination of the Pope, he proclaimed himself as its head, and the Anglican Church accepted this royal supremacy. When Zwingli provoked a rupture with the Church of Rome in German Switzerland, he was contented to allow sovereign authority in matters of religion to pass into the hands of the civil powers. Even Luther, although he reserved a certain measure of liberty and independence to the Church of Germany, yet placed it under the protection and domination of lay sovereigns. In this great question of the relation of Church and State, Calvin aimed at and accom-

[1] Gaberel, i. 326–336. Bungener, pp. 270–275.

plished more than any of his predecessors. Even before he occupied an important position among European reformers, when he heard of the religious supremacy of Henry VIII. in England, he protested strongly against such a system. Notwithstanding his unceasing opposition to the Church of Rome, his judgment was too clear and just to allow him to be blinded to the strength and dignity which that Church derived from the absolute independence of its sovereign, the Pope, and its complete separation from the state. When he became one of the leading reformers, he was anxious that the reformed Church should not lose this grand characteristic; indeed, in calling it evangelical, he claimed for it the independence and authority possessed by the primitive Church in matters of faith and religious discipline. In spite of the repeated opposition of the civil magistrates, and of the concessions which he was sometimes compelled to make, he maintained this principle firmly, and, in all purely religious matters, secured to the Genevese Church the right of self-government, in accordance with the faith and laws made known in the Scriptures.

He also obtained the recognition of a second and no less important principle. In the course of time, and by a successive series of modifications, some of them natural and others factious and illegal, the Christian Church had been divided, as it were, into two distinct parts,—ecclesiastical and religious, or the clergy and the believers. In the Catholic Church all power had fallen into the hands of the clergy; the ecclesiastical governed the religious world; and whilst the latter were adopting the thoughts and opinions of the laity, the former remained more and more separate and supreme. The German and English Reformation had already modified this state of things, and given laymen a certain amount of power in matters relating to religion. Calvin interposed in a much more direct and efficacious manner. He appointed a larger number of laymen than of ecclesiastics, as members of the Consistory, which was the principal moral authority in the reformed church of Geneva and an authority evidently destined to increase; and he thus completely destroyed the line of separation between the clergy and the believers. He summoned laymen and ecclesiastics to deliberate and act together, and in this manner secured a just share of power and influence to all the members of the religious society.

One fact proves the importance that he attached to the active participation of faithful believers with their pastor in public worship. The reformed churches had abolished all the pomp and ceremonies of the Romish Church, and Calvin did not regret them; but although he was devoted to the severe simplicity of evangelical worship, he did not overlook the inherent love of mankind for poetry and art. He himself had a taste for music, and knew its power. He feared that, in a religious service limited to preaching and prayer only, the congregation, having nothing else to do than to play the part of audience, would remain cold and inattentive. For this reason he attached great importance to the introduction and promotion of the practice of psalm-singing in public worship, in addition to the sermons, prayers, and liturgies. 'If the singing,' he said, 'is such as befits the reverence which we ought to feel when we sing before God and the angels, it is an ornament which bestows grace and dignity upon our worship; and it is an excellent method of kindling the heart, and making it burn with great ardour in prayer. But we must at all times take heed lest the ear should be more attentive to the harmony of the sound than the soul to the hidden meaning of the words.'[1] With this pious warning, he strongly urged the study of singing, and its adoption in public worship. 'Some of the psalms which had been translated in verse by Clement Marot were printed, accompanied by a simple and elementary musical notation; and, in order to popularise them, the children were taught to sing these simple tunes in a loud and clear voice. A music master, who was paid by the state, gave three lessons a week to several choirs of children. When they had learnt the psalm thoroughly, they sang it during the service.'[2]

An ecclesiastical organization thus arose in Geneva, created by Calvin, and upheld by his influence. The development of this system, and the completion and modification of its details according to the different necessities of place and time, ultimately formed the presbyterian religion—that is, the religious system adopted in the reformed churches of France, French Switzerland, Holland, Scotland, and several states in the New World. In its origin it was a profoundly Christian and evangelical system; it was republican in many of its fundamental principles and practices, and at the same time it recognised the necessity of authority and order, and originated general and permanent rules of discipline.

[1] Calvin, *Instit. de la Religion chrétienne*, ch. xx.   [2] Gaberel, i. 353.

CHAPTER XIV.

CALVIN'S CIVIL LEGISLATION.

FOR a long time Calvin's able and vigorous scheme of ecclesiastical polity was accompanied by practical success at Geneva. Public order and morality were placed under careful supervision. Gaming-houses were prohibited; and in order to keep the citizens out of taverns, which were at that time greatly frequented, Calvin proposed the establishment of 'clubs open only to members of the association, in which young men, and fathers of families, could meet and discuss matters relating to the war, and other things useful to the commonwealth.' Four such clubs were immediately established. All gross immorality and coarse abuse of the evangelical religion and worship were punished, and so were all drunkards, men and women who led evil lives, and midnight brawlers. In a little municipal republic, with a small population, the character of individual members, and all facts connected with them, were generally so well known that any abuse of power was difficult. The pastors, if they were not active in the discharge of their duty, or did not lead a good life, were suspended, or even banished. There was perfect accordance between the Venerable Company, the Consistory and the Council; and, on the whole, the public approved of and supported all the steps taken in concert by the civil and religious rulers.

But although Calvin's system was righteously conceived and carried out, his thoughts and legislation were influenced by two false notions which soon proved fatal; for when truth and error are blindly united, the evil will assuredly be developed, and will compromise the good. Calvin's religious system for the evangelical church almost entirely overlooked individual liberty. He desired to regulate private life in accordance with the laws of morality and by means of the powers of the State; to penetrate all social and family life, and the soul of every man, and to restrict individual responsibility within an ever-narrowing circle. In the relation of the evangelical church to the State, he asserted and carried out the principle adopted in the Catholic Church, the right of the spiritual power to appeal to the secular arm in order to suppress and punish those offences against religion recognised by the State.; that is, impiety and heresy. Calvin thus denied and violated the rights of conscience and personal liberty in private life and in matters of religion,—a deplorable but natural consequence of his contempt for, and denial of man's freewill in his general doctrine.

In spite of the enthusiasm which had been called forth by Calvin's return, the Libertines, whether sceptical or licentious, of noble or simple birth, soon began to manifest their discontent. They responded to the meddlesome interference and demands of the magistrates, in matters of faith and religious ordinances, by persistent coldness or insolent contempt. 'What a pleasant thing it is to see the delightful liberty that there is in this city!' said a refugee from Lyons, who had not long previously arrived in Geneva: 'Yes!' answered a woman, 'formerly they made us go to mass, and now they make us go to church.' A man was found in the streets on horseback during the hours of divine service: 'Why are you not at church?' said one of the municipal officers: 'Oh!' said he, 'is there room enough in church for my horse and me?' A peasant said, 'My faith and religion are a block of wood, and I am cutting them into chips.' Another heard an ass braying, and called out, 'What a fine psalm he's singing!' A young man presented an account-book to his betrothed, and said, 'Madam, this is your best hymnbook.' These words were repeated, and the speakers prosecuted and punished. One of them was even banished from the city. Disorderly conduct and language were guarded against and repressed with watchful severity. M. Gaberel, the learned and judicious author of the history of the Church of Geneva, whilst he relates these facts with scrupulous impartiality, adds: 'The most vigilant of police-forces failed to discover more than eleven offences against public worship between 1541 and 1546; a country deserves warm praise in which religious feeling leaves so little room for transgression.'[1] The remark is just; nevertheless, it is not so much the number as the nature of these rigorous puerilities which gives such a vexatious character to arbitrary power, and excites irritation that, sooner or later, is sure to become contagious. There is no doubt that there was a

[1] Gaberel, i. 356–367.

great improvement in the moral and social condition of Geneva at this period, that good order and good conduct were restored both in public and domestic life, and that Calvin's government was infinitely superior to that of his adversaries; but his unwarrantable interference in private life, and his contempt for the rights of individuals, furnished his enemies with dangerous weapons and prepared grave perils which he had afterwards to encounter.

These perils from within were augmented by dangers from without, in the attacks of an anti-Christian or sceptical pantheism, which sought to disguise its immorality and anarchy under the name of liberty. At this period pantheistic doctrines were taught on the banks of the Rhine, in some of the great cities of western Europe, as Antwerp and Lille, and they had even penetrated the little court of Nérac, where Queen Margaret of Navarre, who had formerly befriended many reformers, and even Calvin himself, now granted hospitality to some of the advocates of these views, thus showing more liberality than discretion. The sect assumed the name of 'Spiritual Libertines.' Their tenets were soon made known at Geneva, where they obtained prompt recognition from the local and practical Libertines. Calvin was not one who could remain indifferent and inactive in the presence of new germs of impiety and immorality. In 1544 he published a pamphlet *Against that fantastic and furious sect of Libertines who call themselves Spiritual.* 'How is it possible,' said he, 'that I should condemn the Pope and his accomplices, and should nevertheless pardon these men who are much greater enemies of God and more hostile to his truth? For, after all, the Pope does leave some form of religion; he does not rob men of the hope of eternal life; he instructs them in the fear of God, and shows the difference between good and evil; he acknowledges our Lord Jesus Christ to be very God and very man, and recognises the authority of the Word of God. But the whole aim of these men is to confound together heaven and earth, to destroy all religion whatsoever, to efface all knowledge of the spiritual nature of man, to deaden his conscience, and obliterate all distinction between men and brutes.'[1] Queen Margaret complained to Calvin of this violent attack upon men whom she honoured with her protection and favour. He answered: 'My intention, Madam, was in no wise to seek to diminish your honour, or lessen the respect which every believer ought to feel for you. For I say that true believers owe you more reverence than that which is your due from all men, on account of the majesty to which our Lord has exalted you, the royal house from which you have sprung, and your great excellence in the things which pertain to this world. For those who know me are well aware that I am not such a savage, nor so inhuman as to despise and seek to inspire contempt for princes and nobles, and that which belongs to the order and government of this world. But I behold the most pernicious and execrable sect that ever existed in this world. I see what destruction they are causing, and that they are a fire kindled to scathe and destroy everything, a contagion which will infect the whole earth, unless some remedy be found. Since our Lord has called me to the position which I occupy, my conscience constrains

[1] Calvini Opera, vii. 162 (1868).

me to resist them so far as it is in my power. A dog will bark if he sees his master attacked, and should I not be a cowardly wretch if I could see God's truth assailed and stand silent, and utter no word?'[1]

Calvin never remained silent and indifferent on any occasion when he thought that God's truth was assailed, and these occasions were constantly arising. He was labouring to secure the ascendency of Christian faith and morality in the public and private life of the Genevese, in their deeds and words, in their houses and the streets of their city; but at the same time the love of intellectual liberty and practical licence was springing up throughout the republic, and many were most anxious to throw off the yoke of the reformer. Calvin was aided and supported throughout this contest by the two religious organizations which he had instituted—the Venerable Company and the Consistory; he possessed numerous and warm adherents in the various public councils and among all classes of the population; but he had also bitter enemies. Perhaps the most serious dangers he had to encounter arose from those prudent or timid men, who, being short-sighted or weak-hearted, were alarmed at his moral severity and oppressive exercise of ecclesiastical power. After having supported him against his enemies, they would uphold some claim of individual or civil liberty in opposition to him. In the space of three years, from 1546 to 1549, there were seven or eight occasions on which Calvin came into collision either with aristocratic pretensions or popular prejudices, in cases which made a great noise in so small a republic.

[1] Calvin, *Lettres Françaises*, i. 109-117 (1864).

In 1546 a manufacturer of playing-cards, Pierre Ameaux, and his wife Benoite, not only openly declared themselves to be materialists, but carried out the principles they had adopted in their own licentious lives. The woman was summoned before the Consistory, and condemned to imprisonment. Her husband forsook her and obtained a divorce from her, but he continued to lead an immoral life and to declaim against Calvin. 'He is a bad man,' said he, 'a wicked Picard, who has been teaching false doctrines for seven years. It is we who hold the true doctrine, as I can prove. He wants to make himself a bishop, and the magistrates do nothing without consulting him. I could tell you things that would astonish you, and all in good time I will make them known.' Ameaux was summoned before the Consistory, and imprisoned; but the Two Hundred disapproved of the sentence, and elected him a member of the lower Council. There was a division between the two powers. Calvin and the pastors declared that if it was decided that Ameaux's fault was so trivial, and that they were suspected of having preached false doctrine for seven years, they would insist on being brought to trial. The Council hereupon revoked their resolution in favour of Ameaux, and condemned him to the punishment known as the *amende honorable;* that is, he was to walk through all the principal parts of the town in his shirt, bare-headed and with a lighted torch in his hand, and to end by making a public confession and expressing sorrow for his faults, upon his knees.

Theatrical representations were a favourite amusement of the Genevese populace. But they were now rarely indulged in ; and, during this same year, certain performances were proposed. Calvin approved of the first piece, entitled 'A History for the Edification of the People,' 'provided one scene was suppressed, in which shopkeepers were ridiculed and traduced.' Indeed, so great was his toleration that the evening sermon was postponed on account of the length of the theatricals. A month later permission was asked for the representation of a second piece, entitled 'The Acts of the Apostles.' The manuscript of the play was submitted to Calvin, who said, 'Those who desire the performance of this play ought rather to devote their money to works of charity. What I say is not so much by way of censure as of remonstrance; we ought first of all to spend our money for the good of our neighbours.' In spite of this remonstrance, however, the Council sanctioned the performance, adding, 'and, as it will be very edifying, debtors may, for four days, have free admission to see the aforesaid story acted.' One of the pastors, Calvin's colleague, was much more strict, and preached in St. Peter's church against the proposed play in strong terms. 'The women,' he said, 'who mount the stage to perform that false scene are shameless creatures; those who are handsome go to exhibit their beauty, and the ugly ones to show off their finery and their magnificent satins and gold. All this display excites evil thoughts and profligate talk among the spectators.' The subject was again laid before the Council, and Calvin generously supported his colleague, declaring that he held precisely the same opinions as those expressed in the sermon. This time, however, the Council persisted in its toleration, and the play was performed; but, at the request of the pastors, the magistrates refused to sanction any further representations 'until the time was more favourable for them.'

After the theatricals the subject of dancing was discussed. In spite of the ecclesiastical ordinances, a grand ball had been given, accompanied by excesses, in which several of the most important families in the city took part; among others that of the former syndic Ami Perrin, who had at one time been one of Calvin's adherents. Gaberel says: 'A memoir still exists which gives a detailed account of these extraordinary amusements, and from this terrible record it appears that the dances then performed in private houses would not be tolerated at the present day in the height of the most disorderly carnival.'[1] The syndic Amblard had been also present at the ball, but he confessed his fault, listened to Calvin's remonstrances, and still remained his faithful friend; he even declared that it was only just that the rich should be punished as well as the poor. But Madame Perrin was not of such a meek disposition. No sooner had Calvin begun to address her, than she flew into a violent passion, and broke into invective and abuse. 'Oh, you wicked man!' said she, 'you would like to drink the blood of our family; but you will be turned out of Geneva before we are.' Calvin answered, 'Remember that you are a woman, and that you disgrace yourself by speaking in such a manner; you have banished every feeling of modesty from your thoughts and manners, but your temper will not prevent the

[1] Gaberel, *Pièces justificatives*, p. 249. The memorial, addressed to the King of Navarre by Dancau, is in the library of Geneva.

Consistory from doing its duty. If there were as many crowns as there are empty heads in your family, you would not be able to change the current of ecclesiastical discipline. Build a new city if you want to live after your own fashion; but so long as you are in Geneva your efforts to shake off the yoke of the Gospel will be in vain.' In consequence of this scene, Madame Perrin was imprisoned for several days, and from that time the cordial friendship which had united her husband to the reformer was replaced by implacable hatred.

Whatever was the object, and wherever the locality of the contest, whether in street or parlour, against an excited mob, or face to face with angry friends, whether to establish order or to uphold morality, Calvin's indomitable courage never failed. In 1547 a former canon, Jacques Gruet, one of the foremost Libertines, who had, according to the historians, 'concentrated all his hatred upon Calvin,' was one day seen loitering about St. Peter's church and going into it. A paper, evidently addressed to Calvin, was found in the pulpit: 'Pot-belly, you and your companions had better hold your tongues, for if you irritate us too far we will crush you to powder. When men have suffered more than they can bear, vengeance is at hand. . . . We will not have so many masters.' Gruet was arrested, and his papers were seized. Among them were some that were grossly blasphemous, ridiculing and attacking the Christian religion;[1] whilst, on the other hand, there were proofs

---

[1] Papers were found in his own handwriting in which he spoke of our Lord Jesus Christ and his apostles in the most blasphemous and offensive manner. 'The Word of God,' he said, 'is worth nothing,

of his correspondence with the Court of Savoy, and of his willingness to betray the republic, and gratify, at the expense of the national independence, his hatred of Calvin, and the system which he had established. Gruet was tried, condemned, and executed as a blasphemer and traitor to his country. After his apprehension he was repeatedly put to the torture, but he refused to name any accomplices. A warning, however, came from the Pays de Vaud, in consequence of which the Genevese Council was informed that 'more than twenty persons had bound themselves by oath to throw Calvin into the Rhone.' The indignation of the faithful, and the irritation of the Libertines, had reached the highest point ; and both indignation and irritation broke out at a meeting of the Two Hundred on the 16th of December, 1547. They had been called together on account of new complaints made by the pastors of 'the insolence, debauchery, dissolute manners, and enmity which tend to the ruin of this city.' Fresh proceedings had been instituted against the former syndic, Ami Perrin, but he had been acquitted for want of proof against him, though deprived of his official employment. Libertines and reformers were present at the meeting in about equal numbers ; the debate was transformed into a tumult, and violent threats were uttered against the pastors and the Consistory. Some of their friends, terrified at the proceedings, left hastily to warn Calvin and his colleagues not to attend the meeting of the Council.

any more than those who made it. The Gospel is only a tissue of lies; there is less in it than in Æsop's Fables, except false and absurd doctrine.' (Henry, vol. ii. Appendix, 121 ; Gaberel, i. 391.) I have suppressed his coarse and violent language, which would be painfully offensive to every religious and moral nature.

'Wait a few moments for me,' said Calvin, and went out alone, walked direct to the Hôtel de Ville, and entered the meeting unexpectedly. He was received with loud outcries, and it is said that several swords were drawn. He said: 'I know that I am the chief cause of your quarrels, and if blood must be shed to appease them, take my life, for I call God to witness that I am come to expose myself to your swords.' There is sometimes one happy moment in which courage conquers anger; the Council grew calm, the members took their seats, and Calvin continued: 'There is nothing except religion which can make you free, and secure your liberty; but in order to obtain this you must be united, and if my presence is an insuperable obstacle to the maintenance of peace, I will leave the city, and will pray to God that those men who desire to live without Christianity and law may save the republic, and maintain its prosperity.' The reaction was as sudden as the explosion. The Council voted oblivion of the past, and the reconciliation of the opponents. Calvin and one of his colleagues made the first advance: 'Gentlemen,' said they, 'the Lord's Supper is at hand: we wish to unite all hearts, and we desire to offer the hand of friendship to M. Ami Perrin, and we beg, gentlemen, that you will reinstate him in his office of councillor.' 'As for me,' answered Perrin, 'I bring no complaint against any one, I do not wish evil to any one, and I desire to live in peace.' Three months later he was restored to office, and the opponents, whether Christians or Libertines, for a short time imagined themselves to be reconciled.

CHAPTER XV.

DIVISION OF THE RELIGIOUS AND CIVIL AUTHORITIES ON THE QUESTION OF THE LORD'S SUPPER.

BUT however sincere a reconciliation may be, it is seldom so thorough as to put an end to the difficulties which first caused the quarrel. When Calvin proposed that the past should be forgotten, and that there should be peace on the approach of the Lord's Supper, he raised that question which offered precisely the most serious difficulty to the members of the two hostile parties. They were still divided as to whether the religious or the civil authorities had the right of refusing the sacrament to, and pronouncing sentence of excommunication upon, those whom they deemed unworthy. Such a difficulty could not arise in any free country in our own time, or indeed in any country where the meaning of faith and religious liberty are known. The Lord's Supper is administered by the religious authorities under a sense of religious responsibility, and in the name of the religious belief common to the pastors and their flock. It is for them alone to decide those cases in which, for religious reasons, they think it their duty to refuse it ; and the civil power has no right to interfere in this close communion of the conscience of the priest with that of the believer. It is true that ecclesiastics have often abused the right of excommunication, and have thus provoked tyrannical intervention on the part of the civil power—like that of the 'Parlement' of Paris, for example, which occasionally compelled a priest, in olden times, to administer the Lord's Supper to those to whom he had refused it. The magistrates of Geneva, from motives of prudence and to avoid what they called scandal, claimed the same right; and a short time after Calvin's return they maintained that they, and not the Consistory, ought to pronounce sentence of excommunication, and that it was the duty of the pastor to administer the sacrament to all those authorized by the Council to receive it. Calvin immediately declared that he would sacrifice everything and return into exile rather than admit such a claim. Not that he held any fixed and preconceived doctrine on the subject; his point of view was not that of a fanatical theologian, but of a religious ruler. He wrote to Bullinger: 'Since my return to this church we have instituted a kind of religious discipline which is not perfect in itself, and leaves much to be desired, but which, on the whole, accomplishes its aim. A Consistory has been established for the supervision of morals; it has no civil jurisdiction, and can only restrain evil-doers in accordance with the Word of God, and as the chief representative of God,—that is, it can exclude from the Lord's Supper. . . . I know that our friends are not all of one mind upon this subject; there are some learned and pious men who think that excommunication is not necessary under a Christian government, but no sane person would be so infatuated as to condemn and abolish it where it is already established. So far as I am concerned, the teaching of our Lord on this point seems to me perfectly clear, and I believe you will allow that, for us at least, it would be a great disgrace and a fatal defeat, if the edifice of which our Lord has appointed us the guardians was to be destroyed beneath our eyes.'[1] The Libertines at once saw the advantage which they might derive from this disagreement between the Council and the Pastors; they ranged themselves on the side of the Council, and Berthelier, one of their most violent partisans,—a man whose incredulity and immorality were known to all,—presented himself at the Lord's Supper, and was excommunicated by the Consistory. He complained to the Council, which declared that it would not ratify the sentence, and that 'if Berthelier had no impediment in his own conscience which hindered him from approaching the table of the Lord, the Council authorized him to do so.' 'Gentlemen,' said Calvin, 'as for me I would rather suffer death than allow the table of my Lord to be profaned in such a manner.'

The magistrates knew him well enough to feel that these were not mere words. They were intimidated, and sent a private message to Berthelier, saying: 'If you can stay away for the present, you will do well.' But, unlike the magistrates, the Libertine and his friends had no desire to avoid an open rupture. On Sunday the 3d of September, 1553, St. Peter's church was filled by a large and excited crowd; the pastors and elders filled the benches of the Consistory; the Libertines thronged in the vicinity of the communion table. Calvin mounted the pulpit, and preached with

[1] Stähelin, i. 459, 460.

great calmness upon the state of mind and heart necessary for those who would approach the table of the Lord; he ended his sermon by saying: 'As for me, so long as it shall please God to keep me here, since he has given me resolution and I have derived it from him, I shall not fail to exercise it when there is need; and I will rule my life in accordance with the will of my Master, which is quite clear and well known to me..... We are now about to receive the holy sacrament; and if any one who has been excommunicated by the Consistory tries to approach that table, at the risk of my life I am prepared to do my duty.' He descended from the pulpit, and approached and blessed the table of the Lord's Supper. The Libertines drew near, and several among them made a movement forward as if to seize the bread and wine. Calvin spread his hands over the sacred elements, and cried out: 'You may break these limbs, you may cut off my arms, you may take my life! Shed my blood if you will; it is yours! But never shall any one compel me to give things that are sacred to the profane, and to dishonour the table of my God.' The Libertines hesitated; they looked at each other, and looked around them; a murmur which threatened danger was spreading throughout the hitherto silent assembly; they drew back from the table, the crowd opened for their passage, and the sacrament was then administered in silence to the excited and agitated believers.

In the afternoon of the same day Calvin preached again: 'I do not know,' he said, 'if this is not the last sermon I shall ever preach in Geneva; not that

I leave by my own wish, or that I desire to depart from this spot and to give up the authority which I hold. But I take that which has been done to signify that Geneva will receive my services no longer, and will seek to compel me to do what God does not permit. So long as I am free to preach and to serve you, I will do it in the name of the Lord; but if I am forced into an intolerable position, I will not resist the constituted authorities, and I must go.' Calvin's conduct had been energetic, but his language was guarded. He laid claim to his own liberty, asserted his right to act in accordance with the dictates of his conscience, did not urge others to insurrection, and limited his resistance to voluntary exile. He showed himself obedient to the law, and at the same time a faithful pastor. But the people pronounced in his favour. The Libertines drew back. The civil magistrates recognised the difficulty of their position, and did not insist on carrying out their decision. The discussion between the civil and religious powers as to the right of pronouncing sentence of excommunication lasted some time longer; it was occasionally diversified by tumultuous outbreaks, and there was always a tendency towards hesitation on the part of the civil rulers and their compromising allies. At length, on the 25th of October, 1554, the Council induced Berthelier 'to make peace with the pastors;' and on the 24th of January, 1555, the assembled Councils agreed that it was the Consistory which ought to pronounce sentence of excommunication.[1]

[1] Gaberel, vol. i. p. 425

CHAPTER XVI.

DEFEAT OF THE LIBERTINES.

BUT egotism and hatred cannot be extinguished by defeat. The Libertines sought to attack Calvin on other grounds, and succeeded in their attempt; for although the question they raised was on a lower level than the right of excommunication, it was more plausible, and seemed to involve national rights. The persecution of the reformers had become more active and cruel, and it had brought a great number of refugees to Geneva, more particularly from France and Italy. Nobles, burgesses, men of letters, peasants, and artisans, hearing that the Reformation had triumphed in Geneva, and that the pastors were men of great renown, hoped to find in it a safe and sacred asylum. They were warmly welcomed by their zealous Christian brethren; but the local patriots were inclined to be uneasy and jealous: 'We have no certain knowledge,' says M. Gaberel, 'of the number of refugees who fled to Geneva at this time. During the revolution of 1793, the friends of equality wished to destroy all distinction between families living in the same republic, and they therefore burnt the registers in which the names of burgesses and inhabitants had been inscribed ever since the sixteenth century. Fortunately some persons possessed copies of the registers, but these private documents are not complete. The book which records the admission of strangers gives the names of 1,376 persons to whom the right of residing in the city was granted between the years 1549 and 1564; seventy-eight of them were made burgesses during the same period, and paid considerable sums for the privilege of incorporation. The city was in great want of money, in order to rebuild and fortify its walls; therefore the new burgesses were very well received. Indeed, popular feeling was so strong in their favour that one day when a vessel, bringing several refugees, entered the port of Geneva, several of the citizens exclaimed: "That is well; there is a boat-load of money and stone, which will help on the fortifications!"[1]

The strong religious feeling of these refugees was shown by their flight from their own country; they were undoubtedly reliable and zealous allies for Calvin and his party. The Libertines were not slow to perceive this, and from the very first they displayed the most active ill-will towards the new-comers. They found many who were only too ready to join them; there were the old-established burgesses of the city, who were annoyed at seeing strangers invested with the rights, and sharing the advantages offered by their country; and there were men of the lower and labouring classes who dreaded the competition of labourers and artisans who were often much more skilful and industrious than themselves. Appeals were made both to national feeling and personal

[1] Gaberel, i. 426.

interest, in order to keep up this hostility, and the discontented rich fostered the jealousy of the discontented poor. Sometimes their animosity was shown in the sneers uttered by men who had secretly remained Catholics. 'Why, my good friends,' they said to the French refugees, 'you were in a great hurry to leave your country ; the consecrated wafers seem to have stuck in your throat.' At other times it was popular jealousy which broke forth : 'By my faith,' said some, ' these people who ran away from the fire for the sake of the Gospel, raise the price of provisions very considerably.' 'See !' said the women, 'when the Frenchmen are here, there is nothing done for the townspeople ; may the devil break the necks of all these Frenchmen !' Some of the principal Libertines took advantage of the popular ill-will to procure the passing of measures which would tend to weaken the position and influence of the refugees. Calvin wrote to Bullinger: 'They treat barbarously our brothers in the cause of Christ who have fled to us. They subject them to inhuman outrages, and yet the refugees bear it with a gentleness and patience which even those who injure them cannot deny.' Ami Perrin allowed the shops of the French refugees to be plundered ; he proposed to take all arms from them except their swords, which they were no longer to be allowed to wear in public. Some days later he went a step further, and demanded that the refugees should also be deprived of their swords, as he was afraid of some treason on their part in behalf of Henry II. king of France.

The refugees were indignant ; they called upon Perrin to prove that they had any intention of 'throwing themselves again into the power of that Catherine who, with her husband, was bathed in the blood of their brethren.' The first syndic, Jean Lambert, laid their complaints before the Two Hundred : 'Gentlemen,' he said, 'I ask myself in vain, why Captain Perrin and M. Vandel are so furious against the foreign burgesses, saying that they desire to drive the elders from the city and to give it up to the king or to some other prince. Think for a moment if it is at all probable that such an accusation is true! These men came to us from different countries, with different manners, customs, and languages. What plan could be proposed in which they would all agree, or how could they be induced to unite in order to betray and expel us? They have forsaken their own country, their relations and friends, and all their worldly goods, to obey the commands of God ; and now we are told that they intend to throw themselves back again into the power of those princes from whom they have escaped, and that they propose to betray the city which has given them shelter. Certes, Captain, I marvel greatly at your suspicions, for you were quite free from them seven years ago when you wished to admit two hundred dragoons into the city, sworn servants of the king of France. For my part, I hold that we ought to grant every privilege to men who bring us fidelity, honour, and money. The city will be greatly improved if we can get men of good conduct and good report to become burgesses.'[1]

At the beginning of the preceding year[2] a conces-

[1] Gaberel, i. 427–434. Bonnivard, *De l'ancienne et nouvelle Police de Genève*, pp. 127–131.
[2] January 16th, 1554.

sion had been made with which the Libertines might well have been contented. A resolution had been carried stating that eligible members of the Grand Council must have inhabited Geneva and shared its perils during the war of 1536—that is, at the period when the Reformation had been proposed and established. The fresh demands for the exclusion of the refugees, made by Ami Perrin, were rejected; and during the beginning of the year 1555, sixty new burgesses were received. The malcontents declared that 'many of the people regretted that so many new burgesses were admitted from the same country.' The complaints of the Libertines were changed to threats; they stated definitely to the Council that their 'opposition might stir up the people, and that it was absolutely necessary to put an end to these admissions in order to preserve the public peace.'

The Libertines took the initiative in the breach of the peace, and assumed the whole responsibility of it. Restless and defiant, they saw that their influence over the popular mind was diminishing rapidly, and they were driven to attempt a decisive blow by their own passions and by the knowledge of their approaching fall. On the 18th of May, 1555, three days after the Council had rejected their last demands, the leaders of the party supped together at a tavern, 'with many riotous companions,' says Bonnivard; 'they tore the Frenchmen and the receivers of Frenchmen to tatters with their sharp tongues. After the tongue had done its office, the wine induced the feet and the hands to do theirs. "Captain," said one of them to Ami Perrin, "I find you lukewarm, but the people trust you; take the affair into your own hands." "Forward, gentlemen!" said Perrin; "what we do is for the honour of Geneva!" They rushed out, and hurrying to all parts of Geneva, summoned their partisans: "To arms, to arms, all good citizens of Geneva! The French are going to sack the city. To the Rhone with the Frenchmen! Down with every French rascal that shows his head!" One of the bands attacked the Hôtel de Ville; another passed before the house of the syndic Aubert. The magistrate, hearing a great noise, goes down into the street in his dressing-gown, with his bâton of office in one hand and a lighted candle in the other. He is knocked down and trampled under foot, but gets up again, and friends come to his aid. Another of the syndics rapidly calls together two or three companies of militia, and they hasten to the defence of the Hôtel de Ville. The struggle commences, many persons are killed, but the insurgents are everywhere attacked, defeated and pursued. Their resistance was as short as their attack had been sudden and violent; many were taken prisoners, but their leaders, Perrin amongst others, escaped and left the Genevese territory. The insurrection was quickly repressed, and the rioters were severely punished. When they were brought to justice, some of those who had been taken in combat were condemned to death, and executed; others were banished, and a hundred and fifty of their friends withdrew with them to the Bernese territory. But they did not consider themselves defeated. They asked the Bernese Government first to solicit and then openly to insist on their return, thus making Berne the judge between Geneva and those whom she had proscribed. The republic, after that, would only have needed to become the vassal, and then the subject of Berne. In order to allay this storm, much firmness and also much prudence were necessary; for Berne was powerful, and Berne had no love for Geneva. It was Calvin who conducted the whole business, and Berne was compelled to renounce her ambitious pretensions.'[1] The Libertines now carried their animosity and treason elsewhere; they applied to the Duke of Savoy to subdue Geneva : ' See,' said they, pointing to the fortifications of their native city, ' look at those white walls; before long they will be so battered with cannon that there will not be one stone left upon another.' But the city had been put into a good state of defence, and it was not therefore attacked. The Libertines did not abandon their plots, but the Duke of Savoy adjourned his projects. Calvin asked the Council to ordain a Fast-day as a thanksgiving for great mercies, and the pious solemnity took place. After nineteen years of internal struggle the young republic, which in 1536, had so boldly ranged itself under the banner of the Reformation, was able, in 1555, to entertain the hope of living in peace under the influence of its great reformer.

[1] Bungener, p. 339. Gaberel, i. 432-435.

CHAPTER XVII.

CALVIN'S THEOLOGICAL CONTROVERSIES.   SERVETUS.

IT has been often said, that from this time forward Calvin was supreme in Geneva, and governed absolutely. His government has been sometimes called an ecclesiastical theocracy established in the midst of a Christian republic. The assertion is vague and inaccurate. There can be no doubt that the final defeat of the Libertines was a great victory for Calvin, and that it increased his general influence in Geneva enormously. On all subsequent occasions his opinion was relied upon. The civil magistrates often asked his advice. When any important question or grave difficulty arose with regard to the foreign policy of the little state, Calvin was frequently applied to, requested to take part in the negotiations, and to exercise in behalf of Geneva the influence which he had obtained in those parts of Europe where the Reformation had been adopted. But, although Calvin's influence in the republic was very powerful, it is a mistake to say that the government ever assumed an ecclesiastical character. The distinction between the civil and religious powers was strictly preserved, and their domains carefully separated. The civil magistrates recognised the rights of the Venerable

Company, and of the Consistory, in all questions of faith and religious and moral discipline; but they resisted any extension of their power beyond its due limits, controlled it within these limits, and exercised due authority over the pastors themselves. The Venerable Company had transferred one of their pastors to a country parish without asking the Council to authorize this step; they were desired not to act in such a manner in future. The registers of the Council contain the following entry:— 'Nicolas Vandert, preacher at Jussy, does not do his duty in his calling, and does not visit the sick; resolved that he shall be dismissed, and another put in his place.' A little later another pastor was dismissed 'for incontinence.' The Council is informed that Pastor Bernard preaches 'with closed doors,' and thereupon desires him to preach 'with open doors.' Another pastor is warned 'that he is not to speak evil of the magistrates in his sermons.' Even Calvin himself was not beyond the reach of similar admonitions; 'On the 21st of May, 1548, the Council was informed that, in his sermon yesterday, Calvin asserted, with much anger, that the magistrates tolerated many offences. Wherefore it is ordained that he shall be summoned before the Council, and asked what was his intention in preaching to that effect; and if there is any such offence in the city, then the officers of justice shall have orders to see the law carried out.' The mutual recriminations still continued; on the 9th of July, Calvin was denounced because 'yesterday he was very violent in his sermon, speaking against baptism and certain crosses worn upon the clothes.' The Council decides to summon all the ministers before them and remonstrate, telling them that 'they ought not to protest in public, but first of all to bring their grievances before the Council, and afterwards to address the public, if they find that the Council takes no notice of their complaints.' There can be no doubt that the power of the pastors was very great; but that of the civil magistrates was equally great, and they had no hesitation in using it.[1]

Calvin remained the victor in his struggle with the political Libertines; but he was engaged in another contest—a series of theological controversies with the heretical Libertines. He was laying the foundations of the religious system and independence of the reformed Christian Church, but he was also labouring to uphold the Christian evangelical faith within that Church. The three principal and most formidable characteristics of the sixteenth century were its political disturbances, its public immorality, and its ardent outburst of intellectual life, and Calvin was simultaneously resisting all of them. I will not attempt to follow him into the arena where he successfully opposed the numerous speculative theologians who hovered around the great reformers of the century,—Caroli, Bolsec, Castellio, Westphal, Gribaldo, Valentinus Gentilis, Biandrata, Osiander, and many others. But I will select two of the most daring thinkers with whom he was brought into contact, Michael Servetus and Lælius Socinus;

---

[1] M. Amédée Roget, in a little pamphlet on the Church and State of Geneva during the lifetime of Calvin, published at Geneva in 1867, has fully established the truth of these facts, which he quotes from the registers of the Council.

both of them celebrated, one for his tragical end, and the other as the forerunner of his nephew, Faustus Socinus, the founder of the well-known sect of Socinians. Two very different sides of the character of Calvin are displayed in his connexion with these two men; his harsh severity towards those opponents whom he despised, and his moderation and almost gentle tolerance towards those whom he esteemed, and believed to be sincere and humble.

In the year 1509, the very same year in which Calvin was born at Noyon, Michael Servetus was born at Villanueva, a city of Arragon, where his father, a burgess of some eminence, was a notary. He received his early education in a Dominican convent, and his father afterwards sent him to study law at Toulouse, just as Calvin's father had wished him to pursue the same study at Orleans and Bourges. In like manner as Calvin in his youth had received assistance and protection from an ecclesiastic, so also the first patron of Servetus was a priest,—Quintana, father-confessor of the Emperor Charles V., whom Servetus accompanied to Italy, an obscure member of the imperial suite. In spite, however, of this patronage and of his youth, he was strongly imbued with the novel opinions of the time; for when he afterwards recalled the recollections of his visit to Rome, he says: 'I saw there with my own eyes the Pope carried on the heads of the princes of the land, and worshipped in the public squares by a whole people on their knees; so much so that those who could kiss his feet, or even his shoes, thought themselves blessed above all others. O beast, the most murderous of all beasts! O harlot, the most shameless of all harlots! Surely this was the beautiful harlot described in the Book of Isaiah.'[1] A little later, in 1530, Servetus was at Basle, holding communion with the already celebrated reformers who had taken up their abode there, with Œcolampadius, Capito and Bucer. Zwingli, the great reformer of German Switzerland, who was to be struck by death the following year on the battle-field of Cappel, was also at Basle, holding converse with his friends regarding the interests of their common cause. Œcolampadius said: 'I have got a rash, hot-headed Spaniard here, Michael Servetus, who is always raising the most difficult questions, and bothering me horribly. He is an Arian.' 'Brother Œcolampadius,' said Zwingli, 'look after him and be careful; the views of that Spaniard will be the ruin of the whole Christian religion. Unless Christ was truly God and the eternal God, he was not and could not have been our Saviour, and all that the holy prophets and apostles have taught must be false. Try by good and weighty arguments to bring the young man back to the way of truth.' 'I have tried,' answered Œcolampadius, 'but he is so vain, so presumptuous, and so argumentative that I can do nothing with him.' In 1534, four years later, Calvin also visited Basle, and made an impression upon these same reformers, the very reverse of that which Servetus had produced. They foresaw great danger to the reformed religion in one of these young men, and great strength and hope in the other. Their presentiments were not false.

Throughout 1531 and 1532 Servetus was wandering from Basle into Germany, and from Germany back to

[1] Isaiah, chap. xlvii. Henry, iii. 107.

Basle; sometimes in the suite of the confessor of Charles V.; at others alone, and ardently engrossed by the notions which were seething in his brain, and from the realization of which he promised himself a brilliant future. There were no limits to his ambition and presumption; he proposed to inaugurate a very different kind of reformation from that which was going on around him: 'I am neither Catholic nor Protestant,' he said, and he already looked upon himself as the most important, as well as the newest reformer. He returned to Basle in 1531, and brought out his first work on the 'Errors of the Trinity.' It was printed at Hagenau, and he did not hesitate to put his real name on the title-page: 'by M. Servetus, otherwise Reves, a Spaniard from Arragon.'[1] The printer was more prudent; so great was the suspicion which the doctrines of Servetus had already inspired, that he did not put his own name on the book, nor that of the place at which it was published. The work was a violent attack upon the doctrine of the Trinity, written with vigour and a certain glitter of imagination and subtlety of thought, but its rash speculations were vague and superficial. It was received with prompt and severe disapproval both by Catholics and Protestants. Father Quintana spoke of Servetus with contempt, as a young man who had certainly belonged to his suite, and whom he knew by sight, but whom he had never suspected of holding such impious opinions. Even the most gentle of the German and Swiss reformers openly expressed their indignation. Melancthon urged Œcolampadius to

[1] *De Trinitatis Erroribus*, lib. vii. per M. Servetus, *alias* Reves, ab Aragonia Hispanum. In 8vo.

take heed lest such doctrines should be imputed to the Swiss reformers. Bucer denounced the work from the pulpit, and went so far as to say that the author of it deserved to be torn limb from limb. The Government of Basle caused the book to be seized, and even, so it is said, imprisoned the author. But the imprisonment, if it took place, must have been short, for Servetus almost immediately published a second work[1] on the same subject, still in his own name, in which he explained, apologized for, and retracted almost the whole of the first ; not, however, on the ground that his notions were false, but that they were crude and imperfect. Indeed, in addition to the attacks on the Trinity, this book disclosed a much more wild and impious pantheism than the first had done. The second work received little attention, either favourable or unfavourable, but the impression produced by the first was permanent. Servetus saw that he had very little chance of success either in Germany or Switzerland, and he went elsewhere to try and realize his dreams of success and power.

He hoped to do so in France, at Paris. He was there in 1534, and was, at the same time, a student and a professor. He both gave and received lessons in medicine, mathematics, and astronomy, and was soon noted for his rapid insight, brilliant imagination, marvellous powers of acquisition, and wealth of novel theories, often rash, but sometimes ingenious and happy. He conjectured, and almost described, the circulation of the blood, took part with the Greek against the Arabian physicians, speaking of all those

---

[1] *Dialogorum de Trinitate.* Lib. ii. *de Justitia regni Christi*, cap. iv. In 8vo. 1532.

who did not agree with him as 'fools and public pests.' He gave courses of lectures on mathematics and astronomy which were a mixture of science and chimerical conjecture, and he translated Ptolemy's Geography. The extent and versatility of his intellectual powers attracted large audiences; but at the same time his exacting and arrogant character, his overbearing and pretentious manners, his restless and quarrelsome temper soon embroiled him not only with the physicians who were his rivals, but with the whole University of Paris, which distrusted his views and detested his person. He lacked both personal influence and modesty; he was not only violent and abusive to his adversaries, like the majority of even the most eminent learned men in his time, but in every dispute he showed that presumptuous and arrogant self-complacence which inflicts far deeper wounds than open and even brutal anger. His theological heresies and astrological dreams furnished numerous pretexts against him. He was denounced to the 'Parlement' of Paris, and they condemned him to suppress an abusive treatise which he had published, and forbade him to teach astrology, or to prophesy and predict from the stars. Annoyed at this, and lacking stability of purpose, he left Paris and went to Lyons, where he obtained employment as corrector of the press to the celebrated printers Melchior and Caspar Trechsel; he returned to Paris, and left again; went first to Avignon, then to Charlieu, a small town near Lyons, changing his name and residence incessantly; sometimes eager for retirement and sometimes for display; desiring fame, and yet often in great need of concealment. At length, in 1540, he settled at Vienne, in Dauphiné, where the archbishop, Mgr. Palmier, who had attended some of his lectures in Paris took him under his protection.

He lived at Vienne twelve years, concealing his real name Servetus, and adopting that of Villanueva, his native city. He was in high repute as a physician, and conformed outwardly to the Roman Catholic religion; but he was more than ever absorbed in his projected religious reformation, and the great part that he was to play in it. He published numerous works; among others he brought out a translation of the Bible by a learned monk named Xantès Pagninus, then dead. But the Book of Revelations was the special subject of his study. In it he saw the signs of the times, and the approaching fall of Antichrist. 'The Dragon which tries to devour the woman and her child is the Pope; the woman is the Church; her child whom God takes away and saves is the Christian faith.[1] For 1560 days, that is years, the Church has been under the yoke of Antichrist, but now the struggle with the Dragon is about to commence. Michael and his angels will triumph; we shall discover the divine Revelation from the very earliest ages—the great mystery of faith which is beyond all dispute; we shall see the face of God which has never yet been seen. We shall see the glory of his image in ourselves.'[2] Servetus did not assert that he himself was the archangel Michael, but he believed himself to be his ally, and one of our Lord's new apostles. In order to make known all these seething fancies, he prepared a new work entitled *Restoration of Christianity.*

[1] Revelation, chap. xii. [2] Henry, iii. 125-128.

The latest of Calvin's biographers, Stähelin, gives the following account of the doctrines contained in the work of Servetus, 'or rather of so much of them,' he says, 'as it is possible to make out from his involved and mystical language, and the attempted sublimity of his style. The fundamental principle of the whole book is the assertion of the one absolute and indivisible God. It would be impossible to imagine any direct action of God upon the world; he is separated from it by an immeasurable abyss. The instruments which he uses, the links which unite the finite and the infinite, are found in the world of thought. Every thought or idea must be contemplated as a personal reality, having its origin in the being of God, and itself an image of his eternal essence. Perfectly distinct, and yet not separate from God, these ideas animate matter, and thus unite it to God. There are therefore three worlds, each of which has its own separate existence, although they are all closely united one to the other,—God, ideas, and things or beings. All beings are contained in ideas, all ideas in God; God is all things, and all things are God.'[1]

In 1848, two years before the publication of Stähelin's work, M. Emile Saisset, a very distinguished philosopher of the contemporary French school, published in the *Revue des deux Mondes*[2] an account of the doctrine of Servetus, which, although more fully developed, is in perfect agreement with that of M. Stähelin, the theologian of Basle. That doctrine is, in fact, pantheism, with all its pretensions to explain everything in a rational way, and with the chaos

[1] Stähelin, i. 432.
[2] *Revue des deux Mondes*, 1848, i. 605-611.

of logic, mysticism, and mere words, which pantheism offers as rational explanation.

When Servetus was living at Vienne, he was in frequent communication with friends at Lyons, and was within a very short distance, almost within reach, of the religious influence of Geneva, that is of Calvin. I have already said that the two men met in Paris in 1534, commenced a controversy, and appointed a meeting so as to carry it on in public; that Calvin kept this appointment, and Servetus broke it. Whatever may have been the motive of Servetus in so doing, there can be no doubt that some contempt for an adversary who had thus escaped from a contest lingered in Calvin's mind. That which he afterwards heard respecting Servetus from the German and Swiss reformers had certainly confirmed the suspicion and disapprobation with which he was inclined to regard him. But, on the other hand, Servetus could not live so near Calvin without being struck by the importance which he had acquired, the greatness of his work, and the fame of his name. He wished to renew his acquaintance with Calvin, wrote to him, sent him questions, asked his advice, even sent him a copy of the book which he was preparing on the 'Restoration of Christianity;' no doubt for the purpose of finding out beforehand the objections of his formidable adversary. His letters bear the impress sometimes of philosophical inquiry, sometimes of undisciplined temper: 'I am always at work,' he wrote to Calvin, 'trying to revive the life of the Church, and you are angry with me because I associate myself with the angel Michael in such a contest, and because I am

[1] Page 171.

anxious that all pious men should do as I do.
Examine this passage in the Book of Revelations
thoroughly, and you will see that the combat is
waged by men, and that they lay down their lives to
testify of the Christ. It is usual to call them angels
in Scripture, because the regeneration from above
makes us equal to the angels.'

To these letters, which were very numerous between
1540 and 1546, Calvin replied coldly but without
acrimony. He evaded the questions of Servetus
when they appeared insidious, and gave him wise
and earnest advice; but he was evidently careful not
to enter into regular correspondence with him, and
anxious to avoid all appearance of intimacy, even as
an opponent, with a man whom he did not esteem,
and whose views and ideas outraged all his own.
'I was anxious to carry out your wishes,' he
wrote to their common friend Frellon at Lyons;[1]
'not that, from what I see of his present frame of
mind, I have any great hope of doing much good to
such a man, but in order to try once again if there are
any means of subduing him;—which will be when God
has so dealt with him that he is quite different to
what he is now. As he wrote to me in a very haughty
tone, I wished, if possible, to humble him by speaking
more harshly than I am wont to do. I could do no
otherwise, for I assure you that there is no lesson
he is in such want of as one in humility; but it
must come to him from God and no otherwise.
Nevertheless we must put our hands to the work also.
If by God's grace, shown both to him and to us, the
answer you have asked me to send should prove pro-

[1] February 13th, 1546.

fitable to him, I shall have reason to rejoice. But if he continues in his present mind, you will lose time if you entreat me to labour any further on his behalf, for I have other duties which are much more imperative. . . . I pray you to rest satisfied with what I have already done, unless you find him differently disposed.'

Servetus, however, continued to write to Calvin; no doubt hoping either to convince or to perplex him by his persistent correspondence and controversy. At length Calvin grew weary of it, and wrote: 'Neither now nor at any future time will I mix myself up in any way with your wild dreams. Forgive me for speaking thus, but truth compels me to do so. I neither hate you nor despise you; I do not wish to treat you harshly; but I must be made of iron if I could hear you rail against the doctrine of salvation and not be moved by it. Moreover, I have no time to concern myself any further with your plans and systems; all that I can say to you on this subject, is contained in my "Christian Institutes," to which I must now refer you.'[1]

Servetus was deeply wounded by this haughty language: he had made advances which Calvin had resisted, and laid snares from which he had escaped. The prudent reformer with his clear and resolute intellect could not show indifference to the self-confident visionary, who was capable both of lofty sincerity and low cunning, nor was it possible that he could be deceived by him. Even if there had not been any special and profound disagreement between these two men, they were antipathetic by nature, and anything

[1] Henry, iii. 125-133. Stähelin, i. 429-431.

that drew them together and brought them into contact, instead of uniting them, would only cause them to recoil more widely. From this time forward there was an end of all direct correspondence on the part of Calvin. He had previously written to Farel :[1] 'Not long ago Servetus wrote to me, and sent with his letter a volume of his extravagant folly, which he put forward with great ostentation, and I was compelled to read the most unheard-of and bewildering things. He says that, if I like, he will come here; but I will not give him any assurance of my protection, for if he does come and if my authority prevails, I will never suffer him to depart from this city alive.' In September 1548, he wrote to Viret: 'I think you have seen my answer to Servetus. I have declined any further correspondence with such an obstinate and conceited heretic. It is certainly a case in which we ought to follow the precept of the apostle Paul.[2] He is now attacking you, and it is for you to consider how far it is worth your while to refute his dreams. From henceforth he will get nothing more from me.'

Servetus was more annoyed by silence than he could possibly have been by controversy, and he sent back Calvin's copy of the 'Christian Institutes' full of marginal notes, in which he attacked the doctrines it contained. He determined at the same time to put forth his manifesto, his great work on the 'Restoration of Christianity;' which would, so he thought, effect a much greater social and religious revolution in Europe than the Reformation had done. But with a strange mixture of audacity and timidity, although he published it, he did not venture to proclaim himself as its author. He

[1] February 13th, 1546.   [2] II Timothy ii. 23.

tried first of all to get it printed at Basle; not succeeding there he found a printer at Vienne, in the very diocese where he was living under the protection of the Archbishop, who consented to print it under the seal of secrecy. The production was completed in three months, between September 1552 and January 1553, under the superintendence of Servetus himself. Some say that one thousand and others that eight hundred copies were struck off, and bales were forwarded at once to Lyons, Châtillon, Frankfort, and Geneva. The book bore no name, either of author or printer, but, with an infatuation which would be incomprehensible if it were not for the paternal love of an author for his work, the three initial letters of the name and country of Servetus were placed at the end of it; M. S. V.—Michael Servetus, Villanueva.

The public indignation was great; especially in Lyons and Geneva, the former the centre of Catholicism, and the latter of Protestantism. The people of Geneva marvelled that in a city like Lyons, where Cardinal de Tournon and the Roman Inquisitor Matthias Ory resided, no steps were taken to stop the circulation of such a book and to discover and punish the author. There was a French refugee at Geneva, Guillaume de Trie, a zealous Protestant and follower of Calvin, who was in correspondence with a relative at Lyons, Antoine Arneys, who was an ardent Catholic; and, in order to bring De Trie back to the bosom of the Church, Arneys accused the reformers of being without discipline or rules of faith, and of sanctioning the most unbridled licence. De Trie, in his turn, accused the Catholic Church of indifference and inability to repress licence in her own domains; and the name of Servetus, his previous works, his new book, recently printed at Vienne under the very eyes of the Archbishop, and the doctrines taught in the book, were all brought forward in De Trie's letter to the Catholic of Lyons, in proof of the justice of his reproaches. He added : 'In order that you may not think I speak from mere conjecture, I send you the first sheet of the work.' And he did, in fact, send the title-page, index, and first four pages of the 'Restoration of Christianity.'

The Inquisitor, the Cardinal, and the Vicar-General of the Archbishop of Vienne, immediately took the matter in hand. At their request Servetus was summoned to appear before Monsieur de Montgiron, the *Lieutenant-Général du Roi*,[1] in Dauphiné, whose physician he was, under the name of Villanueva. At the expiration of two hours, which even those who uphold Servetus say that he no doubt spent in destroying papers which might have compromised him, he appeared and answered all the questions put to him by a general denial. He said that 'for a long time he had lived at Vienne, and that he had often visited the preachers and other professors of theology. But they would not find that he had ever held heretical opinions or been suspected of heresy. He was willing that his apartments should be searched so as to remove all cause for suspicion, not only that of the court but of any other persons, for he had always desired to live so that there should be no cause for the said suspicion.' His dwelling and papers were searched. The printer

---

[1] The functions of the *Lieutenant-Général du Roi* were military, political, administrative, and, on special occasions, judicial also. This confusion of offices prevailed for a long time in the old French Monarchy.

Arnoullet and his workmen were examined; they were asked if they had seen the manuscript of the book of which the first few pages were shown to them—they answered that they had not, and produced a list of all the books printed by them within the last two years; there was not one of any kind in octavo. The questions put either to Servetus or to those who had assisted him, only led to absolute denial of all that was suggested, and the court decided that there was not sufficient evidence for taking any further proceedings, or for imprisoning the Spanish physician, Monsieur Villanueva.

The falsehood was rash and useless. Too many persons had been engaged in the production of the book, too many copies had been sent away, the initials M. S. V. (Michael Servetus Villanueva) too plainly indicated the author, and Servetus himself had too often boasted of his work, to make it possible that a serious inquiry could have any other result than a discovery of the whole truth. Cardinal de Tournon and the Inquisitor Ory applied to the source from whence they had received warning, for further help. They directed the Catholic Arneys, at Lyons, to write to the Protestant De Trie,[1] at Geneva, and ask for the information and proof which they wanted, and amongst other things for the whole volume of which he had only sent a few pages: 'In order,' so said the letter, 'that the Genevese might see that there were people in France who laid to heart the honour of God and of the Christian faith, and that they were not all as lukewarm as those of Geneva imagined.'

The inquiry at Vienne had taken place about the

[1] According to Stähelin, i. 436, the Inquisitor, Matthias Ory, wrote to De Trie with his own hand.

middle of March; De Trie's answer to Arneys arrived at Lyons on the 26th of the same month. It was as follows: 'When I wrote the letter which you communicated to those who were in it accused of indifference, I did not think that the matter would have gone so far. My only intention was to let you see the fine zeal and devotion of those who call themselves the pillars of the Church, and yet allow such evil to exist among them, whilst they harshly persecute poor Christians who desire nothing more than to serve God in all simplicity. As this was a striking example which had come under my notice, I thought that my letters—as I was writing on this subject—gave me a suitable occasion for mentioning it. But since you have made known that which I had intended to write for your own eyes only, may God so dispose all things for the best, that it may be the means of purging Christianity from such a foul pest. If those you speak of are really as much in earnest as you say, there will not be much difficulty in the affair (even although I am unable at present to furnish you with what you ask for, namely the book), for I can place in your hands that which is more convincing, namely about two dozen papers written by the person in question, and containing some of his heresies. If the printed book was placed before him, he might deny it, but he cannot deny his own writing. . . . But I must confess that I have had great difficulty in obtaining from Monsieur Calvin that which I send you; not that he is unwilling that such execrable blasphemy should be punished, but that it seems to him that, since he does not wield the sword of justice, it is his duty to confute heresy by sound doctrine rather than to seek to extirpate it by any other method. But I have importuned him so greatly, representing that I should be charged with making reckless assertions unless he came to my aid, that at length he has consented to give up that which I send you.'[1]

The packet contained: I. Some pages of a copy of Calvin's 'Christian Institutes,' on the margin of which Servetus had written with his own hand, occasionally using very violent language, some of his theories which were utterly opposed to the Christian dogmas recognised both by Protestants and Catholics. II. Several autograph letters from Servetus to Calvin, in which he brought forward and maintained the pantheistic notions upon which his recent work, the 'Restoration of Christianity,' was based.

Calvin has been strongly blamed for giving up these private letters and marginal notes to the Catholic authorities, who had already commenced proceedings against Servetus. It has been said that he laid the whole plot, and caused Servetus to be denounced, in order to destroy a religious adversary and personal enemy, by the instrumentality of the Catholic Church. His hesitation as to whether he ought to give up the papers and allow them to be sent to Lyons, shows that he had some doubt as to the moral rectitude of his conduct; but it shows an extraordinary misapprehension of his character to imagine that this hesitation was an act of hypocrisy, and that the surrender of the papers was a piece of premeditated perfidy. There are no errors, or rather no vices, with which it is so impossible to charge Calvin as with untruth and hypocrisy. During the whole course of his life he openly avowed

[1] *Revue des deux Mondes*, 1848, i. 822.

his thoughts and acknowledged his actions; he left his native country for ever, and the country of his adoption for a long period, just because he was resolved to assert his opinions, and to act according to his opinions. In his transactions with Servetus, he was brought into contact with a man who, whilst he aimed at becoming the most radical of reformers, lived for twelve years at Vienne as a strict Catholic, and secretly printed and distributed a profoundly anti-Christian book; then, seeing that he was in danger, denied his work and his acts, and protested 'that he had never desired to teach or maintain any doctrine opposed to the Church or the Christian religion.' Calvin felt the greatest contempt for so much untruth and cowardice; he openly condemned the book and the conduct of Servetus from the very first; he considered it both a right and a duty to prove the truth of that which he had affirmed, and to show at Lyons as well as at Geneva that the opinions of Servetus were the same as those put forward in the condemned volume, and that Servetus was really the author of it. 'It is reported,' said he, 'that I have contrived to have Servetus taken prisoner in the Papal dominions, that is at Vienne; and thereupon many say that I have not acted honourably in exposing him to the deadly enemies of the faith. There is no need to insist on my vigorously denying such a frivolous calumny, which will fall flat when I have said in one word that there is no truth in it. . . . If there were any truth in the charge, I should not deny it, and I do not think that it would be at all discreditable to me.'[1]

The effect produced by this information was what might have been expected. The proceedings at Vienne

[1] Bungener, p. 362.

were at once resumed. Servetus was called upon to explain the marginal notes in the 'Christian Institutes,' and the letters he had written to Calvin. He was greatly troubled, and fell into all kinds of strange and contradictory statements and denials : 'He says that, at first sight, it is impossible for him to say if the letter is his or not, because it has been written so long ; however, having looked at it more closely, he certainly thinks that he must have written it; and says that whatever is found in it contrary to the faith, he submits to the decision of our holy Mother Church, from which he has never wished, nor would ever consent to be separated. And if he has written any such things, he says that he wrote them heedlessly, by way of argument and without serious thought.' And then he is said to have burst into tears and uttered the most unexpected lie, denying that he was Servetus : 'I will tell you the whole truth. Twenty-five years ago, when I was in Germany, a book by a certain Servetus, a Spaniard, was published at Aganon (Hagenau) ; I do not know where he was then living. When I entered into correspondence with Calvin, he charged me with being Servetus, on account of the similarity of our views, and after that I assumed the character of Servetus.'[1]

This incoherent mass of untruth and confession caused the proceedings to be carried on in a more serious manner. Servetus was arrested and imprisoned. The gaoler received orders to watch him carefully. Nevertheless he was treated with an indulgence by no means common at that time. He was allowed to have his own servant, to keep possession of a gold chain and some rings which he wore, and to send a demand for the payment of 300 crowns which were due to him.

[1] Henry, iii. 146.

He had undoubtedly many staunch friends; probably the vice-Bailli of Vienne, whose sick daughter he had cured, was one, and possibly Monsieur de Montgiron, the *Lieutenant-Général* in whose service he had been, was another. It was afterwards proved that a servant of the gaoler had said to the servant of Servetus, 'Go and tell your master to escape by the garden.' On the 7th of April, 1553, two days after his imprisonment, Servetus did, in fact, escape in the early morning by a garden which led into the courtyard of the *Palais de Justice*. He hurried across the bridge over the Rhone, and thus passed from Dauphiné into Lyonnais; at least this was the account given by a peasant, who had met him but was not interrogated until three days after his escape.[1]

No traces of him can be discovered between April and July 1553. He was wandering either in French or Swiss territory; and when, at a later period, he was asked where he had intended to go after his escape from Vienne, he varied in his answers, sometimes naming Spain and at others Italy as his proposed place of refuge. I am inclined to believe that from the very first he intended to make his way to a much nearer spot. Be that as it may, whilst he was wandering from place to place, either undecided as to his future course, or waiting for a fitting opportunity of carrying out his plan, sentence was pronounced upon him by the Catholic judges at Vienne; and on the 17th of June he was condemned 'to be burnt alive over a slow fire, at the place of public execution, so that his body should be reduced to cinders as well as his book.'

[1] Henry, iii. 147; Gaberel, ii. 248; *Revue des deux Mondes*, 1848, i. 824.

CHAPTER XVIII.

SERVETUS IN GENEVA. HIS TRIAL AND EXECUTION.

A MONTH later—on the 17th of July—Servetus entered a little inn on thé banks of the lake at Geneva, called the *Auberge de la Rose*. He was alone and unknown: he said that he wanted a boat across the lake, so that he might go on to Zurich. He did not cross the lake, but stayed for twenty-seven days at Geneva, greatly exciting the curiosity of his host, who asked him one day if he was married: 'No,' he said, 'there are plenty of women in the world without marrying.' He seems to have walked out and seen several persons. It is even asserted that he went to church and heard Calvin preach. Calvin afterwards said, 'I do not know how to account for his conduct, unless he was seized by a fatal infatuation and rushed into danger.'[1]

The result shows the infatuation of his prolonged visit to Geneva, but I think that this visit bears equally strong proof of premeditated design. Precisely at this period Calvin was engaged in the contest which I have recently described with the Libertines, on the subject of excommunication from the Lord's Supper. When Servetus entered Geneva, the Libertines had

[1] Henry, iii. 149-151; Rilliet, *Procès de Michel Servet*, p. 20; *Revue des deux Mondes*, 1848, i. 826.

some reason to expect that they might triumph; one of their leaders, Ami Perrin, was first syndic; they believed themselves sure of a majority in the Council of Two Hundred, and almost sure of one in the lesser Council which possessed the executive power. A man of their party, Gueroult, who had been banished from Geneva, had been corrector of the press to the printer Arnoullet at Vienne, at the time when the 'Restoration of Christianity' was published. Thanks to the influence of his patrons, the Libertines, Gueroult had returned to Geneva, and he would naturally be the medium between them and Servetus. I do not find any definite and positive proof of his intervention at this particular time; but taking a comprehensive view of the whole case and the antecedents of all those concerned in it, I am convinced that Servetus, defeated at Vienne, went to Geneva, relying on the support of the Libertines, whilst they on their side expected to obtain efficacious help from him against Calvin.

But neither the Libertines nor Servetus knew the resolute adversary with whom they had to deal. From the moment that Calvin heard Servetus was in Geneva, he did not hesitate for one instant, although he was already engaged in a fierce and perilous struggle. He added a second contest to the first, and resolved to obtain two victories instead of one—the victory of Christianity over a pantheistic visionary, and the victory of religion and morality over a licentious faction. He wrote to one of the syndics requesting him, 'in virtue of the power granted to his office by the criminal edicts of Geneva, to arrest Servetus.' On the 13th of August, 1553, Servetus was arrested. 'I do not deny,' wrote Calvin on the following 9th of September, 'that he was imprisoned at my instance.' But, according to the laws of Geneva, in order that the imprisonment should not be merely temporary, it was necessary that there should be a formal accusation, and a prosecutor who consented to submit to imprisonment, and to hold himself criminally responsible for the truth of the charge. It was Calvin who also provided for this necessity. Nicolas de la Fontaine, a French refugee, his secretary and intimate friend, consented to undertake the painful office. 'I do not conceal the fact,' says Calvin, 'that by my wish, Servetus was apprehended in this city, that he might be compelled to give an account of his misdeeds. And since malevolent and evil-disposed persons gabble all kinds of things against me, I frankly confess that as, in accordance with the laws and customs of this city, no one can be imprisoned unless there is a prosecutor, or some previous knowledge of his crimes, therefore in order to bring such a man to reason, I arranged so as to procure a prosecutor.' The first examination of Servetus took place the day after his arrest, and on the 15th of August his trial commenced.

This theological tragedy lasted for two months and thirteen days. There was great variety in the scenes of which it was composed, corresponding to the different·incidents in the political and social struggle with the Libertines which Calvin was carrying on. I do not intend to give a detailed account of this prolonged trial, but I am anxious that its essential character and principal phases should be clearly apprehended.

At its commencement, and for the first fourteen or fifteen days, Servetus showed no lack either of moderation or skill, although both attack and defence were sharp and keen. He openly assailed Calvin as his personal and hateful enemy, but was careful not to fall into violent abuse of him. He maintained the truth of the doctrines asserted in his own works, but was most anxious to show that they were not contrary to the Christian religion, that he had never wished to separate himself from the Church, and that his aim was to restore Christianity, not to abolish it. The trial was soon transformed into a theological controversy, turning upon points of doctrine; and after the 17th of August Calvin himself took part in it, declaring that he had no intention of screening himself behind those who had commenced or were carrying it on, and that he was prepared to take the prosecution of the prisoner upon himself. He was authorized by the Council to be present at the examinations and take part in the debates, 'either for the purpose of trying to reclaim Servetus, or in order that he might point out his errors more clearly to him.' The scene became more exciting, and gave promise of wider development. Servetus offered 'to show Calvin his own errors and faults before the whole congregation, proving them by arguments drawn from the sacred Scriptures.' Calvin eagerly accepted this offer, declaring that 'there was nothing he desired so ardently as to conduct this trial in the church and before all the people.'

But the Council refused; they wished as a matter of prudence to keep the decision of such matters in their own hands; they were also probably influenced by the wishes of the friends of Servetus, who had every reason to expect that Calvin's words would have much more weight with the people than those of the Spaniard. The discussion between the two adversaries was carried on sometimes by written and sometimes by spoken arguments. For a long time Calvin's keen insight had shown him that the works of Servetus were pantheistic, and that pantheism must destroy historical and dogmatic Christianity. He pressed Servetus closely upon this point, and the Spaniard imprudently acknowledged his doctrine : 'All created things,' he said, 'are of the substance of God.' 'How, wretch!' said Calvin; 'if any one was to strike this pavement with his foot and to tell you that he was treading on your God, should you not shrink with horror at having subjected the Majesty of God to such an indignity?' 'I do not doubt,' answered Servetus, 'that this bench and this table and everything that we see is essentially God.' Again, when it was objected that, according to his views, the devil must be a manifestation of God, he laughed, and answered boldly: 'Do you doubt it? As for me I hold it to be a fundamental maxim that all things are a part and portion of God, and that the collective universe is itself the Deity.'

The Council was both shocked and embarrassed. There were warm partisans of Calvin in its ranks, and eager protectors of Servetus—among others the principal Libertine leaders, Ami Perrin and Berthelier; but there were also some impartial members who were sorry to see Calvin take such a prominent place in the prosecution, and who had no desire to become judges in a trial for heresy. Still they recognised the danger to Christianity of the Spaniard's pantheism, and refused at any cost to appear to sanction it. Moreover, they disliked and suspected

Servetus. He was sincere enough in his adhesion to his own views, but on other points they found him frivolous, vain, arrogant, irresolute, and untruthful. He denied any connexion, even the most indirect, not only with the Libertines of Geneva, but with their agent Gueroult at Geneva, who had corrected the proofs of his book. The falsehood of these disavowals was so obvious, that even those magistrates who hesitated to condemn him, could no longer place any confidence in him. It seems strange that they should have been ignorant of the sentence passed upon him on the preceding 17th of June, after his escape from Vienne, by which he was condemned to be burnt alive; but either they were really ignorant of it, or they wished to appear to be so, for the Protestant Council of Geneva wrote to the Catholic judges of Vienne to ask for 'information as to the crimes which had caused the imprisonment of Servetus in their city, both believing and hearing,' says the letter, 'that it was not without cause, and that you have certain information and charges against him for which he deserves punishment.' It was no doubt by the advice of his supporters that Servetus demanded that the principal reformed churches in Switzerland—Berne, Zurich, Schaffhausen, and Basle—should be consulted on his case; since on similar occasions they had always shown themselves far more moderate than Calvin. The Council granted this request, and Calvin did not oppose it. There can be no doubt that the majority of the Genevese magistrates desired to a certain extent to modify the character of the trial, and make its personal animosity less apparent; they wished to appear the defenders of Christianity rather than the enemies of any special theological system. They adjourned the trial several times, and put off the final decision as if they dreaded to pronounce it.

But there is a time for procrastination and a time for prompt action, a time for courage and a time for prudence. The crisis of the two struggles in which this small state was engaged had arrived, and the great issues involved in them had to be decided. Between Calvin and Servetus, between Calvin and the Libertines—that is to say, between Christianity and Pantheism, between tyrannical austerity and licentious anarchy—there was no longer any possibility of either reconciliation or truce. With the instinct of the man of action, Calvin felt this, and unhesitatingly adopted the most energetic measures in both cases. On the 27th of August, 1553, he uttered the severest censures from the pulpit upon the conduct of Servetus; and on the 3d of September following, as I have previously related, he solemnly refused to administer the communion to the leader of the Libertines, who—in spite of the decision of the Council of State—had been pronounced unworthy of it by the Church. In both cases he thus made a direct appeal to the general body of believers. The trial of Servetus, which was going on at the time of this double excitement, suddenly changed its whole character. All moderation, all prudence were cast aside by the prisoner; led away by the hope of overwhelming an enemy who was fiercely attacked and in danger elsewhere, Servetus became the vehement accuser of Calvin, even unto death. Small pamphlets sometimes took the place of judicial debates. 'Miserable wretch,' said

Servetus, 'you do not know what you are saying; you endeavour to condemn things which you do not understand! Do you think, O dog! that you can deafen the ears of the judges by your howls? Your mind is so confused that you cannot see the truth! . . . . You cry out like a blind man in the desert, because the spirit of vengeance consumes your heart. You have told lies, you have told lies, you have told lies, ignorant slanderer!' Servetus did not confine himself to abuse, but, on the 22d of September, demanded that his adversary should be committed for trial, giving a list of the subjects 'on which Michael Servetus demands that John Calvin shall be interrogated. I demand, gentlemen, that my false accuser shall be punished by the law of retaliation, that his property shall be handed over to me as a compensation for my own, which by his means I have lost, and that he shall be kept in prison as I am, until the trial shall be ended by the condemnation to death of one of us two, or by some other punishment.'

Calvin, in spite of his own violence, was at first overwhelmed by this outburst of passion. He says, 'I was timorous and dismayed before him, as if I had been the prisoner, and had been called upon to answer for my doctrine. In truth, I am afraid that good men will accuse me of too great meekness.'

Servetus soon discovered that his hopes had entirely deceived him, and that the position of his adversary was much stronger than he had imagined it to be. All that the Libertines were able to do for the promotion of their own cause, was, to prolong for sixteen months, the indecision of the civil power on the question of the right of excommunication; but at the end of that time, on the 24th of January, 1555, the civil authorities decided that the right belonged to the Consistory. And as to the unfortunate Servetus, the Libertines who had urged him on, and compromised him in every way from the time of his arrival at Geneva, gave him but feeble support when they saw that the final crisis was at hand. His violent attack on Calvin was not even noticed. On the 19th of September the Council decided to apply officially to the pastors and magistrates of the four churches of Berne, Zurich, Schaffhausen, and Basle for their opinion of the trial. Calvin did not approve of this step, but he had not opposed it; he had, however, written to some of his friends in the cantons, among others to Bullinger at Zurich, and to Sulzer at Basle, in order to point out the very serious nature of the advice for which they had been asked; and it was well known throughout Geneva that his letters would not fail to influence the answers from the cantons. From that time the passionate excitement of Servetus gave place to dejection and anguish. He was in prison, sick and forsaken. On the 10th of October, 1553, he wrote to the Council: 'Most noble lords, for the last three weeks I have implored you to grant me an audience, but have not been able to obtain it. I beseech you, for the love of Christ, not to refuse that which you would not refuse to a Turk who demanded justice at your hands. I have very important things to tell you, which you ought to know. As to the orders which you issued that something should be done towards keeping me clean, nothing has been done, and I am in a more wretched condition than ever. Moreover, the cold torments me greatly, on account of the colic and my other maladies, which give rise to infirmities of which I should be ashamed to write to you. It is a great cruelty that I am not permitted to speak, when I only want to ask that my wants may be supplied. For the love of God, gentlemen, grant this, either out of mercy or justice!' 'The Council sent two of its members to the prison 'with orders,' says M. Rilliet, 'to cause the necessary clothing to be given to the prisoner, so as to remove the hardships of which he complained. But there is no other trace of the result of this interview between the prisoner and the deputies of the Council. Probably it was occupied with topics which Servetus had previously discussed; and that his object was to obtain some influence over the minds of the magistrates rather than to give them any fresh information.' But the appeal which he had made for compassion was of no more use than his violence.

On the 18th of October, 1553, the messenger returned to Geneva, bearing the answers of the four cantons. They were all cautious and guarded, though in different degrees, and at the same time sorrowful in tone, but they were unanimous in the nature of their advice. 'We pray the Lord,' said the Bernese letter, 'that he will give you a spirit of wisdom, prudence, and courage, so that you may secure your own church as well as other churches from so great a danger ; and that at the same time you may do nothing that will appear unseemly in Christian magistrates.' 'We are persuaded,' wrote the church of Basle, 'that you will not fail either in Christian prudence or in holy zeal, but will find a remedy for the snare which has already led away many souls to destruction.' The language of the letter from Zurich was much more definite: 'You must not allow the wicked and false attempts of the said prisoner to prevail, for they are quite contrary to the Christian religion, and cause our churches to be in bad repute.' Schaffhausen gave the same advice as Zurich. There can be no doubt that the four churches recommended severity, although they added a few words so that they might not be charged with the entire responsibility of the decision.

The Council met again on the 23d of October, 1553, and after having read the answers from the Swiss churches, once more adjourned so as to avoid coming to a final decision. Several of the members who were favourable to Servetus had absented themselves, amongst others, the first syndic, Ami Perrin, no doubt in order to necessitate an adjournment. Another meeting was fixed for the 26th of October; and again, when the day arrived, several of the supporters of Servetus did not appear. But Ami Perrin was true to him; he formally demanded that the accused should be acquitted of the charge, and declared innocent; and ultimately moved that the case should be referred to the Council of Two Hundred. Both propositions were rejected. The majority of the Council passed a resolution which was entered in their register in words to the following effect :— 'That,—considering the summary of the trial of the prisoner, Michael Servetus, the report of those who, have been consulted, and his great errors and blasphemies,—it is decreed that he be led to Champel and there burnt alive, and he shall be executed to-morrow, and his books burnt with him.'

At that period there was no hesitation on account of the atrocious torture of such a punishment, and no scruple as to the right of inflicting it. Heresy was a crime, and the stake was the penalty of heresy. In that very year 1553, at Lyons, not far from Geneva, several reformers had suffered martyrdom; among others, five young French students from the theological Institute at Lausanne. The Catholic judges at Vienne had condemned Servetus to the stake. Save for some scattered protests which saved the honour of the human conscience, in the sixteenth century the burning of heretics at the stake was looked upon as the common right of Christianity.

During the whole course of the trial Calvin had never concealed his feeling as to what the sentence ought to be. On the 20th of August, after it had commenced, he wrote to Farel: 'I hope that he will be condemned to death; but I trust that there may be some mitigation of the frightful torture of the penalty.' After the execution of the sentence, he wrote: 'When Servetus had been convicted of heresy, I did not say a word concerning his execution: not only will all good men bear witness to this, but I authorize the bad to speak if they have anything to say.' On the 26th of October, the very day on which sentence was passed, he wrote to Farel: 'The wretch has been condemned by the Council without a division. To-morrow he will be led to the stake. We made every effort to change the manner of his death, but in vain.' Farel hurried to Geneva; he had taken the warmest interest in the case, and had urged great severity; but he was not incapable of sympathetic emotion, and was a man of very strong religious feeling. When Servetus heard of his condemnation, he fell into the deepest despair; he wept, entreated, implored, and cried, 'Mercy! mercy! Farel hoped to bring him to repentance, and save his soul, whilst at the same time his recantation might lead to a mitigation of his sentence. He pressed him to see Calvin; Servetus was not disinclined; Calvin also consented, and obtained permission for the interview from the Council, who sent two of its own members to accompany him on his visit to the condemned prisoner. When asked what he had to say to Calvin, Servetus replied that he wished to solicit his forgiveness. Then Calvin said: 'I protest that I have never carried out any private animosity against you. You must remember that sixteen years ago, being at Paris, I did not spare myself in my efforts to win you for our Lord, and if you would have listened to reason, I would have done everything in my power to reconcile you with all the faithful servants of God. You ran away from the conference, and yet I did not cease to exhort you by letters; but all has been useless, and you have assailed me not so much with anger as with fury. And now I have done with all that concerns myself personally. Ask pardon, not of me, but of that God whom you have blasphemed by trying to disprove the existence of three Persons in one God; ask pardon of the Son of God, whom you have debased and denied as your Saviour.' These words were more likely to wound Servetus than to convince him; they probed his wounds but did not heal them; he remained silent. The repeated exhortations of Farel were of no avail, and Calvin withdrew, following, he says, the rule of St. Paul: 'A man that is an heretic after the first and second admonition reject; knowing that he that is such is subverted, and sinneth, being condemned of himself.'[1]

Servetus was willing to ask pardon, but he would not disavow his opinions. Even in the depths of his despair he preserved all the pride of honest conviction; and although he entreated that his life might be spared, he would not consent to dishonour it by a false recantation. Farel, who accompanied him to the stake, in vain renewed his severe, but at the same time compassionate exhortations up to the very last moment. The dignity of the philosopher triumphed over the weakness of the man, and Servetus died heroically and calmly at that stake, the very thought of which had at first filled him with terror.

[1] Epistle of Paul to Titus, iii. 10, 11.

CHAPTER XIX.

THE TWO OPPONENTS. CALVIN'S LETTER TO SOCINUS.

THIS celebrated trial has become a great historical event, and I have followed its different stages with scrupulous care. I have endeavoured to disentangle its philosophical, social, and political aspects, and to describe them accurately. I have been anxious truthfully to delineate the character, opinions, passions, and attitude of the two opponents. It was their tragical destiny to meet each other and to enter into mortal combat as the champions of two great causes. It is my profound conviction that Calvin's cause was the good one, that it was the cause of morality, of social order, and of civilization. Servetus was the representative of a system false in itself, superficial under the pretence of science, and destructive alike of moral dignity in the individual, and of moral order in human society. In their disastrous encounter, Calvin was conscientiously faithful to what he believed to be truth and duty; but he was hard, much more influenced by violent animosity than he imagined, and devoid alike of sympathy and generosity. Servetus was sincere and resolute in his conviction, but he was a frivolous, presumptuous, vain, and envious man, capable, in time of need, of resorting both to artifice and untruth. In an age full of martyrs to religious liberty, Servetus obtained the honour of being one of the few martyrs to intellectual liberty; whilst Calvin, who was undoubtedly one of those who did most towards the establishment of religious liberty, had the misfortune to ignore his adversary's right to liberty of belief.

I do not think that Calvin ever felt any hesitation or regret as to his own conduct during the trial of Servetus. He believed in his right and duty to suppress heresy in this manner, as sincerely as Servetus believed in the truth of his own opinions; and his most intimate friends, instead of trying to soften him, endeavoured to confirm his severity. Farel wrote, on the 8th of September, 1553: 'You desire to mitigate the severity of his sentence, and in so doing you would act the part of a friend towards him who is your greatest enemy. But I beseech you to proceed in such a manner that hereafter no one shall seek to promulgate new doctrines with impunity and throw all into confusion as Servetus has done. It is absurd to conclude that because the Pope accuses faithful believers of the crime of heresy, and infuriated judges condemn these innocent victims to tortures reserved for heretics, that therefore we must never put heretics to death for the sake of ensuring the safety of true believers. For my own part, I have often said that I was ready to suffer death if I taught anything contrary to true doctrine; and I have added that I should deserve the most frightful torments if I turned any away from faith in Christ.' Even the most advanced advocates of liberty did not go so far as to say that honest error could not be crime.

Servetus himself, when he was accused of saying that the soul was mortal, exclaimed, 'If ever I said that, and not only said it but published it and infected the whole world, I would condemn myself to death.' Nevertheless, either from instinctive justice or influenced by the caution which their position required, many, even of those reformers who were strongly attached to the Calvinistic doctrines, were averse to the capital punishment of heretics; and would not tolerate the reproduction, in their own church, of the cruelty which they protested against in the Church of Rome. These honest scruples were supported by the authority of some of their most illustrious leaders. At the very commencement of the struggle, Luther had said: 'The burning of heretics is contrary to the will of the Holy Spirit.' Calvin himself, not long before the trial of Servetus, reproved a young Italian refugee towards whom he entertained very friendly feelings, for holding opinions which in many respects resembled those of the Spanish physician, but he expressed his disapprobation with almost paternal tenderness. It is not without surprise that I have found among his letters one which, in 1551, he wrote to Lælius Socinus,[1] of Siena, uncle of that Faustus Socinus who, at a later period, founded the Socinian heresy. Lælius Socinus was a young man of great intellectual power, with a strong leaning towards philosophical speculation, and he had passed several years in Germany and Switzerland on friendly terms with all the principal reformers. Calvin wrote to him at Wittenberg: 'You are mistaken in your impression that Melancthon does not agree with

[1] Sózzini.

us in holding the doctrine of predestination. I told you in a few words that I had received a letter from him in which he acknowledges that his opinion is the same as mine. But I can well believe all that you tell me, since it is no new thing for him to avoid speaking plainly on that subject, if for no other reason than to escape troublesome questions. Certainly no one can have a greater objection to paradoxes than I have, and I do not take the slightest pleasure in mere intellectual puzzles. But nothing shall prevent me from openly avowing those things which I have learnt from the Word of God, for he is a master in whose school we learn nothing that is not useful. The Bible is my only guide, and I shall always endeavour to order my life in accordance with its pure doctrines. I earnestly desire, my dear Lælius, that you may learn to govern your faculties with the same moderation. Do not expect any answer from me so long as you put forward such strange questions. If it gives you any pleasure to float in the ether of speculation, pray do so; but you must allow me—a humble servant of Christ—to confine my meditations to those points which may help to establish or confirm my faith. From henceforward I will pray for you in silence, and will importune you no further. But truly I am deeply afflicted that the fine talents which God has given you should not only be employed in vain and barren researches, but debased and destroyed by pernicious speculations. I repeat with all earnestness that which I told you long ago: if you do not try to subdue your passion for investigation and speculative inquiry, it is to be feared that you will bring upon yourself bitter misfortune. It would be great cruelty towards you if I treated with apparent indulgence that which I look upon as a most dangerous error. I would rather pain you a little now by my sincerity, than leave you, without any protest, to be led into danger by your over-inquisitive mind. I hope that the time may yet come when you will be glad that you received such a harsh warning. Farewell, my very dear and greatly honoured brother; and if my strictures seem more severe than they have any right to be, you must remember that they arise from my love towards you.'[1]

Assuredly no orthodox theologian could have spoken with more affectionate earnestness, or more forbearance, to a man who was incessantly expressing doubts as to the divinity of Christ, the truth of redemption, expiation, original sin, and the majority of the Christian doctrines. It is true that Lælius Socinus was young; he had published nothing; and he showed very great respect for Calvin, who had never been called upon to enter into any controversy with him.

Nothing is more easy, and at the same time more vulgar and unworthy, than to speak with irony and contempt of the inconsistencies of even the greatest among men. We ought rather to congratulate ourselves on these inconsistencies, as an involuntary homage paid to truth. They show that truth is so deeply rooted and so powerful in the human mind, that it keeps or makes a place for itself even when we might expect it to be destroyed by the most noxious errors. Man often creates the gloom which darkens his own soul,

[1] Calvin's Letters, published by M. Jules Bonnet and translated into English, ii. 330. (Philadelphia, 1858.)

but it is not in his power to shut out altogether the light which comes from God.

At length, to the honour of humanity and the promotion of its moral and social well-being, rays of divine light have shown us the right of the human conscience to liberty of belief. In that very city of Geneva where, three hundred years ago, the fire was kindled for Servetus, the members of that same reformed religion which Calvin then established, met together, not long ago,[1] in the various churches of the city, to commemorate the three hundredth anniversary of the death of the great reformer. One of the most eloquent and pious speakers present, M. le pasteur Coulin, alluded to the trial and execution of Servetus, and pronounced a just and righteous sentence upon that lamentable act. He said: 'Even if Calvin's system had been exempt from any possible error, if it had been, as he sincerely believed that it was, truth itself, he should not have attempted to compel men to accept it. He forgot that those around him did not understand, or reason, or form conclusions as he did. That was his mistake, and it is a very grave one. Assuredly truth is the queen of the intellect, and whosoever believes in truth is a champion bound to promote the establishment of her reign. But man is so constituted that truth can and will consent to govern him, only on condition of his own free adhesion to her rule. God has placed a something inviolable within us for the reception of truth, which most shows our own greatness when we maintain the supremacy of truth. If truth is a queen, conscience is her throne. This is why that which has

[1] On the 27th of May, 1864.

truly been called liberty of conscience is the essential condition of the reign of truth. Seek truth, show it, prove it; exhibit in turns the splendour of its beauty, the majesty of its strength, the charm of its excellence. Urge all around you to bow before truth, and pay homage as to a queen. But if you cannot prevail with them, then, in the name of truth and of the most sacred interests of the glory of truth, remember that there are still two things even in the most bitter enemy—a free conscience which ought to be respected, an erring brother who may be loved. These two things Calvin did not recognise; in his blind zeal he wished the conscience either to acquiesce or to abdicate its function. It is impossible to assert too strongly that every outrage upon the liberty of conscience of the individual, is a blow that truth receives upon the face, which dishonours her. Make every allowance for the spirit of the age, for the prevailing prejudices which not even a man of genius can altogether escape; make allowance for all the necessities of the time and the pressure of circumstances; make allowance for whatsoever you choose: but the fact still remains that the laws and measures by means of which Calvin endeavoured to ensure unity of conviction in Geneva are a stain upon his memory, an element condemned beforehand in his work, upon which time ought to pass a just sentence.'

CHAPTER XX.

CALVIN'S INFLUENCE OVER THE REFORMED CHURCHES. HIS PRESBYTERIANISM.

AFTER the termination of the trial of Servetus in 1553, and of the contest with the Libertines in 1555, Calvin obtained, not repose, but victory and unopposed supremacy. He had need of it, for his health, which was naturally weak, had become exceedingly infirm. He had frequent attacks of quartan fever, violent headaches, disease of the liver, attacks of gout, and he was threatened with consumption. There was no longer any one in his home to watch over him with that tender assiduity which is almost as necessary for the health of the soul as for that of the body. He had lost his wife, Idelette de Bure, on the 6th of April, 1549. She had borne him three children, but they all died young, and in their conjugal solitude she had shown that entire and unselfish devotion which gives everything, and asks for nothing in return. She had three children by her first husband, Störder; when she was very ill, one of her friends urged her to speak to Calvin about them : 'Why should I ?' said she ; 'that which concerns me is to have them virtuously brought up : if they are virtuous, he will be a father to them ; if they are not, of what use is it for me to commend them to his care ?' But Calvin anticipated her maternal solicitude, and without waiting until she spoke, he promised to treat them as if they were his own children: 'I have already commended them to God,' she said. 'That does not prevent me from also taking care of them,' said Calvin. She answered: 'I know well that you will never forsake those whom I have confided to the Lord.' She died as she had lived, showing pious and tender confidence in God and her husband. In the letters written during his lifetime to his two most intimate friends, Farel and Viret, Calvin often spoke of her, briefly but affectionately, and with entire satisfaction. When she died he spoke of his grief more openly than he had ever done of his happiness. He wrote to Viret: 'I have lost the excellent companion of my life, who would never have forsaken me, either in exile, poverty, or death. So long as she lived she was my faithful assistant; she took no thought for herself, and was never either a trouble or a hindrance to her husband. I control my sorrow as far as it is in my power; my friends also do their duty; but it is of very little use either for them or me. You know the tenderness—not to say the weakness—of my heart. I should give way utterly if God had not stretched out his hand to hold me up. It is he who heals the broken-hearted, who consoles the wounded spirit, who strengthens the trembling knees.'[1]

From the time that he lost his wife until his own death, that is from 1549 to 1564, Calvin lived alone in his little house at Geneva. He had been deprived of that domestic happiness which is a rest

[1] Henry, i. 416–423; *Bulletin de la Société de l'Histoire du Protestantisme Français*, iv. 644–649.

alike to body and soul; he took no part in any ordinary pleasures, but gave himself up entirely to the duties which he had undertaken, and to the work to which he was devoted. These duties and labours extended far beyond the narrow bounds of the city in which he lived. His ambition was loftier than that of the most mighty princes, and his proposed sphere of action more vast than that of the most extended kingdom. His ruling passion, the strongest desire of his soul, was the re-establishment and organization of the Christian Church in accordance with the intention of its divine author, and on the foundation laid by the apostles. He wished to build up a Christian Church, free and independent in its evangelical unity and universality. He believed that neither the separation of nations, nor diversity of origin and language, nor difference of political rule, ought to affect the great Christian society. For Calvin, as for St. Paul, there was no longer either Jew, or Greek, or Barbarian; either Swiss, or French, or Italian, or English, or Slave. He saw only the human being, called to become a faithful Christian and to live in close relation to Christ, keeping his faith and fulfilling his law. Calvin was convinced that Christ had revealed in the Gospel all the essential principles of Christian society, that is of the Christian Church; and he believed that these essential principles were three in number:

I. The union and united action of ecclesiastics and laymen within the Church, and in its internal government; no human theocracy and no ecclesiastical tyranny.

II. The mutual independence and limited alliance

of Church and State. The Church perfectly free in her spiritual rule, but at the same time acknowledging and supporting the temporal rule of the State.

III. The spiritual and moral authority of the Church over the religious and moral life of its members, to be maintained, if necessary, by the power of the State.

The application and development of these principles was to be found, according to Calvin's views, in the self-government of the Church by a mixed body consisting of pastors and members. There would then be the mutual and valuable influence of the Church in the State, and of the State in the Church, each according to the nature of its own power, and within the limits of its own rights.

He believed that such a system was in harmony on the one hand with the Gospel, and on the other with the condition and requirements of European society in the sixteenth century. He saw in it the abolition of abuses, which time, and the crimes or follies of men, had introduced into the Christian religion; and he hoped by means of it to restore the spirit as well as the spontaneous organization of the early Christian Church. He expected to introduce into this system the degree of freedom and of restraint necessary to accomplish the great aim of Christianity, namely the discipline and salvation of the human soul.

This was the Reformation according to Calvin's view, and he endeavoured to realize it in the system known as Presbyterianism.

He watched its establishment in Switzerland, France, Holland, England, Scotland, Germany, and Poland with inexhaustible interest and unshaken

fidelity. He had abundant means of knowing all
that was going on throughout Europe in reference
to the Reformation. Numerous refugees had sought
a place of safety in Geneva; he himself had made
many expeditions into France, Germany, and Italy;
and the friendships which he had formed, and
his numerous correspondents had brought him into
close connexion with many foreign reformers. He
knew how far the Reformation had succeeded in
different countries, what progress it was making,
and what obstacles it had met with, so that
he could modify his course of action according to
circumstances. Where there was no band of reformers ready to unite and openly proclaim themselves a religious society, as for example in Italy,
Calvin endeavoured, in his letters and by his advice,
to sow the first seeds of the Reformation; and
to make known the fundamental doctrines of the
reformed faith. Wherever he found the rudiments
of a Christian association and a reformed church, he
endeavoured to promote its organization in accordance with the principles of the system established at
Geneva. As a mother country provides for the early
wants of her colonies, so he sent models for con-
fessions of faith and rules of discipline, as well
as founders and preachers for the distant churches;
and he watched over the progress of these local
works with paternal solicitude. Many of the French
churches were originally organized by Calvin, and received their first pastors from him. Letters reached him
from all parts asking for light or guidance in the prevailing religious fermentation. M. de Beaulieu wrote
to Farel from Geneva on the 30th of October, 1561,

saying: 'I cannot tell you how many persons there are in this city who have come from Lyons, Nismes, Gap, Orleans, Poitiers, and elsewhere, and who are asking for labourers in the new harvest. Many have told me that if four or five thousand pastors could be sent out, there would be no lack of work for them.'[1]

In the midst of the stormy vicissitudes of the Reformation in England and Scotland, Calvin's influence was also felt. He wrote to the young king of England, Edward VI., to Queen Elizabeth, and to all the most important persons in the kingdom, political or ecclesiastical. He addressed the prudent and versatile Cranmer, as well as the fiery and intractable Knox, and to each he gave the advice best calculated to promote the general interests of the Reformation. After Knox had been banished from Frankfort in 1555, he went to Geneva, where he was appointed pastor, and remained until 1559, making himself fully acquainted with the doctrine and discipline of the Presbyterian Church. In this vast and varied exercise of his influence, Calvin was never led astray by political bias or prejudice in favour of any system or sect. He thought Knox took too prominent a part in the struggles of the nobles and people in Scotland; that he was unduly hostile to the Anglican Church, its liturgies and forms of worship: 'I hope,' he wrote, 'that in those things which concern ceremonies, your severity, which is displeasing to so many persons, is somewhat abated. No doubt we must take care that the Church is purged from all those evils which have been introduced by error and superstition. We must take heed lest the divine

[1] Henry, iii. 483.

mysteries be changed into childish mummery; but when that is done, you are well aware that there are many things which, without being approved, may yet be tolerated. I am profoundly grieved at the dissensions of your nobles.'[1]

John Knox, the Scotch reformer, was one of the most eminent and influential of Calvin's allies, and, I do not say disciples but coadjutors. By character, as well as position, Knox was a master, not a disciple. He was four years older than Calvin, and like Calvin he had been drawn towards the Reformation in early life; but when he began to play an important part in it, he was led by the state of public feeling, and probably by his own inclination also, to take part in the political as well as the religious struggles of his age and country. He was the champion of a party as well as of a cause, and was quite as eager to subdue his enemies in the State as to insure the predominance of his doctrines in the Church. Often active and influential in his own country, at other times proscribed and wandering on the continent of Europe, he was tossed to and fro by divers fortunes. He became personally acquainted with Calvin, and understood and admired him from the very first. One of those close and intimate friendships sprang up between them which unite men of the same temperament, whatever may be their difference of disposition and habit. Whenever Knox was compelled to leave Scotland, he sought refuge in Geneva; he took the warmest interest in the labours, the trials, and the struggles for success in which Calvin was engaged, and watched his skilful organization of the reformed Genevese Church When

[1] Calvini Epistolæ, ix. 150. (Amsterdam, 1667.)

he returned to Scotland, he corresponded constantly with Calvin, consulted him on numerous occasions, and set great store by his advice, although he always preserved his own independence of thought and action. Knox was as resolute and persevering as Calvin, but more fiery, more violent, and without that respect and consideration for established authority which was so characteristic of Calvin even when he was opposing it. And yet, with all their difference of predilection and method, the work of the two reformers was essentially the same. Although he was no less independent than his great ally, Knox was powerfully influenced by Calvin's example, and he transported the presbyterian system to Scotland, which, after three centuries of trial, still flourishes there as it does in Geneva. The Scotch Church has lately passed through the severe ordeal of division into a Free and an Established Church, and, to its great honour, without danger to the State or to religion.

But to return to Calvin : in France his moderation and liberality were carried very far. He aimed at establishing the reformed churches on the presbyterian basis, but he expressly warned their members never to take the initiative in appeals to force or insurrection. His correspondence with the principal French reformers was a constant exhortation to prudence, patience, submission to the civil powers and religious independence. He desired to see neither aggression nor vengeance on the part of the Protestants. He strongly condemned the conspiracy of Amboise,[1] and the sanguinary reprisals of the Baron

---

[1] The conspiracy of Amboise was planned among the French Reformers in 1559 and 1560, and carried on by a gentleman of Perigord,

des Adrets.[1] No doubt the precepts and practice of St. Paul were always present to his mind, and that he both preached and practised obedience to the powers that be, in things that did not interfere with faith in Christ and the will of God. In all that concerned religion no innovator was ever bolder than Calvin, and at the same time less revolutionary. None was ever more scrupulously indifferent to all other aims than the propagation of the Gospel, the organization of the evangelical Church, and the reformation of man's moral nature. I do not know how far his logical forethought was able to penetrate the future, or if, whilst he was prosecuting his work of religious emancipation, he foresaw that what he was doing would bring forth, as a natural consequence, such immense political and social changes. I am inclined to believe that he did not concern himself about it in any way, that his essentially judicious and practical mind was exclusively occupied by his mission and by the immediate present, and that he did not seek to penetrate the darkness of future centuries, and the far-off designs of God.

Calvin's conscientious conviction of the necessity of submission was so great that he would sometimes

---

named Godefroi de la Renaudie, in the name of the principal Protestant leaders, especially that of the Prince de Condé. Its object was to take all power from the hands of the Guises, to 'have them punished by law,' and to secure for the reformers, not only religious liberty, but the chief power over Francis II. in the government of France. It was discovered in March 1560, and repressed and punished with great severity.

The Baron des Adrets (François de Beaumont) was a Protestant gentleman of Dauphiné, who lived from 1513 to 1586, and who was notorious at that period for his cruel reprisals upon the Catholics in the religious wars of France.

say a man ought not to employ force even to effect his escape from prison and to save himself from martyrdom. After all, he said, it was martyrdom which had contributed so powerfully to the triumph of the early Christian Church; and when the cause of God had need of martyrs, it was man's duty to submit.

This excessive severity and pious enthusiasm did not, however, prevent him from using all the influence which he possessed, and exerting all his power, both moral and political, in behalf of those reformers who were persecuted, imprisoned, and on the eve of martyrdom. He was not satisfied with doing all that was in his own power, writing, preaching, importuning and harassing the persecutors; he induced all those governments that were favourable to the reformers, and able to exert influence which would be beneficial to them, to intercede on their behalf. He sent agents, legal help, indirect protectors, money and assistance of all kinds. And when he had been unable to succeed in averting persecution or diminishing its severity, when the day of martyrdom arrived, he employed all his Christian zeal in sustaining the courage of the victims, lavishing upon them proofs of his own sympathy, and teaching them to put their trust in God and his Divine justice. The persecuted reformers at Nismes in 1537; the Waldenses, cruelly ill-treated and tortured in Provence and Dauphiné in 1545; the martyrs of Lyons in 1552; the church of Paris and the victims of the attack upon the reformers in the Rue St. Jacques in 1556 and 1557; and in many other places and on many other occasions, the fugitives and martyrs of the French reformation received warm help and fraternal consolation from Calvin. We may say that he changed the words of Dante, and that, when he had been unable to save those for whom he had laboured, he opened the doors of the eternal future, saying to them, ' Do not lose all hope, ye who enter here!'

But Calvin's solicitude was not confined to the fugitives only, and to the patent and manifest sufferings of the French reformers. He had too deep a knowledge of human nature and the world not to know the secret aspiration, hidden grief, and ignoble strife which vex and torment the soul, and are found in every social condition, the most exalted as well as the most humble. In many such cases his watchful care and influence were also felt. The Duchess Renée of Ferrara was not the only woman nor the only great lady with whom he kept up a zealous correspondence through life. He wrote numerous letters to important personages, renowned leaders or vacillating friends of the Reformation; to the King of Navarre, Admiral de Coligny, the Duke de Longueville, M. de Soubise, and the Baron des Adrets. In addition to these, the numerous published collections of Calvin's letters, and the repositories which contain those that are still unpublished, are full of others addressed to M. and Mme. de Falais, M. and Mme. de Budé, Mme de Cany, Mme de Rentigny, the Marchioness of Rothelin, Mlle. de Pons, Mme. de Grammont, and a host of other persons who were important or interesting in his eyes. Some of them were more or less closely connected with the great cause which he had at heart; to others he was drawn by their spiritual condition, and by the value which he set upon their faith, conduct, and salvation.

Calvin was one of those rare great men who are rich both in heart and intellect, who can no more look with indifference at the fate of an individual than at that of a kingdom, and who feel for the joy and sorrow of the human heart, as well as for the storms which agitate a nation. He was as deeply interested in the faith and sorrows of one simple woman as in those of all Christendom, and could apply himself as eagerly to the enlightenment of a single conscience as to the moral reformation of a whole city. Moreover, he knew that sooner or later, far or near, the influence which he thus acquired over single individuals would be so much gained for the authority which he desired to exercise over the general cause of the Reformation, and thus the sympathetic zeal of the Christian helped the social mission of the founder of a church.

CHAPTER XXI.

CALVIN THE AUTHOR. HIS CHURCH CATECHISM. HIS RESPECT
FOR THE INTELLECT.

AT the same time that he showed this indefatigable activity in his personal relations, Calvin continued to communicate with all the reformed churches, and the whole European public, by means of his written works. He revised and completed his great book, the 'Institutes of the Christian Religion.' He wrote commentaries on all the books of the New Testament, and on some of the more important of those in the Old Testament; among others on the Pentateuch, the Psalms, and several of the Prophets. Historical and philological criticism was at that time in its infancy, and we do not find any striking evidence of its existence in Calvin's Commentaries, but they show the most intelligent appreciation of the moral and religious signification of the sacred volume, and of the practical applications which Christians ought to draw from it. He also published, either as sermons or special dissertations, various works in support of the theories which he had already put forth on certain great questions, such as the Lord's Supper, free-will, predestination, and others. He carried on with great ardour all the theological controversies in which he had engaged, whether they were with Catholic adversaries of the Reformation, with Protestant opponents of his own special doctrines, or on the subject of the disagreements between the reformers themselves. In these different scenes of action he sometimes displayed a noble spirit of conciliation, and at others the greatest intolerance and most unmeasured violence. I do not intend to give any detailed account of his different works. They were collected at Geneva in 1617, and at Amsterdam from 1667 to 1671, in two folio editions; the second of these is far better than the first, but they are both incomplete and often faulty. Several learned French and German editors, among others the eminent historian and Professor of Theology at Strasburg, M. Edouard Reuss, are preparing a new edition, published at Brunswick. The first seven volumes, quarto, have already appeared, and this edition will be in every respect infinitely superior to all that have preceded it. I mention these large collections in order to give the reader some insight into the numerous and varied literary works with which Calvin was occupied, and which must be added to his extensive correspondence, political struggles, daily labours, preaching and religious instruction.

I will pause for a moment to consider one of these numerous works ; not only on account of its high moral value, but because it formed part of the important system of public instruction which Calvin inaugurated at Geneva after he had established the Reformation. It is entitled, ' *Catechism of the Church of Geneva, for the instruction of children in Christian Doctrine; written in the form of a dialogue in which the minister asks questions and the child answers.*' It was published in 1545.

This catechism aimed at much more, and was quite on a different plan from that published by Calvin in 1538, consisting of a certain number of paragraphs in which the fundamental doctrines and rules of the Protestant Church and Christian life were briefly stated. In the Catechism of 1545, Calvin changed the form, and extended the plan of the work. By the arrangement in questions and answers, the book became a true catechism, fitted for the instruction of youthful Protestants. It was fundamentally a treatise on dogmatic theology, in which all the doctrines of Calvin's great work, the 'Christian Institutes,' were reproduced in the form of elementary instruction. The peculiarity of such a method is that all the information is given by the pupil, *the child*, as Calvin says, and that the only aim of the master's questions is to bring out this information in a logical and scientific form. The child thus seems to be teaching the master, and certainly shows how far the master has been already well taught. It is a very anomalous position, and becomes still more so when the master's queries lead the child to discuss some of the most difficult theological questions, and to uphold doctrines which are disputed even among the most eminent theologians. Calvin made his catechism serve not only for instruction in the fundamental doctrines of Christianity, in its historical, spiritual, and moral truths ; but also for the propagation of those parts of his theological system which were beset with difficulty and controversy. In my eyes this is a very grave defect ; at the same time, however, Calvin's catechism has one important characteristic, admirably suited for its purpose :—it is not philosophical discussion, it is religious instruction. I open some of the most highly approved catechisms, Protestant or Catholic, and I find as the very first question, at the beginning of one of them, 'What is God?'[1]—in another, 'Are we certain that there is a God, and by what proofs may we convince ourselves of his existence?'[2] These questions involve philosophical research. Calvin proceeds in a very different manner: he does not seek God, he knows him, possesses him, and takes God as his starting-point. God the creator, man his creature, and the relation of man to God, these form the fundamental facts and natural basis of the history, doctrines, and laws of Christianity. Calvin's catechism commences thus: 'What is the chief end of human life?'—'To know God.' And this first assertion is the mainspring of all the principles and religious duties which are afterwards presented, not as the discoveries of the human mind, but as communications made by God in order to meet man's aspirations, and enable him to regulate his life. It is neither a scientific method, nor is the catechism a philosophical work: it contains the assertion of a real, immemorial, universal and historical fact, and explains the consequences of that fact. It is the natural and legitimate method of mparting religious instruction, inherent in the very first principle of all religion ; it is specially in harmony with the origin and history of Christianity, and no one has ever recognised its power or proved its efficacy more fully than Calvin.

[1] *Instruction Chrétienne*, used in the Church which has adopted the Confession of Augsburg, and said to have been revised by one of its most eminent representatives, the late M. le Pasteur Verny, p. 1.
[2] *Catéchisme de Montpellier*, i. 10, 11 (1769).

Although Calvin gave the first place in his heart and thoughts to theology, he was not exclusively engrossed by it. He knew too much of human nature and human society not to give great consideration to their different claims and wants. Moreover, he entertained great respect for the human intellect, and looked upon its full development as essential to the accomplishment of the destiny of man and the glory of God. Literature and social science, all great intellectual labour and all large utterance of thought, had great value in his eyes, and attracted him powerfully.

Geneva was not exclusively occupied by its republican efforts to obtain national independence, but from the very commencement of the fifteenth century was influenced by the revival of literature which then took place, and the prevailing taste for classical studies. In the year 1428, François de Versonnay, a citizen of Geneva, founded a college there, in the following words:·'I look upon instruction as a useful work; it dispels ignorance, disposes the mind to wisdom, forms the manners, instils virtues, and is favourable to the good administration of public affairs. Nevertheless, up to the present time, Geneva has been entirely deprived of this benefit for want of a public building, conveniently situated, and able to hold all the pupils. To remedy this defect I have set aside part of the worldly goods which Providence has granted me.' And the college was thereupon founded. Grammar and Aristotle's Logic were taught in it, and the liberal arts, that is poetry and a knowledge of the works of ancient authors. It prospered for several years; but towards the end of the fifteenth century, and during the commencement of the sixteenth, civil discord, danger from without, and want of means caused it to fall into decay. Several attempts to restore it were fruitless; and on the 3d of January, 1531, at the height of the troubles of the Reformation, 'the Rector having left the city, and no application being made for an appointment which on account of the small number of pupils was not at all profitable, the Council decided upon closing the school until fresh orders were given concerning it, as the children were very destructive.'[1]

With the exception of a few attempts made by Farel towards the re-establishment of the College, this was the condition of public education in Geneva, when Calvin returned from Strasburg and took up his abode there in 1541. In the following year, 1542, he proposed to the Council: 'In the first place to extend and improve the College, and also to establish an academy in which the citizens and strangers might pursue more advanced and important studies.' He thus from the first disclosed his whole plan; which was that the College should consist of an elementary and a classical school, and that there should be an *academy* or university above it. But the times were stormy; political and theological contests were all-absorbing; there was a lack both of men and means, and sixteen years passed before any step was taken beyond the purchase of a house for the projected university. At length in 1558 the theological disputes were terminated, and the Libertines, who were completely defeated, had withdrawn from the contest. Calvin again submitted his proposition to the Council, asking them to take measures for pro-

[1] Gaberel, i. 493-498.

curing the necessary funds, and offering to assist in obtaining them. The Council summoned the notaries, 'in order to give them express commands that for the future, in drawing up wills, they should exhort their clients to leave a legacy for the support of the College.' They also set apart for this purpose a portion of the fines inflicted in the courts of justice. Calvin himself made a house-to-house collection, explaining fully the nature of the two establishments for which he was soliciting contributions. At the end of six months he presented the sum of ten thousand and twenty-four florins to the Council.[1] The work was immediately commenced, and the buildings were planned and laid out. Calvin had only just recovered from a very serious illness, but he insisted on being carried to the building, where he exhorted the workmen, and watched their progress from day to day; as active and influential in the public streets as in the Council chamber. The old college building was prepared for the reception of pupils. An unforeseen event was the means of providing Geneva with professors for the *academy* or university. The Government of Berne quarrelled with the majority of the pastors and professors of Lausanne on the subject of the right of excommunication. Many of the most eminent among them—Beza, Viret, Chevalier, Tagaut, and Berault—left Lausanne, and asked hospitality from Geneva. Calvin received them all gladly, and those who would be of use to the new university, with special warmth. Beza, who was already celebrated, was appointed rector of the university and professor of theology; Chevalier was

[1] From 1,200*l*. to 1,600*l*.—some 30,000 or 40,000 francs.

named Professor of Hebrew, Tagaut of philosophy, and Berault of Greek. When all was thus completed, professors and material means provided, a solemn festival on the inauguration of the new institution was fixed for the 5th of June, 1559. Laymen and ecclesiastics, pastors, professors and students, magistrates and burgesses, assembled in St. Peter's church; Calvin was there, weak and exhausted by the sufferings which he had undergone for many months, and from which he was only beginning to recover. After an address, in which the magistrates congratulated their city on becoming 'at the same time the mother of science and of piety,' Beza spoke first, and as rector, addressed himself especially to the students: 'I implore you, in the name of God,' he said, 'not to be unfaithful to yourselves. There is a celebrated saying of Plato's that knowledge, if separated from justice and virtue, is only skill and not truth. Nothing is more natural than that pagan philosophers should have been unable to conform fully to all that this maxim implies. But you—how can you excuse yourselves if you fall short of it?—you who have sucked in the pure knowledge of God and of his truth with your mother's milk. You are assembled here, not like the Greeks, to take part in the exercise of intellectual dexterity or to behold the display of noble physical powers, but to undertake the earnest study of the highest truths and the most excellent sciences, to fit yourselves for glorifying the name of God, for becoming the blessing and ornament of your country: you have come here that at the last day you may, with all confidence, give an account to the Lord of the holy combat to which he has called you.' Calvin rose, added a few words, 'brief, clear and weighty, according to his custom;' he thanked God for the success of the work, expressed his gratitude to all who had given help, and closed the meeting by a prayer, in which he invoked the protection of God on the institution.

Calvin's prayers were answered from the very first by the success of the academy. 'There was a hall in the cloisters of St. Peter's church, in which classes were held, and the number of pupils attending them was so great, that the Council set apart the chapel of Notre Dame la Neuve, which was, after that, called the *auditorium*. A hundred and nine students received instruction from the new professors, and more than eight hundred theological students, consecrated to the propagation of the Gospel in France or Germany, gathered around Calvin.'[1] This brilliant beginning was followed by permanent success ; Calvin's system of public education has existed and prospered in Geneva for more than three centuries. He was not able at first to give it so large a development as he desired. He wished to establish schools of law and medicine in the University, and also of all the higher studies, but he could find neither the necessary professors nor the funds. At a later period, however, the University of Geneva was honoured by the presence of many men, illustrious in the world of science; Isaac Casaubon, Joseph Scaliger, and Hottoman were there, as professors of Greek, of philosophy, and of law. In our own day, Bonnet, De Saussure, Pictet, and De Candolle have shed upon Geneva the light and fame of their studies in natural science. The educational

[1] Gaberel, i. 507.

establishments of Geneva were so vigorous, and so firmly rooted in their native soil, that they withstood the effect of revolutions which changed the face of the country. My mother, guided by her great intelligence and entire devotion to my education, took me to Geneva in 1799, in order that I might obtain a classical and complete education, for which there was not at that time any facility in France. Geneva had then become a French Department; but the college, the university, the lecture-halls for literature and philosophy, had survived the fall of its national existence. The republic of Geneva had disappeared, but the religious reformation and the system of public education established by Calvin, the theological and scientific professorships which he had founded, were still in existence, and doing good work. Internal revolutions have again changed the face of Geneva, but Calvin's work goes on; his anniversary is still celebrated, and a new building has been recently dedicated to the cause which he promoted, and to the honour of his name.

CHAPTER XXII.

THE END.

IN 1559 his work was completed, so far as human work can be completed, but Calvin had almost reached the limit of his strength—I mean his physical strength, for his intellectual and moral powers remained undiminished to the last. His health of body drooped and failed, but his intellect remained clear and his will unshaken. His soul was one of those which lack time on earth for full development, and return again to God without having expended all the store of wealth and power with which at their creation he has endowed them. On the 2d of February, 1564, Calvin gave his last lecture on theology, and on the following Sunday, the 6th, he preached his last sermon. He had an attack of bleeding from the lungs whilst he was in the pulpit, and all speaking in public was after that prohibited. He was still constantly engaged in study or writing, and when his friends urged him to take a complete rest, he said: 'Then you wish that when the Lord comes he shall not find me watching.' On Easter Day, the 2d of April, he was carried to the church and received the sacrament from the hands of Beza. He expressed a wish to be carried to the Hôtel de Ville on the 27th of April, in order that he might once more pay his respects to the Syndics and the Council. But they prevented this by visiting him in a body at his own house. He thanked them 'for having condescended to show him so much more honour than he had any claim to, and begged them to excuse him for having done so much less than he ought to have done, both in public and private life; and he thanked them also for having patiently borne with his great vehemence and other sins, of which he repented, and which he trusted that God had forgiven.' He then with much gentleness offered them very judicious advice as to the government of the republic, 'and having begged them to pardon all his faults, which could never have seemed so great in any eyes as they had done in his own,' he held out his hand to say farewell. Beza says : 'I do not think that any parting could have been more sad for these gentlemen. On account of his office they all looked upon him, and with good reason, as speaking to them from God, and they had an affection for him as for a father, since he had known and trained many of them from their youth upward.' On the 28th of April all the evangelical ministers in the city and neighbourhood were assembled in his room, and Calvin addressed his last counsels and last farewell to them, speaking with solemn and affectionate familiarity, like a chief who takes leave of his companions when he is about to set out on some great enterprise : 'It may seem to you,' he said, 'that I say too much, and that I am not really so ill as I make people think; but I assure you, that although I have often been ill before, I have never felt as I do now, nor have I ever been so weak. When I am moved in order to be placed on my bed, my head swims, and I faint immediately. There is also this shortness of breath, which troubles me more and more. I am in all things unlike other sick people, for when they are near death their mind grows weak and wanders ; whilst as for me, it is true that I am as it were benumbed, but it seems as if God intended to shut up all my senses within me and keep them there. And I think that it will be very difficult for me to die, and will cost a great effort, and I may lose the power of speech whilst I still possess all my faculties. But I have given warning of this, and have said what I wish should be done with me, and for the same reason I desire to speak to you before God takes me.' He then reminded them of all the principal incidents in his political and religious career, the struggles which he had been called upon to maintain for the Gospel and the Reformation, and ended by saying: 'Gird yourselves up and take courage, for God has a use for this church, and will maintain it. I tell you God will keep it in safety. . . . You have elected Monsieur de Bèze in my place: take care that you comfort and support him, for he will have a great responsibility. As for him, I know that his will is good, and he will do what he can. See also that there are no bickerings and no angry words among you ; for I know that oftentimes, when taunts are uttered, we see nothing but smiles at the time, but there is great bitterness in the heart. It is all of no use, and moreover there is a want of Christianity in it. You must guard against it, and live in all true peace and friendship. I had forgotten one thing. I beg you to make no changes, and to introduce no novelties. People are always seeking novelty. Not that I am thinking for myself, or speaking from ambition and a desire that what I have begun shall continue, and that people shall cling to it and not seek that which is better, but because all changes are dangerous, and sometimes injurious.'

These last words were preserved by one of the ministers present, who closes his account of the interview by saying: 'He took leave kindly of all his brother pastors, who went up to him one by one weeping, and shook hands with him.' . . . 'Which caused me such anguish and bitterness of heart,' adds Beza, 'that I cannot recall it now without exceeding sorrow.'

There was still another last farewell about which Calvin was anxious. He wished to take leave of his old friend Farel, who twenty-eight years previously had induced him to stay at Geneva, and thus had decided the work of his life; and for whom he entertained an affection, which was perhaps the deepest and most tender feeling he ever knew. On the 2d of May he received a letter in which Farel, hearing of his illness, announced his intention of visiting him. Calvin immediately dictated the following answer: 'Fare thee well, my very dear and good brother! and since it pleases God that you shall remain behind me, live in the memory of our union, the fruit of which awaits us in heaven, for it has been profitable to the church and to God. I will not have you fatigue yourself for me. I draw my breath with very great difficulty, and from hour to hour I expect breath will fail me. It is enough that I live and die in Christ, which is gain to those that are his, both in life and death. I commend you to God,

together with our brethren who are in your parts.'
Nevertheless Farel arrived; came on foot, say some,
from Neufchâtel to Geneva, in spite of his seventy-five
years of age. The two friends supped together, just
those two. Farel preached on the morrow, and then
returned at once to Neufchâtel, saying in his heart, as
he said a few days later in a letter to Fabri: 'Why
was I not taken in his place, and many years of health
granted him for the service of the church and of our
Lord Jesus Christ? Praises be to God a thousand
times for his inestimable grace in allowing me to meet
this man and detain him, against his will, at Geneva,
where he has begun and completed more than any
tongue can tell!' After the departure of Farel,
Calvin only saw some of his colleagues, the Genevese ministers, for a few moments. They were
to dine together in his house on the 19th of May;
he remained in his own chamber, which was quite
close to the dining-room, and said, 'with the most
joyous face in the world,' says Beza: 'The wall
that is between us will not prevent my being with
you in spirit.' Both by day and night many persons, some of whom had travelled a great distance,
came to Calvin's door, asking to see him or at
least to have tidings of him. Beza says: 'On the
27th of May, 1564, he seemed to speak with less
difficulty and more vigorously; but this was a last
effort of nature, for towards night-time, about eight
o'clock, all the signs of approaching death suddenly
set in. I was sent for immediately, and ran to the house,
together with some of my brethren, but I found that he
had already given up the ghost. He had died peacefully, without any last struggle, had been able to

speak clearly to the very last moment, and had been in full possession of his judgment and all his senses; he had not moved either hand or foot, and so he looked asleep rather than dead. Thus, in an instant, our sun set on that day; and the greatest light of this world, and the glory of the church, was withdrawn and taken back into the heavens. We may well say that in our time it has pleased God to show us in one single man both how to live and how to die.'

'On the following day and night,' says Beza, 'there was great lamentation throughout the city, for the people mourned for the prophet of the Lord; the poor flock in the church wept for the loss of their faithful pastor; the academy deplored its true head, and all in common bewailed their beloved father and their chief comforter next to God. He was placed in a simple wooden coffin, and about two hours after mid-day, in accordance with his own wish, was carried in the usual manner, without any pomp or ceremony, to the public cemetery called Plain Palais. There he lies to this very day, waiting for the resurrection which was his own constant hope, as he taught us to make it ours. I say that all was done quite simply, according to the custom of our church in the burial of any person whatsoever; so that a few months later, when certain new students who had come to the college went, one day, to the cemetery to visit Calvin's tomb, they found that they were mistaken. They expected to see some lofty and magnificent monument, and there was only a simple mound of earth, and it was just like all the other graves. And this may serve as an answer to those who have long accused us of making an idol of Calvin.'

In the registers of the Consistory, under date of the 1st of June, 1564, a cross follows the name of *Calvin*, †, and by the side of it are these words, 'He went to God on the 27th of May in this year.'

Men are called great and obtain a place in history under different titles. With some it is exalted station, and glory, and great power during their lifetime which makes them great; with others the importance and permanence of their works; with others again it is moral elevation of nature and beauty and purity of life. The greatness of Calvin arises from all these sources; he is great by reason of his marvellous powers, his lasting labours, and the moral height and purity of his motives. When Pope Pius IV. heard of his death, he said: 'The strength of that heretic consisted in this, that money never had the slightest charm for him. If I had such servants, my dominions would extend from sea to sea.' It is true that Calvin's disinterestedness was a very prominent characteristic, but it was by no means his chief or only one. He was never influenced or governed by any interest, any desire, any personal pleasure other than the triumph of his faith, and the success of his labours for a moral as well as a religious reformation. Although he took a leading part in a great revolution, he had neither revolutionary ideas nor passions. He was essentially a lover of order, he knew the conditions as well as the claims of power, and had received from nature the gift of exercising authority. Upon principle he neither recognised nor admitted the claims of liberty, either in human nature or human society. In his eyes man was God's instrument and not a 'fellow-worker with God,' as St. Paul says. God, as he thought, had preordained the destiny of every man, and of the whole human race. The mission of the civil powers was therefore to recognise and carry out the law of God in all its precepts and towards all its subjects, in private as well as in public life, both in the family and in the state. But, in point of fact, and in spite of his doctrines on free-will and predestination, Calvin contributed largely to the progress of liberty in the Christian world, for he both claimed and used it in opposition to the religious and civil tyrants of his period. He separated Church and State, but he united laymen and ecclesiastics in the government of the religious society, and he placed the soul of man not under the direction of a priest but under the direct influence of the law of God made known in the Scriptures. As a moral philosopher he was inaccurate and inconsistent, but he was strictly consistent in the practical application of his theories to his own conduct and his duties towards his fellowmen. He honoured men but did not trust them; had an ardent desire for their moral welfare, but did not dare to leave their part in its accomplishment in their own hands; and he obtained the devoted affection of the best men and the esteem of all, without ever seeking to please them.

Earnest in faith, pure in motive, austere in his life, and mighty in his works, Calvin is one of those who deserve their great fame. Three centuries separate us from him, but it is impossible to examine his character and history without feeling, if not affection and sympathy, at least profound respect and admiration for one of the great reformers of Europe and of the Great Christians of France.

GUIZOT.

VAL. RICHER, 1869.

NOTE TO ST. LOUIS.

The Punishment of Blasphemy, p. 144.

One of my learned colleagues, M. Natalis de Wailly (*Académie des Inscriptions et Belles Lettres*) has pointed out that the punishment of branding a blasphemer on the lips with a red-hot iron (p. 144) was probably resorted to on account of some peculiarly heinous offence, and was an isolated case; that it cannot be considered as due to any general and permanent decree applied to all cases of 'that vile oath,' blasphemy, because there is an enactment of St. Louis (*Recueil des Ordonnances des Rois de France*, i. 99) which decrees that adult blasphemers shall be punished by a fine, or in default of fine, by the pillory and imprisonment. Blasphemers under fourteen years of age were to be whipped. M. de Wailly's remark is just, and I hasten to acknowledge that in this matter the piety of St. Louis did not systematically lead him to exercise general and excessive rigour.

LIST OF THE MOST IMPORTANT OF THE WORKS REFERRED TO IN THIS VOLUME.

ST. LOUIS.

Bibliothèque de l'École des Chartres.
Dom Bouquet's *Recueil des Historiens des Gaules et de la France*, vol. xx.
Faure (Félix), *Histoire de Saint Louis*. Paris, 1867.
Histoire littéraire de France, vol. xvi.
Joinville. Edition published by Mr. N. de Wailly. Paris, 1867.
Jubainville, *Histoire des Ducs et des Comtes de Champagne*.
Paris (Mathieu), *Histoire de l'Angleterre*. Folio edition, 1644.
Recueil des Ordonnances des Rois de France, vol. i.
Rémusat (Abel), *Mémoires de l'Académie des Inscriptions et Belles Lettres*.
Tillemont (le Nain du), *Vie ae Saint Louis*, édit. par De Gaulle (*Soc. de l'Histoire de France*). 1847-51.
Topin (Morin), *Aiguesmortes*. 1865.

CALVIN.

Beza, *L'Histoire en bref de la Vie et Mort de Calvin*, par Th. de Bèze. Lyons, 1565. (*Archives curieuses de l'Histoire de France.*)
―― *Histoire des Églises réformées de France*.
Calvin, *Œuvres de Calvin*. Brunswick, 1863.
Drelincourt, *La Défense de Calvin*. Genève, 1667.
Gaberel (Jean, *ancien pasteur*), *Histoire de l'Église de Genève*. Genève, 1853.
Guizot (C. F. G.), *Méditations sur la Religion*. Paris, 1868.
―――――――― *Histoire de la Civilisation en France*. Paris, 1868.
Henry (Paul), *Das Leben Johann Calvins*. Hamburg, 1835.
Martin (Henri), *Histoire de France*, vol. xxiv.
Stähelin (Lic. E.), *Johannes Calvin* (*Hagenbach*). 1860-63.

www.ingramcontent.com/pod-product-compliance
Lightning Source LLC
Chambersburg PA
CBHW020218240426
43672CB00006B/350